THE SUSTAINMENT BATTLE STAFF
& MILITARY DECISION MAKING PROCESS (MDMP) GUIDE

Brigade Support Battalions (BSB),
Sustainment Brigades (Sus Bdes), and
Combat Sustainment Support Battalions (CSSB)

Version
3.0

Dr. John M. Menter, COL (Ret)

ISBN: 0692387366
ISBN 13: 9780692387368

TABLE OF CONTENTS

★★★

BRIEFING FORMATS

OTHER GUIDANCE, TERMS, & PLANNING CONSIDERATIONS

This Guide is designed to assist the logistics planner at any level from the Brigade Support Battalion to the Sustainment Brigade, to move through the Military Decision Making Process (MDMP) from receipt of a higher headquarters mission, analysis of the mission, development of courses of action, completion of operations orders/plans, preparation and execution of briefings to decision-makers, and continuous planning through current and into future operations.

The techniques adopted in this guide and used throughout the process have been developed through several years of experience working the MDMP. They have been adjusted and tweaked over time and are in use with various sustainment organizations as well as the emerging guidance published with ADP/FM 3-0 (Unified Land Operations), ADP/ADRP 5-0 (The Operations Process), ADP/ADR 3-90 (Offense and Defense) and the newly revised FM 6-0 (Commander and Staff Organizations and Operations) replacing ATTP 5-0.1. It is expected that this guide is a living document, subject to frequent, necessary changes as doctrine, techniques, and experiences change.

As a final note, when the term "Brigade Support Battalion" is used, it also applicable to the Aviation Support Battalion (ASB)– the sustainment structure associated with Combat Aviation Brigades.

- Editor

This Book is dedicated to
The Logistician's Logistician
My Wife "Jeanette" who
without which this work
would not have been possible

The Author would also like to express his sincerest
appreciation and thanks to those folks involved with the Mission
Command Staff Training Program, who have significantly
improved ARNG unit sustainment capabiliites both at home and
OCONUS. Last and by no means least, my sincerest
thanks and appreciation to Ben Terrell and Roy Pond, whose
inputs at the" dead of night" keep the Author on course
and the replenishment mission on track.

"The more I see war, the more I realize how it all depends on administration and supply... It takes little skill or imagination to see where you would like your army to be and when; it takes much knowledge and hard work to know where you can place your forces and whether you can maintain them. A real knowledge of supply and movement factors must be the basis of every leader's plan; only then can he know how and when to take risks with those factors, and battles are won only by taking risks."

Napoleon Bonaparte

A.C.P Wavell <u>Speaking Generally,</u> (London, 1946), page 78-9.

WHY DO WE NEED A SUSTAINMENT MDMP GUIDE?

★★★

"If Logistics were easy – It would be called Tactics"
Famous Fort Leavenworth Saying

"Forget Logistics and you lose."
LTG Frederick M. Franks

Although the military decision making process (MDMP) is at times a cumbersome and time consuming process, the benefits of performing MDMP to standard far outweigh the time and energy consumed participating in the process. Planning success at the Brigade and higher staff level requires sufficient time to perform MDMP, having the right personnel involved in the process, and coming to the table with the necessary tools to effectively integrate the war fighting functional areas (WFFA) into the overall plan. This is especially important for the combat service support (CSS) "Sustainment warfighting functional area", specifically for the Brigade Combat Team (BCT) and its organic Brigade Support Battalions, which now under transformation has a robust Support Plans Officer logistics "planning staff". How well the Sustainment WFFA Subject Matter Expert (SME) is integrated into the MDMP is a direct function of having the right personnel with the appropriate tools participating throughout the process, or at a minimum, during key events. This guide will assist the sustainment planner whether the Brigade S-4, Support Operations Officer (SOO)/ Support Plans Officer (SPO), or the Battalion S-2/3. In any event, integration of the Sustainment/CSS WFFA in the Brigade/CSSB or Sustainment Brigade MDMP is essential to ensuring current, mission specific, and future support requirements are identified. In addition it is crucial to allocating resources to accomplish the specified and implied tasks, and synchronizing key logistics events with the brigade's course of action.

"Sustainers" as logisticians are now referred to, accomplish this planning in several ways, but they must come to the MDMP with the available tools. These tools include (but are not limited to) personnel and logistics estimates (using the Logistics Estimate Worksheet, OPLOG Planner, 'Quick Logistics Estimation Tool' or historical data), a draft OPORD/OPLAN Para 4, Annex F, a Brigade/Division Concept of Support (CoS), and sustainment (aka CSS) synchronization matrix. With these tools, participants have the capability to understand the brigade's current situation and to analyze/adjust future requirements based on a complete picture of the logistics battlefield. Sustainers must ensure that the MDMP methodology includes a discussion of sustainment operations throughout the depth of the battlespace.

The MDMP timeline is one of the biggest challenges sustainment planners must overcome because of the possibility of multiple key events happening simultaneously. Here, the Brigade DCO/XO must deconflict critical events to maximize participation by his sustainment planning staff. Such events include sustainment rehearsals (if conducted), Sustainment/Movement Control Work Group Battle Rhythm meetings, daily operational meetings, and future planning cycles. Either of these conducted without a "Sustainer" will only spell disaster, usually at a key event or time. Remember, under modularity, your "margin of error" is now razor thin.

Finally, let's address some of the misconceptions Sustainers might have regarding the MDMP process. Most BSB/CSSB or

Sustainment Brigade Commanders, SPOs and BCT S-4s argue that it is just too hard to accomplish current operations as well as plan future missions. Most believe having an assistant S4 planner at the brigade Main Command Post (MAIN) is sufficient to plan and synchronize logistics support. The belief is that these planners have a rudimentary understanding of modular sustainment functions and their roles in COA development and analysis. There is also a common belief by many brigade sustainers that a brigade plan is merely a guide for how the BSB will support the BCT. Once the BSB receives the BCT order, they will perform their own MDMP and determine how they will "really" support the mission. In addition, most logisticians believe that their ability to improvise mitigates the risk of not participating in the MDMP. Finally, in the absence of active participation in MDMP, sustainers always have the "CSS rehearsal" to put the plan together. But what happens if the rehearsal isn't conducted (as we all know is what usually occurs....)

Conducting the Sustainment MDMP is essential in integrating the Sustainment War Fighting Functional Area (WFFA) into the organizations plan and for ensuring a synchronized and supportable course of action. Successful integration is a result of having the right personnel, available tools, correct MDMP doctrine & methodology, and synchronized timeline throughout the process. If this guide can assist sustainment planners in accomplishing this process, then it has accomplished its intent and mission.

Dr. John M. Menter, CPL, Mar 2015

CHAPTER 1

ARMY TRANSFORMATION & THE BIRTH OF MODULARITY

1. Background. Beginning shortly after the advent of September 11th, 2001, the US Army began a complete reorganization of its structure in light of the changes to the world brought about by the end of the Cold War to create a force that was *light enough* in order to be rapidly transported to any part of the world, *yet heavy enough* to withstand enemy armor heavy counterattack operations. Army Transformation initially started in the mid 1990's as "*Force XXI*", these changes and reorganizations gained momentum as the US Army began offensive operations within Afghanistan (Operation "*Enduring Freedom*" – or *OEF*) and Iraq (Operation "*Iraqi Freedom*").

> *"When the army is landed, the business is half done"*
> *- Maj. Gen James Wolf at the Battle of Quebec, 1759*

a. The Strategic Army Corps. Ever since the late 1950's, Army planners (in conjunctions with their US Air Forces counter-parts) envisioned the creation of a "*Strategic Army Corps or STRAC*" comprised of a Corps like structure that could be transported to hotspots anywhere in the world within a week. In time STRAC was a designation given to the <u>XVIII Airborne</u>

Corps at Fort Bragg, North Carolina. The designation was, in reality, the assignment of an additional mission rather than a true designation. The additional mission was to provide a flexible strike capability that could deploy worldwide on short notice without declaration of an emergency. The 4th Infantry Division (Mech) (then stationed at Fort Lewis, WA), and the 101st Airborne Division at Fort Campbell, Kentucky, were designated as STRAC's first-line divisions, while the 1st Infantry Division (Mech) at Fort Riley, Kansas, and the 82nd Airborne Division at Fort Bragg were to provide backup in the event of general war. The 5th Logistical Command (later inactivated), also at Fort Bragg, would provide the corps with logistics support, while Fort Bragg's XVIII Airborne Corps Artillery would control artillery units.

Although STRAC's mission was to provide an easily deployable force for use in a limited war or other emergency, its ability to deploy overseas was limited by airlift constraints. Without the declaration of a national emergency allowing DoD unconstrained use of the US flagged airlines of the Civil Reserve Air Fleet (CRAF), the required lift assets would not be released to support a STRAC deployment. The concept of STRAC was tested to a limited basis during the Berlin Crisis (1961) with the deployment of the 3rd Armored Cavalry Regiment to Germany within 30 days, and was ready for full implementation during the Cuban Missile Crisis (1962). Ultimately STRAC died a quiet death in the late 1960's with the XVIII Airborne Corps continuing to assume the role of a rapid response force for the duration of the 20th Century.

b. Exercise REFORGER (from REturn of FORces to GERmany). The REFORGER exercises were designed to prove U.S. Army's ability to move large conventional military forces rapidly from the continental United States to Central Europe in the event of a conflict with the Soviet Union. The first exercise was conducted in 1967, when due to the increasing pressures and cost of the Vietnam War, the United States Army announced plans to withdraw 28,000 troops (roughly two divisions) from Europe in 1968. To demonstrate its continued commitment to NATO, the US agreed to a large scale force deployment of not less than three brigades of a single division to Europe in an annual exercise. Thus was born REFORGER, which both tested the ability of conventional forces to fight in a conventional war scenario and demonstrated American determination.

REFORGER was not merely for show—in the event of a conflict, it would be the actual plan to strengthen the NATO presence in Europe. In the instance of armed conflict within central Europe, it would have been referred to as **Operation REFORGER**. Important components in REFORGER included the Military Airlift Command, the Military Sealift Command, and the Civil Reserve Air Fleet.

While REFORGER clearly demonstrated American resolve and support for NATO, it wasn't until REFORGER '83 that an American Division (1ˢᵗ Cavalry Division) became the "First unit to train as a 9,000 man division-size element in Northern Europe." This was the first U.S. unit deployment to Holland and Northern Germany since World War II. By April 1993, the last REFORGER was undertaken (a mere shadow of the original), conducted largely as computer-driven logistical exercise. This last exercise included only a portion of one unit from the United States.

For REFORGERs training value, it became clear that extensive preparation of pre-positioned equipment and stocks within Europe was required before the arrival of any rapidly deployable US force. The US Navy's Military Sealift Command's (and to a lesser extent the US Air Force's Military Airlift Command) ability to rapidly move large (and heavy) forces from the United States to Europe (or anywhere within the world for that matter) remained largely untested until August 1990 with the commencement of *Operation "Desert Shield."*

A US M60A1 tank moves through a village in
West Germany, as part of REFORGER '82 Exercise

c. Army Division 86, Army of Excellence (AOE), and *"Force XXI"*. At the conclusion of the Vietnam War and shortly after the Arab-Israeli "Yom Kippur War", then Chief of Staff of the Army, General Creighton Abrams, chaired a board of senior officials to focus on the next series of key weapons systems that the Army would require to fight future foes. Out of this was born the M1 *"Abrams"* Main Battle Tank, the M2/3 *"Bradley"* Infantry Fighting Vehicle, the AH-64 *"Apache"* Attack Helicopter, and the MIM-104 *"Patriot"* Air Defense System, and the M270 Multiple Launched Rocket System (MLRS), with all being fielded with the decade of the late 1970's and early 1980's. With the fielding of new systems coupled with a revised doctrine dismissing the former embraced "Active Defense" which had been the cornerstone of tactical operations within NATO, change was in the air and was coined "Army (or Division) '86.

In short, within the Division 86 heavy divisions, much of the structure of which survived into the early 1980s Army, numbered approximately 20,000 men. Divisions were organized as 6 tank battalions and 4 mechanized infantry battalions in its armor version, 5 and 5 in its mechanized infantry form. It added a significant new component in an air cavalry attack brigade (complete with the division's aviation assets and cavalry squadron), and it expanded the division artillery into batteries of 8 howitzers. It departed the World War II and ROAD triangular principle by strengthening each maneuver battalion from 3 line companies to 4 and adding TOW missile companies and other changes. Within the Division Support Commands (DISCOM), the Maintenance, Transportation, Quartermaster, and Medical Battalions were reconfigured into three Forward Support Battalions (each with Supply & Transport, Maintenance, and Medical Company) and a Main Support Battalion. These organizational changes could only work by adding additional combat service support structure to the organization. Before long, tactical units became "too fat" for use in a global contingency outside the plains of Germany.

By the early to mid 1980's, it also became apparent that pre Army Division 86 existing unit Tables of Equipment (commonly referred to as a "TOE") were insufficient to accommodate the logistical requirements needed to sustain readiness. Typical of this insufficiency were US armor battalions and cavalry squadrons equipped with the new M-1 tank. Fuel consumption quadrupled and soon overwhelmed the capacity of the unit's support platoon. Newer (and more complex) systems required more extensive maintenance organizations and sophisticated mechanics. Changes were not simply of a logistical nature – newer systems had an impact on doctrine as well as the Army began adaptation of its just release *Airland Battle* concept. These newly fielded systems scheduled for production and fielding in the 1980s presented an even greater leap ahead in combat power as demonstrated during Brigade Combat Team rotations at the Army's National Training Center, Fort Irwin, California.

The Army of Excellence (or "*AOE*") model followed shortly after as the US Army's effort to remedy this situation by the design and creation of a new, strategically deployable light infantry division limited in strength to approximately 10,000 personnel, globally deployable in approximately 500 airlift sorties.

Creation of the AOE light infantry division embodied a noteworthy turn in the history of Army tactical organization. With it, the Army fashioned a division for use primarily in the contingency world, with only a collateral mission for reinforcement of heavy forces and only then where terrain and circumstance called for it. Ordinarily it would fight in components as part of an integrated heavy/light or light/heavy force. The light infantry division gave the Army a new and necessary flexibility. Force structure decisions followed which converted two non-mechanized infantry divisions to the new type and added two more in the Active Army and one in the reserve components for a total of five light infantry divisions. Army division totals in the AOE reorganization went from 16 Active Army and 8 Army National Guard to 18 and 10, respectively.

This organization, while functional for the time being, did have its problems. Primary criticisms of the light infantry division were that it was too light, lacked tactical mobility, long range artillery, a roust anti-armor capability, and that its likely adversaries in the increasingly heavily armed third world would out gun, outmaneuver, and defeat it. This was clearly demonstrated at the Fort Irwin high desert training area in March 1983 during an exercise when the 40th Infantry Division (Mech) (California Army National Guard) overran a newly deployed brigade of the 82nd Airborne Division. But in the context of the more powerful corps to which it belonged, the AOE heavy division found general acceptance. There was recognition that the corps together with its divisions retained, as a unit, very strong combat power and that it constituted the right doctrinal answer.

Accompanying the debate of the light division was evolving support for the utility of heavy/light or light/heavy mixes of forces. Such mixes made good tactical sense where mission, enemy, terrain, troops, and time available - the "METT-T" considerations of doctrine - dictated the need and the wisdom of mixed forces. From the logistician's point of view, it was a nightmare, with CSS units insufficiently equipped to hand non-routine unit attachments. Heavy units lacked transport support for attached light infantry, while light infantry units could not substantially maintain attached armor/mech units. It was often said within the light infantry community that AOE was "nothing more than the Army's turning a soldier into a pack mule."

In August 1990, Iraq invaded its neighbor Kuwait. This aggression prompted an immediate response from the United Nations of which the United States took the lead in assembling coalition forces in Saudi Arabia to defend the Saudi's and eject Iraqi forces from Kuwait. Within a short time, it became readily clear that the concept of rapidly moving US forces from the continental United States to the Middle East "ala REFORGER" was broken beyond repair. Instead of a rapid response of heavy forces beyond deployment of the XVIII Airborne Corps (*Operation Desert Shield*), it would take almost six months to generate sufficient combat power to begin *Operation Desert Storm.* The weight problem of these heavy forces envisioned to fight in central Europe had come home to roost.

In 1993, the US Army's Training and Doctrine Command (TRADOC) had written a new, more versatile, fundamental operational doctrine to fit the new strategic circumstances of a smaller, primarily U.S. based force projection Army to reflect the redraw of forces from Germany and the overall draw down of the US Army in the wake of the Cold War ending. That design project, titled Force XXI, began on 8 March 1994 when Chief of Staff of the Army, General Gordon R. Sullivan, directed the start of a major campaign effort to create a new and highly effective fighting force for the 21st century. Progressing toward incremental realization at the year 2000, the Force XXI redesign was the last of the major operational Army reorganizations of the 20th century and would supersede the Army of Excellence which had been implemented in the mid-1980s. It was the first force redesign effort in which a full panoply of newly-emergent, computer-driven constructive and virtual simulation methods, equipment, and software were joined to actual live field simulation to test and analyze new military unit designs. In addition, the multiyear Force XXI design effort was the first to invent and embody for those fighting units a linked, instantaneous common operating picture and situational awareness of the close and distant events of the unfolding battle. "Digitization" was the rubric given this revolutionary emerging capability.

One of the key structure changes of Force XXI was the creation of "*Forward Support Companies*" out of the combat arms maneuver battalions and attaching them to the Brigade's Forward Support Battalions. Here, the battalion's Support and Maintenance Platoons were pulled out of the unit and combined into a separate structure acting as a single unit. Combat Arms battalions shrank from four companies to three, along with the removal of a corresponding service support slice from the Headquarters Company.

FORCE XXI was the structural organization largely in place throughout most of the US Army as it entered the 21st Century. For all it's innovations in digital Command and Control (C2), leveraged automation systems, and logistics support restructuring, FORCE XXI was still a large, heavy division-centric force that still lacked strategic deploy ability.

d. Army Transformation & Modularity. Two major but entirely separate actions occurred at the close of the 20th Century that would ultimately intertwine to undermine the FORCE XXI structure. The first was the publication of a book in 1996 by Colonel Douglas MacGregor named "*Breaking the Phalanx: A New Design for Landpower in the 21st Century[1].*" Here, MacGregor basically wrote that with technology and resourcing, today's maneuver brigades would dominate the

---

1   Breaking the Phalanx: A New Design for Landpower in the 21st Century by Douglas A. Macgregor, Center for Strategic and International Studies (Washington, D.C.) Published by Greenwood Publishing Group, 1997, ISBN 0275957942, 9780275957940

battlefield with division's reduced to simple Command and Control (C2) Centers (after all, this is how the Israeli Army fights with their brigades). Massive divisional structures would give way to smaller, more agile (and easily transportable) Brigade Combat Teams. Needless to say, MacGregor's thesis was met with mixed reviews within the Army community, much of which still dominated by the Cold War Generals in charge. But in 2000, George Bush was elected President and with him came a new Secretary of Defense - Donald Rumsfeld. One of Rumsfeld's first orders of business was the restructuring of the US Army to a more agile, easier deployable, brigade-centric force to distant theaters within the world (the lessons of the ill fated 55 day deployment an Apache2 Attack Helicopter battalion from the 11th Aviation Brigade in Germany to Albania in support of Operation *"Allied Force"* in Kosovo, April 1999 bore this out). It was fate that these two

---

2   Planning for Task Force Hawk didn't start until March 30th 1999; even though, the planning for Operation Allied Force had begun in the winter of 1998. Gen Clark and Admiral James O. Ellis, discussed how to utilize the Apaches to augment the Air Force assets posed to strike in 4 days. The Army's planners would be strapped for time to put together a plan to deploy a mission that had never been employed by an AH-64 Apache unit Instead of supporting ground troops the Apaches would be supporting Air Force missions. Gen. Clark's vision for the unit was to destroy the Yugoslavian units stationed in Kosovo supporting the Serbian police force. The Yugoslavian units were not formed in their typical company or battalion sized formations but rather spread out through the countryside. This made acquiring the targets and relaying the information to bomber units who couldn't spot them easily. It was projected that the Apache units would be able to identify and eliminate these targets more efficiently, due to their effectiveness during Operation Desert Storm. By March 22, 1999, Army planners finished with the initial plans for operation. These plans projected that the forces would be deployed to Macedonia, but the Macedonian government refused to allow offensive NATO operations to be spared from their country. "Army planners in Germany learned the mission would probably be cancelled on the Friday before Easter." Many soldiers would be given their first day off in weeks; however, on April 3rd, Gen. Clark decided to deploy the task force. It was announced on April 4th, by the Department of Defense that Task Force Hawk would be deployed to Albania to assist in Operation Allied Force. The original size of the task force was estimated at 2000 but had to be increased due to the lack of force protection that was present in Macedonia.

personalities would meet as philosophical equals in regards to Army reorganization. Transformation gained additional momentum in Oct 2001 when Army Planners in planning Operation *Enduring Freedom*, struggled to find a suitable, yet adequate (hence modular) structure to support US – SOF operations in Afghanistan in the wake of the September 11th World Trading Center bombing by Al Qaeda. By 2004, a new (and radical) unit organizational structure was at last developed and released that would use the best of FORCE XXI, but focus at the Brigade-centric level, thus giving arise to what is today referred to as "Army Transformation."

Under Army Transformation, traditional divisional brigades are reorganized into Brigade Combat Teams[3], designed to operate without outside support for three days with only supplies and fuel aboard their vehicles when they roll away from the aircraft delivering them to an area of operations.

Key to the success of transformed Brigade Combat teams required their deployment capability to go anywhere within the world within 96 hours, a full division within 120 hours, and five divisions on the ground within 30 days. Every piece of equipment belonging to the newly formed Brigade Combat Team had to be transportable within either a C-130 or C-17 aircraft, and required minimal RSO (Reception, Staging, & Onward Movement) support. From this point, the Brigade Combat Team would leave the Aerial Point of Embarkation (APOE) to operate without any further support for a minimum of three days. Additionally, BCTs are designed for field-level maintenance self-sufficiency with no reliance on EAB field maintenance support.

---

3   The idea of a Brigade-centric force was not uncommon – most divisional brigades undergoing a combat training rotation at the National Training Center, Fort Irwin from 1985 to 2000, would add addition transport & maintenance (from the base division's Main Support Battalion), a military intelligence company (for the division's MI Battalion), signal assets (from the division's Signal Battalion), and so on, often swelling up from a base strength of 1,700 to 4,000 soldiers per rotation.

Along with the reorganization of Active/Reserve Component divisional combat brigades, the ARNG Separate Enhanced Brigades (eSBs) were also transformed into modular Brigade Combat Teams, each composed of two maneuver battalions, and one reconnaissance (i.e. 'Cavalry') Squadron, along with a Fires Battalion (105 mm for IBCTs and SBCTs, 155mm for ABCTs) (See Fig 1-1 below) which continue to evolve to this day. As of this writing, there are fielded:

> AC: *33 BCTs (12 Armored, 14 Inf/Light, 7 Stryker), aligned into 10 Divisions
> ARNG: **28 BCTs (7 Armored, 20 Inf/Light, 1 Stryker), aligned/affiliated within 8 Divisions
> * 2 More BCTs are scheduled for deactivation TAA 18-22.
> ** Under TAA 18-22, the ARNG could go down to a low of
> 315K (5 Armored, 18 Inf/Light, 1 Stryker)

As the US Army emerges from over ten years of the Global War on Terror (GWOT)/Overseas Contingency Operations (OCO), the typical paradigm of downsizing rears its head as the US Armed Forces downsize to a new (acceptable?) strength under the doctrine of Unified Land Operations (ULO). Is Army Transformation and modularity complete? As of this writing, the Brigade Combat Team described above is again reorganizing, transforming the Special Troops Battalion into the new Brigade Engineer Battalion (losing its Military Police platoon, but picking up an extra Engineer Platoon). This new BEB structure is fortunate in picking up its own Forward Support Company. Additional, whether an Armored, Infantry, of Stryker Brigade, the good news is the aforementioned Brigades will all pick up an additional maneuver battalion, bringing to the brigade back to three maneuver battalions (as it was in the Army of Excellence days). The bad news is the Brigade Support Battalion will lose its bulk water and fuel capability; more mouths to feed, more vehicles to fuel, with less capability to accomplish this task. Debate continues to this day was to the size of the Cavalry Squadron (back to the Brigade Reconnaissance Troop or eliminated entirely) as well as determining the very size of the Brigade HQ's (upwards of losing 50+ personnel from its MTOE). Sustainers will be challenged in meeting these new manning requirements in future operations.

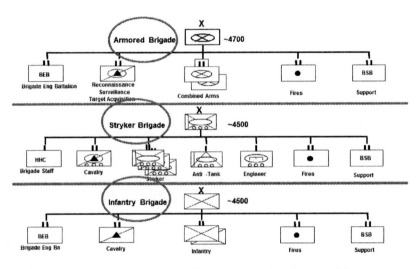

Figure 1-1 Brigade Combat Team Organization and Structure

2. What has changed under "Transformation" for the Logistician?

Over the past decade since the inception of Army Transformation and Modularity, many organizational structural designs and naming conventions (UEx, UEy to name a few) have taken place. While the Operational side (Army, Corps and Divisions) remain in hierarchy similar to their past counterparts, the logistics redesign is revised, largely to reduce layering, redundancy, while expanding capability. (See Figure 1-2).

What is Different...What is Changing
The "New" Look of Sustainment

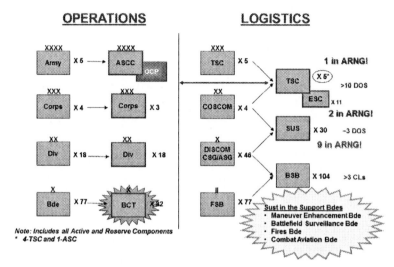

Figure 1-2 The New Look of Sustainment Support

First item to note is the elimination of the Corps/Area Support Groups, and the Corps/Division Support Commands (COSCOM/DISCOM), transferring and realigning these unit capabilities into the new "Sustainment Brigade" (More on the Sustainment Brigade capabilities below). Per Para 1-3, ATP 4-93[4], the role of the Sustainment Brigade is defined as follows:

> *"The sustainment brigade is a flexible, modular head-quarters organization capable of conducting multiple missions, and is a key organization in linking sustainment support from the operational to tactical levels... The Sustainment Brigade provides the sustainment needed by Army forces to enable operational reach, freedom of action, and prolonged endurance, thereby enabling Army forces to conduct decisive action."*

---

4   9 August 2013Final

Additionally, the old AOE Theater-Army Command (TAACOM) is replaced with a more streamline Theater Sustainment Command (TSC)[5]. To assist the TSC Commander, the Expeditionary Support Command (ESC) is created to assist in the coordination and conduct of distribution operations within the theater/area of responsibly.

Breaking this down further, Figures 1-3 & 1-4 depicts roles and responsibility migration of material management functions from AOE to Modular structures.

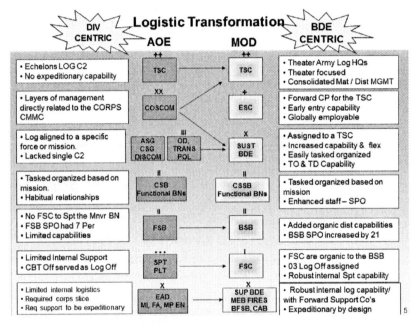

Figure 1-3 Migration of Logistics Functions AOE to Modular

The total migration of material management sustainment functions from AOE to transformed – modular sustainment structures is outlined below in Figure 1-3.

---

5   TSCs may also be known as SC(T), while ESCs are sometimes referred to as SC(E)., however neither nomenclature are in use today.

Materiel Management Functions
From the Army of Excellence (AOE) to the Modular Force

AOE	Category	Modular Force
• Property Book Management – Division: DMMC – Non-Division: Embedded PBO at Brigade • Asset Visibility: DMMC/CMMC/TMMC	Class VII Property Accountability Asset Visibility	• Property Accountability: BDEs (BCTs and SPT BDEs) with embedded PBOs • Asset Visibility: Division/Corps/Army Service Component Command (ASCC) G–4
• DMMC, CMMC, TMMC – Overlapping redundancy	General Supplies Class I, Water, Class IIIB	• TSC, ESC (if utilized), SUST BDE DMC manages stocks • BCT requirements sent to TSC/ESC DMC through supporting SUS BDE
• DMMC (DAO): Coordinates and controls Class V use within the Division • CMMC: Managed Corps CSAs/ASPs • TMMC: Managed Theater TSA/ASPs • TMMC ICW ASCC G–3: Establish CSRs	Class V	• BSB BAO: Coord BCT requirements • Div/Corps G–4: Planning and oversight • TSC/ESC/SUST BDE: Manage stocks, issues MROs to CSSBs ASAs • TSC ICW ASCC G–3: Establishes CSRs/Stockage Obj/NICP requisitions
• DMMC/CMMC/TMMC with duplication at Division/Corps/Theater G–4	Maintenance/ Readiness Management	• BSB: maint mgmt/readiness for its BCT • Division/Corps G–4: Monitors readiness information for CDR, establishes priorities, write plans/orders
• Managed by hierarchal MMCs (DMMC, CMMC, TMMC) • Each level conducted manager reviews with SARSS–2 boxes • SARSS data communicated to hierarchal boxes (SARSS–1 to SARSS–2A/D to SARSS–2A/C)	Demand Supported Class II, IIIP, IV, IX	• SUST BDE single face to the customer • Overall centralized management at the TSC/ASC or ESC (if utilized) • Time sensitive RIC GEO functions pushed to SUST BDEs as required • SARSS–1 data communicated to CTASC directly

Figure 1-4 Migration of Material Management Functions

Combat Sustainment Support Battalions (CSSBs) are an inherent key structure functioning as the workhorse of the Sustainment Brigade. They are the distribution link between the theater base, Aerial /Sea Points of Entry/Departure (A/SPOE/D) and the supported units. Developed as an outgrowth of the AOE Corps Support Battalions, CSSB are multifunctional in nature with no two CSSB tasked organized alike. Per Para 3-1, ATP 4-93 (Sustainment Brigade):

> *'The role of the CSSB is to provide logistics support on an area basis to Army forces at EAB, or if required by its higher headquarters, to joint and multifunctional forces. This includes providing support to brigade combat teams, functional and multifunctional support brigades operating within the CSSB area.'*

Per Para 3-2, with the loss of bulk water generation and bulk fuel holding from BCTs, a new type of CSSB (Corps and Divisional) is developed to provide this support forward:

> *'When supporting BCTs and functional brigades, the CSSB may be specifically organized with a multi-capable quartermaster supply company (QSC) and a composite truck company. These companies provide water-purification, petroleum storage, and troop transport (IBCT only) to the BCT. When supporting multifunctional and functional brigades performing Corps missions such as out-of-sector operations, the CSSB will also be specifically organized with the same multi-capable quartermaster supply company and composite truck company to augment the support brigade logistics capability. Other CSSBs are organized with functional logistics a units based on mission requirements.'*

During operations in Iraq and Afghanistan, CSSBs often times operated as a headquarters for groupings of contractor organizations (i.e. 'White') responsible for delivering commodities and support. This concept was further modified in the closing days of *Operation Enduring Freedom* (OEF), where CSSBs served as the lynch pin for the CENTCOM Material Recovery Element (CMRE), identifying and coordinating the drawdown, recovery, and disposition of material and property from Afghanistan to the Continental United States (CONUS).

The sustainment support structure found within the modular brigade is the Brigade Support Battalion (BSB). One of the single greatest impacts on the transformed brigade size organizations was the placement of both a network support (i.e. signal) unit within the Brigade's Special Troops Battalion and a dedicated logistical support structure – the Brigade Support Battalion (BSB). While remarkable that this capability is now found within these newly transformed Brigade structures – not all BSBs are alike. (see Chapter 2 on BSBs)

The creation of the BSB addresses an issue plaguing divisional Brigade Commander's since the creation of the Forward Support Battalions in the mid 1980's; who owns the unit and who is the Brigade Logistician? Followers of the FM 63 series will tell you the FSB is owned by the DISCOM Commander and that the FSB Cdr is the Brigade Logistician. Maneuver Commanders will cite the FM 71-123, counter claiming that the Brigade Commander owns the FSB and the Brigade S-4 is the Brigade Logistician. Under transformation, the BSB is established as an integral component of the Brigade with its commander as the Brigade's Sustainment Operator. Like it's FORCE XXI predecessor, BCT & Support Brigade BSBs come with a Forward Support Company for each of the Brigade's organic battalions

On a final note regarding transformed sustainment and support to organizations, it is important to note that:

1) There is one TSC assigned per theater AOR. All TSCs are aligned with a corresponding Army Service Component Command (ASCC).

2) Intitially as modularity came on line (and abundant rsources were available), Sustainment Brigades worked for either the TSC or the ESC Commander. They are not assigned to Corps or Divisions (hence why they own their own Distinctive Unit Insignia – DUI). This has changed recently. By July 2015, all Active Component Sustainment Brigades will be aligned with an associate division headquarters, with Army National Guard Sustainment Brigades following suit thereafter. Soldiers within these sustainment brigades (to include subordinate units) will now wear the supported division patch. Finally, these units will be redesignated so the sustainment brigade is called a '*division sustainment brigade*' and is numbered the same as its supported division. (Ex: the 4th Sustainment Brigade supporting the 4th Infantry Division is now referred to as the 4th Division Sustainment Brigade)

3) There is no rule of allocation of Sustainment Brigades required to support a Corps or Division. Allocation is based on requirements and workload. Concurrently, subordinate combat sustainment support battalions are organized with any combination of subordinate units from the force pool.

4) Medical organizations are designed and tailored to support the force. They are not subordinate to the Sustainment Brigade, but rather to the Medical Deployment Support Command (MDSC) via the locally assigned Medical Brigade. Human Resource – HR (Personnel and Finance) units are also modular configured and scalable based on METT-TC. *It is important to note that Medical Brigades do not work for (but in conjunction with) Sustainment Brigades.*

6) All modular transformed brigades (combat and multifunctional) possess a Brigade Support Battalion[6]. The same cannot be said for "functional" (i.e. Engineer, Military Police, Chemical, Ordnance/EOD, & ADA) brigades. Support relations need to be coordinated and established for these structures. Most if not all sustainment (formerly known as "Combat Service Support") battalions work for a Sustainment Brigade. The only exception is the Brigade Support Battalion.

7) Most maneuver (formerly known as "Combat Arms") and maneuver support (formerly known as "Combat Support) battalions have attached Forward Support Companies. Military Police, EOD, Civil Affairs/Psyops, ADA & SOF battalions do not. Like functional brigades, support relations need to be established for these structures.

---

6   The exception here is the Battlefield Surveillance Brigade which possesses a Brigade Support Company (BSC) in lieu of a Brigade Support Battalion. Within the Combat Aviation Brigade, the BSB is referred to as the Aviation Support Brigade or "ASB".

3. Changes in Latitudes, Changes in Attitudes – the revision of Combat Service Support into the new Sustainment Doctrine.

As CSS structure transformed from the rapidly obsolete AOE into modular 'sustainment' type formations (see Figure 1-3 above), it was inevitable that CSS doctrine would need to change as well to reflect the leveraged capabilities inherent with the creation of the new distribution-based units/nodes and the employment of logistics automation.

Logistics Transformation

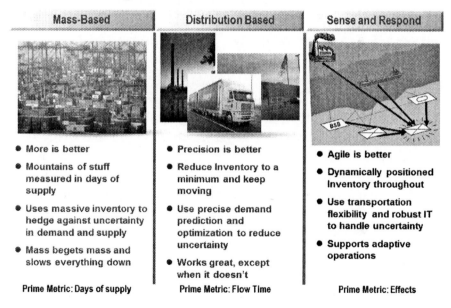

Mass-Based	Distribution Based	Sense and Respond
● More is better	● Precision is better	● Agile is better
● Mountains of stuff measured in days of supply	● Reduce Inventory to a minimum and keep moving	● Dynamically positioned Inventory throughout
● Uses massive inventory to hedge against uncertainty in demand and supply	● Use precise demand prediction and optimization to reduce uncertainty	● Use transportation flexibility and robust IT to handle uncertainty
● Mass begets mass and slows everything down	● Works great, except when it doesn't	● Supports adaptive operations
Prime Metric: Days of supply	Prime Metric: Flow Time	Prime Metric: Effects

Figure 1-5 Continued Evolution of Military Logistics

One goal of a transformed logistics[7] system is to eliminate reliance on stockpiles located at each echelon from the Brigade to

---

7   A general definition of logistics is "the process of anticipating customer needs and wants; acquiring the capital, material, people, technologies, and information necessary to meet those needs and wants; optimizing the goods-or service-producing

the Theater level (the so called massed based "Iron Mountains"). These stockpiles are vulnerable to enemy attack, difficult to move, and reduce the tactical commander's flexibility.

Operation Shield/Desert Storm typified the difficulties associated with the length of time required to assemble the required amount of supplies to support 3rd US Army's offensive operations into Kuwait[8]. Support to the Persian Gulf provided an example of the problems facing the defense distribution system throughout the 1990s. Although combat performance had been justifiably esteemed across the board, there were significant problems in logistics support. Distribution times were long, variable, and unpredictable, due largely to inefficient processes, clogged ports, and a myriad of other problems. The result was materiel often took more than 35 days to get out of the United States.

The answer would evitable would be found within the civilian sector which had undergone a revolution throughout the late 1980's, creating in distribution based systems, slimming down warehousing operations and replacing it with "velocity management." Thus was born *"Supply-chain" Management* logistics.

What is *Supply-Chain Management?* It is the system relationship among transportation, inventory requirements, warehousing, exterior packaging, materials handling, and some activities or cost centers involved. More important, technological improvements in inventory management, bar coding, transport tracking allowed for cost saving by reducing warehouse inventory and giving customers the ability to track in bound shipments, allowing for "just-in-time" deliveries.

---

network to fulfill customer requests; and utilizing the network to fulfill customer requests in a timely way."

8   As documented in "Moving Mountains – Lessons in Leadership and Logistics from the Gulf War" by LTG (R) William G. Pagonis (Boston, Harvard Business School Press, 1992) ISBN 0-87584-508-8

Put another way, *Supply-Chain Management* can be viewed as a pipeline or conduit for the efficient and effective flow of products, materials, services, information, and financials from the supplier's suppliers through the various intermediate organizations/companies out to the customer's customers or the system of connected logistics networks between the original vendors and the ultimate final customer. By the time the US Armed Forces began to adapt these practices in the late 90's and the beginning of the 21st century, they had been honed to a fine (and efficient) science by such companies as General Motors, Target Stores, nearly all major grocery store chains, and the master practitioner of the supply-chain management concept – Wal-Mart!

How does this apply within the military environment? Distribution in the new logistics system substitutes speed for mass. This transformed logistics system combines situational understanding by way of the Common Operational Picture (COP) and capabilities with efficient delivery systems to form a seamless distribution pipeline. The supply pipeline becomes the warehouse and represents inventory in motion. (Figure 1-6)

The logistics imperative of increased velocity reduces both organizational and material layering (thus the elimination of the Division and Corps Material Management Centers or "MMCs"). Logisticians control the destination, speed, and volume of the distribution system. With In-Transit Visibility (ITV), Total Asset Visibility (TAV), advanced materiel management, and advanced decision support system technology, logisticians will have access and visibility over all items within the distribution pipeline.

It is this technology that allows logisticians to divert, cross-level, and mass logistics assets anywhere, anytime to support the maneuver commander. Logisticians maintain situational awareness of the battlefield via the Logistics Common Operating Picture, otherwise known as the *"LCOP"*, which greatly facilitates logistics planning and execution.

Military Distribution Simplified

Sustainment	+	Movement	+	Force Protection	=	Distribution
LOG REPORTING		TMR/STMR		Convoy Security Process		
Distro Matrix		Distro Matrix		Distro Matrix		
Critical Reports		Critical Reports		Critical Reports		
Manifesting		Manifesting				
STAMIS		MSR/ASR Status		MSR/ASR Status		

Figure 1-6 Military Distribution Simplified[9]

On a final note, with the recent 22 February 2011 publication of FM 3-0 (Operations), the US Army's longstanding love affair with the term "Combat Service Support" as an oversimplified definition of logistics has come to an end. The new term used to denote the Army's replenishment process of her units is "*Sustainment*". Per Para 4-47, FM 3-0, Sustainment is defined as:

> "*The sustainment warfighting function is the related tasks and systems that provide support and services to ensure freedom of action, extend operational reach, and prolong endurance*. The endurance of Army forces is primarily a function of their sustainment. *Sustainment determines the depth and duration of Army operations*. It is essential to retaining and exploiting the initiative. Sustainment provides the support for logistics, personnel services, and health service (excluding force health protection, which is a component of the protection warfighting function) necessary to maintain operations until mission accomplishment. Internment,

---

9   LTC James H. "Cotton" Henderson, *The Process of Military Distribution Management*, (Bloomington, Authorhouse, 2006) p. 6.

resettlement, and detainee operations fall under the sustainment warfighting function and include elements of all three major subfunctions. FM 4-0 describes the sustainment warfighting function, and FM 4-02 discusses the Army Health System."

Such is the magnitude of this change that FM 4-0 "Combat Service Support" was in rewritten in 2009 to reflect this change and was released as FM 4-0 "Sustainment". In 2011, the U.S. Army Combined Arms Support Command (CASCOM) published Army Doctrinal Publication (ADP) 4-0 "Sustainment" in order to further define and refine this emerging concept, targeting this publication towards middle and senior leadership of the Army, officers in the rank of major and above who command Army forces in major operations and campaigns or serve on the staff's that support those commanders.

A comparison of the old "Combat Service Support" FM with the new "Sustainment" FM is provided below.

COMPARISON OF OLD TO THE NEW

Topics of relevance in the current version will migrate to the draft

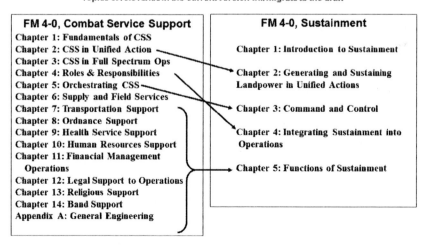

Figure 1-7 FM 4-0 "CSS" versus the new FM 4-0 "Sustainment"

Since its inception in late 2009, FM 4-0 continued to be modified along with its newly published sister publication ADRP 4-0 'Sustainment' in order to bring it in line with the evolution of contemporary military operations as the U.S. Army has moved from the concept of *'Full Spectrum Operations'* to its newly conceived 'Unified *Land Operations'* as defined within the doctrine supporting ADP 3-0 and ADRP 3-0.

SUSTAINMENT COMPARISON BETWEEN FM 4-0 (2009) and ADP 4-0 (2011)

FM 4-0, Sustainment (2009)	ADP 4-0, Sustainment (2011)
Chapter 1: Introduction to Sustainment	Chapter 1: Sustainment Warfighting Function
Chapter 2: Generating and Sustaining Landpower in Unified Actions	Chapter 2: Sustainment Principles
Chapter 3: Command and Control	Chapter 3: Sustainment in Support of Unified Land Operations
Chapter 4: Integrating Sustainment into Operations	Chapter 4: Sustainment of Decisive Action
Chapter 5: Functions of Sustainment	Conclusion

Figure 1-8 FM 4-0 (2009) versus the new ADP 4-0 "Sustainment"

It is not inconceivable that within the near future, perhaps within the decade, U.S. Army (as well as joint Service components) sustainment operations will mirror those performed by their civilian counterparts. However it is now defined in light of new technology and the completion of Army Modularity transition, the old time tested adage still rings true today:

Famous Saying:
Amateurs talk Tactics; Professionals talk Logistics
(now Sustainment)

CHAPTER 2

THE SUSTAINMENT BRIGADE, COMBAT SUSTAINMENT SUPPORT BATTALION (CSSB), & THE BRIGADE SUPPORT BATTALION (BSB)

*"We can get along without anything but food and ammo.
The road to glory cannot be followed with much baggage."
- Maj. Gen Richard Ewell, 1862*

1. Background. With the Army completed its reorganization from the AOE/FORCE XXI based TOEs into a modular "plug & play" based organization, sustainers were presented a series of new structures, ideally suited to support the emerging Brigade Combat Teams and the newly created Support Brigades (Maneuver Enhancement, Combat Aviation, Battlefield Surveillance, and Field Artillery Brigades). Each sustainment structure tasked organized in support of the combatant's mission, equipment, troops, terrain, time and civilian (METT-TC) considerations. These are the Sustainment Brigade, Combat Sustainment Support Battalion, and the Brigade Support Battalion[10].

---

10 For Combat Aviation Brigades, the BSB is referred to as the Aviation Support Battalion (ASB).

2. The Key Sustainment Organizations

a. The Sustainment Brigade. Sustainment Brigades are created as a logistical structure to bridge the gap between Brigade Combat Teams (BCTs)/Support Brigades and the Theater Sustainment Command/Expeditionary Sustainment Command in the wake of the elimination of the AOE Division Support Commands (DISCOMs) and Corps Support Commands (COSCOMs) and their affiliated Corps/Area Support Groups in order to create a more efficient and streamline distribution operation. Sustainment Brigades possess only one assigned organic unit – a Special Troops Battalion (STB), with all other subordinate units assigned per METT-TC. Sustainment Brigade's provide:

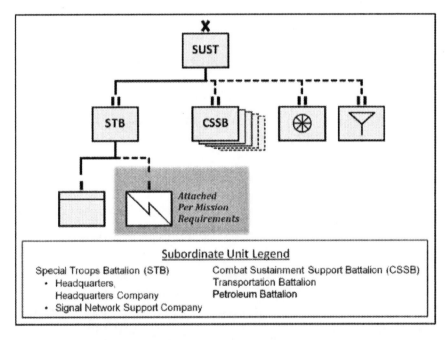

Figure 2-1 Generic Sustainment Brigade Mission and Capabilities.

Mission: Plans, synchronizes, monitors, and executes sustainment operations. Conducts distribution operations within assigned AO. Conducts Theater Opening and/or Theater Distribution

operations when directed. Provide support to joint, interagency, and multinational forces as directed.

Capabilities
- **Scalable tailorable brigade providing full spectrum support**
- **Configures for, distributes to, and retrogrades to and from maneuver BCTs, other Support Brigades, and to joint forces as directed**
- **Supports Theater opening or Theater distribution operations with augmentation**
- **Provides postal, replacement operations, strength management, casualty operations and essential personnel services as directed.**

* Distribution and distribution management of material to BCTs/Spt Bdes as part of a theater-wide distribution process. Sustainment Brigades were designed to be part of a single, distribution-based logistics system within the AOR.

* Area (GS) customer support to units within an assigned Area of Operations (AO), Mission Command by either the TSC[11] or affiliated ESC.

* Mission Command HQ's with a functioning Distribution Management Center (DMC) to manage the flow of logistics to the BCTs or assigned force.

Sustainment Brigade Missions. (See Figure 2-1) Sustainment Brigades, when task organized with CSSBs, Transportation Battalions, Movement Control Battalions, POL Supply Battalions and on occasion, a Transportation Theater Opening Element (TTOE)[12], are capable of conducting the flowing missions:

---

11   Starting July 2015, all AC Sustainment Brigades will be aligned with an associated AC Corps/Division HQ's. Shortly thereafter ARNG Sustainment Brigades will follow suit aligning with appropriate ARNG Div HQ's. USAR Sustainment Brigades are assigned against Regional Readiness Commands (RRCs) or ESCs.

12   TTOEs are programed to be removed from the force during TAA 18-22

* **Theater Opening (TO)** (Figure 2-2) consist of Mission Command of theater opening, Theater RSO,[13] initial theater sustainment contracting, establish rapid & effective port clearance, and provide physical security and force protection. Depicted below is a typical Sustainment Brigade organized for a Theater Opening (TO) mission:

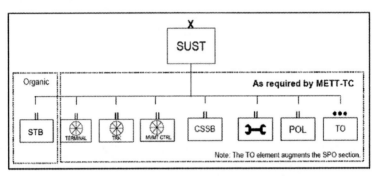

Figure 2-2 Sustainment Brigade assigned with a Theater Opening mission.

* **Theater Distribution (TD)** (Figure 2-3) consists configuring/ reconfiguring loads, storage of bulk supplies and ASL items, direction of the distribution of all supplies and services, provision of airdrop assistance, SOF operations, and theater ground distribution network maintenance. The TD also provides Total Asset Visibility (TAV)/In-Transit Visibility (ITV) over assets within the pipeline, operates regional hubs, movement control operations, and on order (O/O) deploys an EEE to establish a robust distribution operations beyond the theater base. Depicted below is a typical Sustainment Brigade organized for a Theater Distribution (TD) mission:

---

13 RSO defined is **Reception** (unloading, marshalling, and transporting), **Staging** (assembling, holding, and organizing), and **Onward Movement** (movement and delivery)

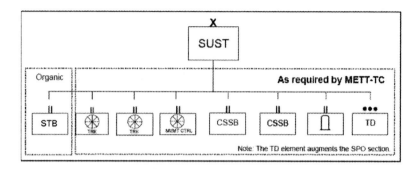

THEATER DISTRIBUTION ELEMENTS

*Figure 2-3 Sustainment Brigade assigned with a
Theater Distribution mission.*

  * **Operational & Tactical Sustainment Operations.** (Figure 2-4) The workhorse mission for the majority of Sustainment Brigades, Operational/Tactical Sustainment operations provide; supplies field service, field and selected sustainment level maintenance, recovery, and field feeding. Additionally, Sustainment Brigades missioned with operational/tactical sustainment may plan and conduct LSA (base) & base cluster self-defense, provide sustainment management information and advice to commanders and staff within its AOR, exercise technical supervision over operations for all sustainment units, and provide logistics systems management, plans, policies, and procedures for logistics automation systems. Sustainment Brigades assigned this mission are highly involved in providing local/regional contractual support. Other sustainment operations may include operations as part of an Army, Joint, Interagency, and Multinational (JIM) forces. Depicted below is a typical Sustainment Brigade organized for a basic tactical sustainment missions:

SUSTAINMENT ELEMENTS

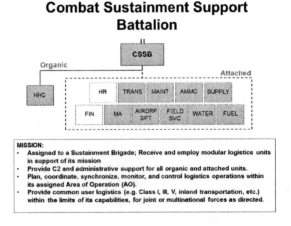

Figure 2-4 Generic Sustainment Brigade assigned with an Operational/ Tactical sustainment mission.

b. Combat Sustainment Support Battalion (CSSB). (See Figure 2-5) An integral component of the Sustainment Brigade, CSSBs, are also organized and configured per METT-TC conditions. In many regards, they may be thought of as a cross blending of the robustness of the Divisional Main Support Battalion coupled with the multifunctional capability of the Corps Support Battalion.

Combat Sustainment Support Battalion

MISSION:
- Assigned to a Sustainment Brigade; Receive and employ modular logistics units in support of its mission
- Provide C2 and administrative support for all organic and attached units.
- Plan, coordinate, synchronize, monitor, and control logistics operations within its assigned Area of Operation (AO).
- Provide common user logistics (e.g. Class I, III, V, inland transportation, etc.) within the limits of its capabilities, for joint or multinational forces as directed.

Figure 2-5 Generic Combat Sustainment Support Battalion.

Overall, the CSSB is a flexible, responsive, modular sustainment organization that is tailored to execute logistics sustainment throughout the depth of its assigned AO. Under the mission command of the Sustainment Brigade, a CSSB may consist of some or all of the functional companies shown: supply, ammunition, fuel, water, transportation, cargo transfer, aerial delivery, mortuary affairs, maintenance, and field services. CSSBs are capable of receiving and missioning HR and Finance management units, but these functions are typically assigned to the Sustainment Brigade's Special Troops Battalion (STB). The organic structure contains a command group and staff sections consisting of a S1 Section, S2/3 Section, S4 Section, S6 Section, Unit Ministry Team (UTM), and a Support Operations Team. This tailored sustainment framework enables the employment of a unit capable of quickly adapting to changing tactical conditions.

The CSSB is structured to optimize the use of sustainment resources (through situational understanding the LCOP) and therefore, minimizes the sustainment footprint in the AO.

Supported units rely heavily on CSSBs to meet sustainment requirements beyond their internal capabilities. It is important to note that CSSBs are tasked to support one to three, brigade sized maneuver or non-maneuver elements. The CSSB is the Sustainment Brigade element that provides the distribution link between the theater base, APOD, SPOD and the supported units. Its structure includes cargo transfer and movement control assets, fused with supply functions based on mission of assignment. The CSSB performs the function of transporting commodities to and from the maneuver BCTs/maneuver support brigade BSBs, and to/from theater repair or storage facilities. It maintains the flow of replenishment using Expeditionary Support Packages (ESP), to include retrograde of unserviceable components, end items and supplies. It also monitors distribution of sustainment replenishment that is throughput directly from the theater base by assets of the Corps Sustainment Brigade tasked with the theater distribution mission and, assisting with transportation coordination and delivery if necessary. Additionally, the CSSB augments/supplements supported units during the normal replenishment cycle, delivering sustainment that is not being throughput directly to units. The CSSB has organic maintenance capabilities for self-sustainment.

A typical CSSB mission statement reads:

> *"To provide mission command of assigned and attached units providing area support sustainment operations and limited distribution operations within its assigned area of operations."*

To accomplish this, CSSBs usually possess the following capabilities:

- Provide equipment maintenance support, tailorable to units assigned in its area of support.
- Provide Class I support.
- Provide transportation support within the area for local haul.
- Provide multiple SSA capability with Class II, III(P), IV, VII and IX.
- Distribution operations within an assigned AO.
- Establish and operate a Convoy Support Center (CSC).
- Provide field services including shower, laundry and clothing repair.
- Pack/Unpack containers during container operations.

In past operations, CSSBs may be configured for heavy, light, or area support operations.

In heavy operations, CSSB are configured with mostly heavy lift transportation elements (MDM, PLS,) heavy POL haul (M969 5K or M1062 7.5K tankers) and heavy equipment transporter (HET M1070s) systems. This configuration was typical of CSSBs employed in Iraq during the period 2005 until the cessation of combat operations in mid-late 2010.

In light operations, CSSB are configured with mostly to support troop lift transportation elements (LT/MDM) limited POL/Water haul and airdrop operations. This was typical of CSSBs employed in Afghanistan during the early years of Operation Enduring Freedom (OEF).

In area support operations, CSSB are configured with a balanced support mix for both light and limited heavy units as well as any aviation elements operating within the AO. This configuration was typical during the drawdown of Operation *Iraqi Freedom* (OEF) and Operation *New Dawn* (OND), and is also found in CSSBs employed in Afghanistan during the surge period of 2010. In a few instances during the closing days of Operations New Dawn, CSSBs were entirely composed of contractor (i.e. 'White') elements in lieu of typical 'Green' military organizations.

Regardless of the configuration of the CSSB, in all cases these organizations may be further augmented with contractor/LOGCAP support, depending on the level of security and maturity of the area of operations. During the OEF drawdown and into OND, it was fairly common to have a CSSB HQ's over seeing pure 'white' contractor operations with no attached 'green' sustainment units.

To accomplish their respective support missions, CSSBs are task organized with a number of functional company sized sustainment organizations. The following is a listing of the various company, platoon, and section units that might be found with the battalion:

*Transportation Units/Truck Companies. Transportation elements of the CSSB provide mobility of personnel ad all classes of supply (less Class VIII which is handled through medical channels). They are designed, equipped, and trained to meet Army sustainment needs by performing integrated transportation operations in support of '*Decisive Action*' operations (per FM

3-0, *Unified Land Operations*). Based on mission requirements, transportation units may include: Combat Heavy Equipment Transporter (M1070) Company, Light or Light/ Medium Truck Company, Medium Truck Company, Palletized Load System (PLS) Truck Company, Movement Control Battalion (MCB) or subordinate Movement Control Team (MCT). Truck Companies essentially provide transportation for movement of break bulk cargo, containers, bulk water/POL, heavy lift combat systems, reconfigured loads on flatracks, and of course, personnel.

* **Quartermaster Support Company (QSC).** Aside from the transportation elements, the QSC is the workhorse organization of the CSSB. QSC's provide Mission Command of two to four subsistence or area support platoons, providing food service and supervision/common tools for unit level maintenance. The QSC when typically task organized with one subsistence platoon and three area support platoon can provide the following support:

- Receive, store and issue a cumulative 94 STONs of CL I/ day
- Provide refrigeration for perishable rations and augment subsistence personnel at CL I issue point.
- Deliver perishable subsistence to CL supply points
- Receive, store, issue and account for 208 STONs of CL II, III (P), IV, and IX supplies.
- Each area support platoon can operate in two different locations.
- Provide limited configuration loads support.

* **Petroleum, Oil and Lubricant (POL) Supply Company (PSC).** The mission of the POL Supply Company (PSC) is to receive, store, issue, and distribute bulk POL products in support of Theater, Corps or Division operations. Based on task organization, PSCs provide the following support:

In tactical sustainment support, the PSC is authorized three (3) 50,000 gallon platoons with the capability to:

- Store 1.8M gallons of fuel.
- Receive/issue 600K gallons daily.
- Area Support Sections stores/receives/issues 360K gallons
- Distribution Sections transports 146,250 gallons daily.
- Establish and operate six hot refueling sites.

In operational sustainment support, the PSC is authorized three (3) 210,000 gallon platoons with the capability to:

- Store 5M gallons of fuel.
- Receive/issue 900K gallons daily.
- Area Support Sections stores/receives/issues 360K gallons.
- Distribution Sections transports 146,250 gallons daily.
- Establishes and operates six hot refueling sites.

CSSB's responsible for large POL storage and distribution may have a **POL Quality Analysis (QA) Team** attached. This team operates a local petroleum laboratory that performs complete specification and procurement acceptance testing of petroleum products received from supported units. The POL QA team capabilities include:

- Technical assistance for the storage, handling, identifying, sampling and quality evaluation of POL products & containers, for all US and Allied forces within the unit area of operations.
- Petroleum quality surveillance testing outside FOB conditions.
- "B-Level" quality surveillance testing on ground and aviation fuels, with limited "B-level" testing of packaged POL products using information to make recommendations for correct use, recycle and discard of product.

* **Quartermaster Field Service Company (FSC)**. The Quartermaster Field Service Company (also known as the SLCR Co) provides direct support (DS) shower, laundry, and clothing repair support for approximately 21,000 soldiers on an area basis. During mid-heavy combat operations, military personnel provide most if not all field service support in forward areas, while contractors/Host Nation Support (HNS) and LOGCAP providing much of the support in low combat/stability operations. Quartermaster Field Service Companies are capable of providing:

- Laundry services totaling 315K lbs of laundry/week based on 15 lbs/soldier per week in support of 21,000 troops.
- Each SLCR section can support 500 troops per day/3500 troops per week.
- Distribution for individual laundry with organic distribution assets providing 24-hour laundry service.
- Limited light textile repair.
- Unit level maintenance on organic equipment.
- Food service for assigned and attached personnel.
- Delousing service when deemed necessary by medical authority.

* **Support Maintenance Company/Component Repair Company**. The US Army's two level maintenance system uses modular designed field level maintenance units called *Support Maintenance Companies* (SMCs) and sustainment level maintenance units called *Component Repair Companies* (CRCs). These units are often supported by *Collection and Classification* (C&C) *Companies* that have the capability to attach classification teams forward, at the direction of the Distribution Management Center (DMC), to expedite component and end item repair & salvage into the distribution system. Each type of maintenance organization is built from a company HQs that is capable of commanding platoon/team level units. All of these maintenance units are found within CSSBs within a Sustainment Brigade.

First unit is the Support Maintenance Company (SMC) whose mission is to provide area support to all units within the Sustainment Brigade area of operations. It provides Corps & Division area support field maintenance, supports field level theater opening packages, and is capable of accepting modules (platoon, sections, and teams) from CRCs and C&Cs. Its mission is to provide mission command of cellular platoons, modules, and teams performing field maintenance (on system repair and replacement) and return to user operations. SMC capabilities include:

- Co HQs element that normally does not exceed 250 personnel
- Unit can integrate civilian augmentation (approx 10% of the overall unit strength) from the Logistics Support Element) as required.
- Provide mission staging operations.
- Conduct tactical and operational area field maintenance support.

The second maintenance support type unit is the Component Repair Company (CRC)[14]. Its mission is to provide sustainment level support to the theater supply system. CRCs are employed in any location within the distribution system beginning at the national source of repair. CRCs provide component repair capability and return the repaired item to the supply system, normally operating in conjunction with a Supply Support Activity (SSA). A CRC may attach platoons, sections, teams to an SMC or other sustainment units.

---

14   Scheduled to be removed from the force in TAA 18-22

The last maintenance support type unit is the Collection & Classification Company. C&C Cos establish and operate collection and classification facilities for the receipt, inspection, segregation, disassembly, preservation, and disposition of serviceable/unserviceable Class VII & IX material (except items unique to cryptographic material, missile systems, aircraft, airdrop equipment, unmanned aerial vehicles, and medical equipment) and similar foreign material.

* **Quartermaster Collection Company – Mortuary Affairs (MA)** provides mission command (MC) administrative, logistical, field feeding support, and unit level maintenance management to the company. These units are task organized with two (2) Forward Collection Platoons (FCPs) and one (1) Main Collection Platoon (MCP) capable of:

- Processing 240 remains and personal effects/day from up to twelve locations. This includes evacuation of remains to the MCP.
- MCP can process 400 remains daily.
- Coordinate evacuation of remains and personal effects to the Theater Mortuary Evacuation Point (TMEP).
- Operate a Mortuary Affairs Decontamination Control Point (MADCP) when supported by a chemical decontamination company.

* **Quartermaster Mortuary Affairs Company (MAC).** The MAC provides MC, administrative, logistical, and field feeding support and consolidated unit level maintenance for organic units. These units are organized with two personal effects platoons, two evacuation/mortuary platoons, and one collection platoon. This unit's capabilities are:

- Receiving, storing, safeguarding, inventorying, processing, and ensuring proper disposition of personal effects for approximately 500 remains.

- Standing up and operating a Theater Mortuary Evacuation Point (TMEP), which can process and evacuate up to 500 remains per day.
- Standing up and operating an in-theater mortuary when augmented with civilian personnel.
- Setting up and operating five Mortuary Affairs Collection Points (MACP) to receive, process, and coordinate 100 remains and personal effects per day from five separate locations. This includes the evacuation of remains to CONUS/OCONUS military mortuaries.

* **Quartermaster Water Purification and Distribution Company (WPDC).** The WPDC provides MC for two to four platoons for company level administration, unit supply, food service and unit maintenance. These units are typically task organized with two water purification platoons (using 6 3K/day ROWPU systems) and two water storage and distribution platoons. In this configuration, the WPDC is capable of:

- Producing 360K gallons of potable water using a fresh water source per day. (6 systems operating 20hrs/day) or 240K gallons of potable water using a salt water source per day.
- Water storage for 168K gallons of water.
- Static storage of 160K gallons of potable water at one location or 80K gallons at two locations.
- Distribution of up to 66K gallons of water per day based on 75 percent availability of equipment and two trips per day.

CSSB's assigned to Sustainment Brigades responsible for supporting airborne operations or airborne delivery support may be assigned the following quartermaster companies:

* **Quartermaster Heavy Airdrop Supply Company (QHASC).** The mission of the QHASC is to pack parachutes & temporarily store and/or rig supplies and equipment for airdrop operations conducted by Joint (Army, Air Force, USMC, etc) Services. The QHASC is capable of:

- Airdrop of 200 short tons (STONs) of the following classes of supply on a daily basis: Class (including water) – 20 STONs, Class II – 10 STONs, Class III (P) – 10 STONs, Class IV – 20 STONs, Class V – 110 STONs, Class VII – 10 STONs, Class VIII – 10 STONs, and Class IX – 10 STONs.
- Personnel parachute support to include packing and unit maintenance for up to 450 soldiers during a 45 day period.
- Assists aircraft loadmaster in loading of supplies and equipment into aircraft and in release of supplies and equipment from aircraft in flight.
- Providing technical advice and assistance in recovery and evacuation of airdrop equipment.
- Provide technical/rigger inspection of airdrop equipment upon initial receipt from supply source.
- Can perform the Army portion of the joint inspection of airdrop loads.

* Aerial Delivery Support Company (ADSC). The ADS Company's mission is to provide mission command, company level administration, and logistics support, for two to four Aerial Delivery Support Platoons. This company is task organized with three (3) Aerial Delivery Support platoons to provide the following services:

- 1200 personnel parachutes per day/High altitude low opening (HALO) 39 parachutes/cargo and small extraction parachute pack.
- 225 ST per day (containerized delivery system or type V heavy drop platforms).

- Field level maintenance of airdrop equipment/limited receipt, storage, and issue of air items.

All phases of the company's mission are directed through the unit's aerial delivery office. This office plans, coordinates, and supervises aerial delivery operations and directs company missions.

Often times, smaller aerial delivery units are required, especially in the event company size aerial delivery support units are unavailable. In this event, the **Aerial Delivery Support Platoon** is used. This platoon has the mission of packing parachutes and temporary storage and rigging of equipment and supplies for airdrop by the Army, Air Force, or other services. It provides personnel and cargo parachute supply, parachute packing, and field level maintenance of airdrop equipment. It is assigned to an Aerial Delivery Support Co (ADSC) HQ or an Aerial Delivery Office, and is capable of:

- 400 personnel parachutes per day/HALO 13 parachutes/ cargo and small extraction parachute pack.
- 75 ST per day (Containerized delivery system or type V heavy drop platforms.
- Field level maintenance of airdrop equipment/limited receipt, storage, and issue of air items.

Finally, CSSB's assigned to a Sustainment Brigade responsible for a Theater Opening (TO) mission, may be assigned the following quartermaster companies:

* **Quartermaster Force Provider Company**. The Force Provider Company HQ's provides the necessary mission command for one to six Force Provider Platoons operating in up to six (6) independent Force Provider Modules, with each modular capable of supporting 550 soldiers. With modules combined, it supports a brigade size force of 3300 personnel. The Force Provider Company may be assigned to either a TSC or CSSB, and may be detached to operate separately in an austere environment. The Force Provider Platoon provides one Force Provider module, supporting 550 soldiers, with climate controlled billeting, food service support, shower and latrine facilities, laundry service, and MWR facilities.

 * **Quartermaster Heavy Material Support Company (HMSC).** The mission of the Quartermaster Heavy Materiel Support Company (HMSC) is to receive, store, maintain, de-processes (as required), and issue Class VII items of equipment, (excluding aircraft and medical, marine, and railway mission-oriented equipment). It may also receive, store, issue, and classify Class VII that results from theater two-level maintenance and retrograde actions. The HMSC's capabilities encompass the following:

- Receives, warehouse, and issue approximately 1,400 tons of Class VII material per day. Initially, these items may be a part of the PWRMS.
- De-process approximately 300 tons of Class VII equipment to ready-for-issue status per day. The unit's de-processing platoon is staffed for a single 12 hour shift since approximately 80% of the Class VII items received into the theater are already been de-processed. The supply operations office and supply platoon are capable of operating 24 hrs/day.
- Provide in storage maintenance (not to exceed the unit maintenance) on all material warehoused by the supply platoon.

c. The Brigade Support Battalion (BSB). As mentioned earlier, Brigade Combat Teams (BCTs) are self-contained, ready-to-fight structures capable of world-wide deployment in 96 hours. To enable self-sustainment, BCTs have a Brigade Support Battalion (BSB) as an organic part of the unit structure to accomplish internal sustainment. The BSB provides the brigade with the self-sustainment capability to support internal needs for fuel, ammunition, Force Health Protection

(FHP), maintenance, water production and common supplies, thus reducing the need for reliance on higher logistics organizations for anything other than replenishment operations for up to 72 hours (3 DOS) of high intensity combat. The overall ratio of combat soldier to support is 3:1

Sustainment operations are founded on a distribution-based, centrally managed, force-projected concept of support that is fully integrated in the brigade concept of operations and scheme of maneuver. To meet the challenge of supporting the warfighting mission and meet time objectives, the brigade (either BCT or Spt Bde) employs a sustainment force (in the form of the BSB) that possess a self-sustainment capability to support internal needs for fuel, ammunition, FHP, maintenance, water production, and common supplies.

The BSB consists of a Headquarters and Headquarters Company (HHC), a Distribution Company, a Field Maintenance Company (FMC), a Medical Company[15], and three (3) or four (4) Forward Support Companies (FSC)[16]. The BSB combines situational understanding with efficient delivery systems to form a distribution pipeline, reducing most stockpiles. Supplies are tailored and packaged for specific supported units based on a specific time and location. Total asset visibility, including in-transit visibility, through sustainment MC systems, gives sustainment personnel visibility over all assets and infrastructure capacity in the Area of Operations (AO). Reliance upon distribution-based sustainment operations allows the BSB to place a smaller footprint on the battlefield. (See Figure 2-6)

---

15   The Medical Company is not allocated to BSB supporting Combat Aviation Brigades (CAB), Maneuver Enhancement Brigades (MEB), Field Artillery Brigades, or Battlefield Surveillance Brigades (BsfB).

16   Staffing has approved establishment of FSCs within Stryker Brigades BSB MTOEs.

BSB ORGANIZATION

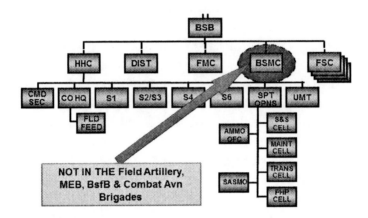

Figure 2-6 Organization of the Brigade Support Battalion.

Success in battle is dependent upon the unity of effort between the maneuver brigade and the BSB. The maneuver (combat) commander succeeds or fails by how well the sustainment operators within the BSB understand the sustainment characteristics of responsiveness, simplicity, flexibility, attainability, sustainability, survivability, economy, and integration, and their applicability to the mission of the Brigade Combat Team.

The modular Brigade Support Battalion versus the AOE Forward Support Battalion. The AOE FSB was the first such multifunctional support in the Army's force structure since the early 1980's. They are somewhat similar in that they are both multifunctional units that provide dedicated logistics and FHP to a brigade. (See Figure 2-7)

The FSB, a subordinate element of the Division Support Command (DISCOM), provides Direct Support (DS) to brigade and division units operating in the brigade area. It provided all logistical support, and ties together the entire spectrum of supplies, maintenance, and services for the maneuver brigade.

The FSB is organized with a Headquarters and Headquarters Detachment (HHD), Supply Company, Maintenance Company, and Medical Company.

By contrast, the BSB, organic to the brigade it supports, provides support to a brigade level combat team. The BSB is organized with an HHC, Distribution Company, Field Maintenance Company (FMC), Brigade Support Medical Company (BSMC), and a Forward Support Company (FSC) for each of the brigade's maneuver battalions. The FSCs perform the functions previously performed by the maneuver battalion support platoon and maintenance platoon, both of which no longer exist.

COMPARISON

BSB versus FSB

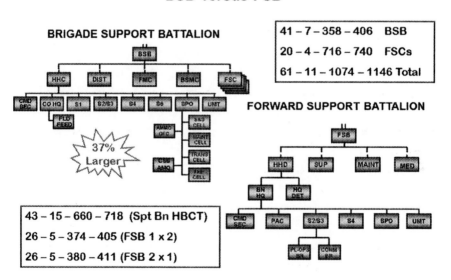

*Figure 2-7 The Brigade Support Battalion vs
The Forward Support Battalion*

The FSB and BSB are similar in that they both are fixed multifunctional units that support brigade-size units. However, there are some distinct differences. The most significant difference is in the relationship between the battalion and the brigade it supports. The FSB was assigned to a DISCOM and provided DS to the brigade it supported, essentially being in the awkward position of having to serve two masters (per the old FM 63 series Manuals). On the other hand, the BSB is organic to the brigade it supports. Organizationally, the BSB is more robust and has more organic capability than the FSB (*See Figure 2-7 above and 2-8 below*). An example is the addition of the FSCs to support the brigade's maneuver battalions. Additionally, the BSB has a more robust supply and distribution capability in its Distribution Company, than the FSB's Supply Company, with organic transportation assets in addition to separate platoons for supply and fuel and water. The FSB Supply Company did not have a distribution capability for supplies other than Class III(B). The company had to rely on the DISCOM's Main Support Battalion's (MSB) Co B (Transportation Motor Transport Company) to deliver supplies to the BSA for transloading to supported unit vehicles. Additionally, the Distribution Company has the capability to purify and distribute water, while the FSB had no organic water supply or production capability, often times having to receive a ROWPU support team from the MSB.

For maintenance operations, the two battalions provide support in the same manner, but have slightly different organizations. In addition to the Company Headquarters, the FSB's Maintenance Company has three sections (Maintenance Control, Service/Recovery, Class IX Support), two platoons (Automotive/Armament and Ground Support Equipment), and a number of System Support Teams (SSTs) that support tank and mechanized infantry units. On the other hand, the BSB's Field Maintenance Company is organized with a Company Headquarters, Maintenance Control Section, and two platoons (Area and Base). The Area Support Platoon contains the company's recovery and mechanical maintenance (automotive and track) capability, while the Base Support Platoon contains the electronics and missile, ground support equipment, and armament repair capability. The BSB's Field Maintenance Company does not have the SSTs like the FSB because of the presence of the FSCs in the battalion; the FSCs have Field Maintenance Teams similar to SSTs. Additionally, when workload exceeds its organic capability, the FSB Maintenance Company may receive augmentation from a Sustainment Brigade Support Maintenance Company.

Force health protection between the two battalions is provided essentially the same, but with organizational variations. The major difference is in the BCT BSB's BSMC, which has a Preventive Medicine Section, a Behavioral Health Section, and a Brigade Medical Supply Office to manage Class VIII resupply and medical equipment; the FSB's Medical Company does not have these capabilities. Additionally, unlike the FSB Maintenance Company, the Medical Company does not receive augmentation from the MSB's medical company (it no longer exists), when patient load exceeds its organic capability, instead, must transport casualty overflow to the nearest practical Support Brigade Medical Company (SBMC) or Combat Support Hospital (CSH).

Increased Sustainment Capability w/I BCT

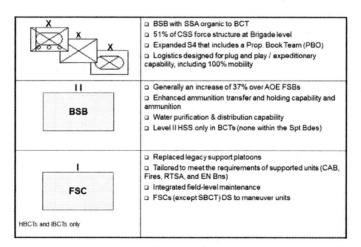

X (BSB)	□ BSB with SSA organic to BCT □ 51% of CSS force structure at Brigade level □ Expanded S4 that includes a Prop. Book Team (PBO) □ Logistics designed for plug and play / expeditionary capability, including 100% mobility
I I BSB	□ Generally an increase of 37% over AOE FSBs □ Enhanced ammunition transfer and holding capability and ammunition □ Water purification & distribution capability □ Level II HSS only in BCTs (none within the Spt Bdes)
I FSC HBCTs and IBCTs only	□ Replaced legacy support platoons □ Tailored to meet the requirements of supported units (CAB, Fires, RTSA, and EN Bns) □ Integrated field-level maintenance □ FSCs (except SBCT) DS to maneuver units

Figure 2-8 BSB Increased Sustainment Capabilities

Brigade Support Battalion Mission. The mission of the BSB is to provide sustainment support to the brigade and is responsible for sustainment operations throughout the brigade. It distributes all supply classes; performs field maintenance and recovery; and provides health services support (HSS)[17] for force health protection. It carries the sustainment stocks that exceed the organic carrying capability of the brigades maneuver battalions of three days of requirement for high intensity operations. The BSB also provides organic field feeding to the brigade through field feeding teams in the HHC, BSB, and the FSCs, and provides area support (supply, maintenance, and medical) to FOB/BSA tenant units. The BSB may function in a highly dispersed manner, with some BSB elements close to the maneuver units and others within the support area in a non-contiguous battlefield. The BSB commander serves as the senior logistics advisor for support to the brigade. His battle staff monitors and manages sustainment operations through on-site supervision, recurring reports, and an array of digital Mission Command information systems.

To accomplish its mission, the BSB is composed of four companies; the Headquarters Co, Distribution Co (Co A), Field Maintenance Co (Co B), and in BCT BSBs – Forward Medical Co (Co C).

* Headquarters Company. The role and organization of the Company Headquarters is similar throughout each company assigned to the BSB. The Company Headquarters is comprised of a Company Commander, Company Executive Officer, First Sergeant, Supply Sergeant, CBRN Specialist, Armorer, and various support personnel.

Besides the common responsibilities, the Company Commander is also responsible for commanding and controlling the company; developing the headquarters occupation plan; ensuring local headquarters security, including constructing

---

17   As noted, this function is not provided outside BCTs or within Support Brigades.

defensive positions, arranging and moving the headquarters, training, morale, welfare and recreating (MWR) activities for the headquarters; billeting; field sanitation, supply for the headquarters, field maintenance for organic equipment; and coordinating health service support.

The Company Headquarters also has a field feeding section, which provides food service support to all elements of the battalion and separate companies/elements within the brigade not supported by another organization.

Due to the similarities in role and organization the Company Headquarters will not be addressed when discussing the Distribution Company and the Field Maintenance Company. The mission and organizational structure of the BSB Headquarters and Headquarters Company is essentially the same despite the composition of the brigade to which it is assigned. All HHCs are comprised of a Command Section, S1 Section, S2/S3 Section, S4 Section, S6 Section, Support Operations Section, Unit Ministry Team (UMT), and a Company Headquarters Section with a Field Feeding Section. The minor exception to this rule is the Stryker Brigade Combat Team (SBCT); the assets found in the Support Operations Section comprise a Distribution Management Cell.

* The Distribution Company (Co A). The Distribution Company is fundamentally organized in the same fashion despite the composition of the BCT to which it is assigned. Each Distribution Company is comprised of a Company Headquarters Section, Transportation Platoon, Supply Platoon, and a Fuel/Water Platoon. The mission and composition of both the Supply Platoon and the Fuel/Water Platoon are the same throughout each BCT. The variance lies in the Transportation Platoon; BCTs categorized as 'Infantry' will have a higher number of truck squads than 'Armored' BCTs due to a limited wheeled vehicle equipment density within each maneuver battalion. Likewise, as in the case of the Field Artillery Brigade, truck squads are equipped with wheeled assets that provide the same capability/maneuverability as the maneuver battalions within the BCT.

Distribution Companies are comprised of three platoons – transportation platoon, supply platoon, and fuel/water platoon – the Distribution Company provides direct transportation support to the brigade, provides Class I, II, III(P), IV, V, VI, VII and IX receipt and distribution support, maintains limited Class II, III(P), IV, and IX ASL, purifies, stores, and distributes potable water within the brigade, and receives, stores, and issues bulk petroleum.

Transportation Platoon. The Transportation Platoon provides direct transportation support to the BCT. Platoon assets serve as the basis for logistics package (LOGPAC) operations between elements of the brigade and the FSCs co-located with line companies forward of the BSB within the TF Support Areas (TFSAs). The Transportation Platoon transports Class I, II, III(P), IV, V, VI, limited VII, and bottled water in configured loads during LOGPAC operations. The Supply Platoon typically transports class IX.

The platoon is comprised of a platoon headquarters and three truck sections, the Transportation Platoon is highly mobile and equipped with truck assets, such as the Heavy Expanded Mobility Tactical Truck – Load Handling System (HEMTT-LHS), Containerized Roll-In/Roll-Out Platform (CROP), and Container Handling Unit (CHU) to allow it to keep up with the maneuver elements and operate in all weather conditions and environments. The BSB Transportation Cell within the Support Operations Section is the tasking authority for the Transportation Platoon assets, and uses Movement Tracking System (MTS) and/or FBCB2 to communicate with the platoon and manage transportation assets.

Supply Platoon. The Supply Platoon manages the distribution of all classes of supply for the brigade, less bulk water, Class III(B), and Class VIII. The Supply Platoon is task-organized into three primary sections, each of which is responsible for the following functions:

- General Supply Section – The General Supply Section receives, stores (limited), and issues Class II, III(P), IV, and VII in support of the BCT. It receives Class I and bottled water from the Sustainment Brigade at the Field Ration Issue Point and distributes rations in conjunction with the Transportation Platoon to the FSCs. Configured loads are transferred from the incoming modes of transportation to flatracks in the supply marshalling area for distribution to units.
- Class IX Section – The Class IX Section receives, stores (limited), and issues Class IX to the BCT, maintains the brigade's Class IX authorized stockage list (ASL), and provides direct exchange for reparable items.
- ATHP Section – The Ammunition Transfer/Holding Point (ATHP) Section supports the ammunition requirements of the BCT, operating the BCT ATHP within the BSA. The ATHP serves mainly as a transload point, conveniently located to facilitate rapid issue.

The Supply Platoon also contains a Platoon Headquarters Section; co-located with the Platoon Headquarters Section is the Stock Control Section. Utilizing SARSS or GCSS-A, the Stock Control Section facilitates on-site item management. Key functions of this section include operating SARSS or GCSS-A for ordering and receiving; maintaining a current listing for all on-hand commodities; and delivering issued assets (LOGPAC) and picking-up retrograde (turn-ins to maintenance and/or for disposal).

Fuel & Water Platoon. The Fuel and Water Platoon is responsible for the purification, storage, and distribution of bulk water, as well as the receipt, blending, storage, and distribution of Class III(B) to the BCT, the Fuel and Water Platoon consists of two primary sections – the Class III Section and the Water Support Section.

The Class III Section provides reinforcing Class III (B) resupply to the FSCs and area support to brigade units through receipt, storage, and issue of bulk petroleum. This section also provides retail capability to individual BSB vehicles and supply point distribution to BSA tenant units. The entire section is fully mobile, with the modular tankrack fuel farm providing the ability to displace even when it contains fuel. The Class III Section is further equipped with a fuel additive injector, giving it the capability to receive commercial Jet A1 fuel and blend it to the single battlefield fuel, JP8.

The Water Support Section purifies stores and distributes potable water to the BCT. This section is equipped with organic purification equipment - the Tactical Water Purification System (TWPS) and the Lightweight Water Purifier (LWP) - both of which can operate up to 20 hours a day (shutting down for four hours for maintenance). This equipment provides the Water Support Section the capability to purify up to 24,000 gallons of water per day from a fresh water source. Water purification does not occur at levels below the BSB; the Water Support Section is the only BCT asset for potable bulk water. Water is distributed to brigade units during LOGPAC operations.

Distribution Company Operations – the "Concept of Support." (See Figure 2-9) Replenishment of general supplies within the BCT is a combination of MSO, SRO, and CRO. First, let's define what is an MSO, SRO, and CRO operation.

- Mission Staging Operations (MSOs) are intense time-sensitive operations, which include all preparations for an upcoming mission – planning, troop leading, rehearsals, training, reconnaissance and surveillance, reconstitution – to ensure mission success. MSOs are planned deliberate operations that can last 1-3 days and require support from both the tasked Sustainment Brigade and the BSB.
- Sustainment Replenishment Operations (SRO) is defined as quick, in-stride sustainment operations that

are conducted within a unit's battle rhythm with a duration of 3-7 hours. An SRO can be either a deliberate or hasty operations as dictated by OPTEMPO.

- Combat Replenishment Operations (CROs) are brief or pit-stop like events to rearm, refuel, provision essential supplies, and support maintenance function by cross leveling and use of on-board spares with duration of up to 3 hours.

The BCT deploys to a theater of operations with three combat loads of supplies using organic assets – one at using-unit level, one at FSC-level, and one at BSB-level stored by the Support Platoon. Each combat load is configured based on mission and supported unit composition. Within the FSC, general classes of supply configured as combat loads remain uploaded on the vehicles used to distribute them. The FSCs provide combat replenishment from these combat loads to supported units via logistics packages (LOGPACs) during CRO. The Distribution Platoon of the FSC is responsible for conducting LOGPAC operations and interfaces directly with each line company.

During SRO, the BSB Distribution Company conducts replenishment operations (ROs) via LOGPACs of the FSC's combat loads. The FSC Company Commander sends a request for replenishment of Class I, II, III, IV, V, VII, or IX through either BCS[3] or FBCB2 to the BSB S4. The request is passed through the Support Operations Office to the Distribution Company; upon receipt of the request, the Company Commander tasks the appropriate platoon to conduct the LOGPAC mission. Direct coordination occurs between the FSC and the Distribution Company for date, time, and location of delivery.

MSO operations are conducted with the support of the Quartermaster Supply Company (QSC) of the Sustainment Brigade, the FHP units of the Medical Brigade, and supported BSBs. The QSC area support platoons build configured loads from modules and bulk supplies received from both theater distribution Sustainment Brigades and CONUS. Depending upon the quantity of supplies to be replenished and the location of the supported BSBs on the battlefield, configured loads are either transported forward via LOGPACs to supported BSBs during MSO or issued during extended pauses in tactical operations from the Sustainment Brigade MSO site. The overall concept is depicted as Figure 2-9.

DISTRIBUTION
CONCEPT OF SUPPORT

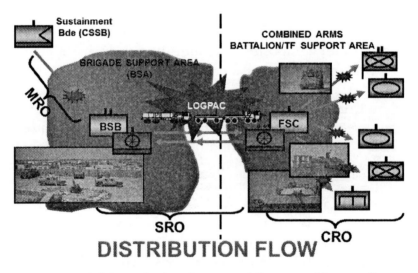

Figure 2-9 Distribution Company "Concept of Support"

* Field Maintenance Company (Co B). The BSB maintenance concept centers on the Modular Logistics Concept that replaces the AOE four-tiered system of organizational, direct support, general support, and depot-level support maintenance with a two-tiered construct that is centrally managed. The two tiers are field and sustainment maintenance; field maintenance is a combination of organizational and direct support maintenance and includes tasks that directly return a system to an operational status whereas sustainment maintenance includes tasks that support the supply system. The two-tiered system ultimately provides greater capability per maintainer and reduces the number of maintainers within an area of operations (AO), thus reducing the logistics footprint.

The Field Maintenance Company is fundamentally organized in the same fashion despite the composition of the brigade to which it is assigned. The mission of the FMC remains the same - provide field maintenance support to the brigade (either BCT or Support), to include recovery, automotive/ armament, ground support, electronic maintenance, and maintenance management. However, within both the IBCT (Infantry) and the SBCT (Stryker), the FMC is comprised of a Company Headquarters Section, Maintenance Control Platoon, and Maintenance Support Platoon. The Maintenance Control Platoon functions in the same manner as the Area Support Platoon of the ABCT and is comprised of a Platoon Headquarters Section, Recovery Section, and Wheeled Vehicle Repair Section. The Maintenance Support Platoon is organized in the same manner as the ABCT Base Support Platoon. The Platoon Headquarters Section, Missile/Electronics Repair Section, Ground Support Equipment Repair Section, and the Armament Section perform consolidated maintenance on low-density equipment for the BCT, to include the BSTB/BEB, Brigade Headquarters, and FSCs. The organizational structure of the FMC assigned to the Field Artillery Brigade is identical to that of the ABCT FMC.

The FMC provides field maintenance support to the brigade, to include recovery, automotive/armament, ground support, electronic maintenance, and maintenance management to brigade elements located in the LSA/FOB and reinforcing maintenance support to the FSCs. Comprised of a Maintenance Control Section, an Area Support Platoon, and a Base Support Platoon, the Field Maintenance Company also serves as a source for maintenance advice for the brigade and acts as the central entry and exit point into the brigade for low density equipment.

Maintenance Control Section (MCS). The Maintenance Control Section (MCS) serves as the management cell for all field maintenance and recovery mission activities within the BSB, the Brigade Headquarters, and as tasked for support to the FSCs. It is important to note that although the Maintenance Control Section serves as the management cell for these activities, the BEB contains a Maintenance Section within its HHC that is responsible for providing wheeled, tracked, and generator maintenance to the BEB and Brigade Headquarters.

The MCS further provides technical inspectors, monitors job orders, and maintains limited combat spares (PLL and shop stock). The technical inspectors are responsible for all aspects of quality assurance, technical inspection, and quality control maintenance activities of the company. The MCS currently utilizes SAMS-E, SAMS-1, SAMS-2 (to be replaced by GCSS-A), and FBCB2 to assist in mission accomplishment. The MSC receives missions from either supported units via call for support (CFS) messages transmitted through FBCB2 or the Support Operations Section as taskings for reinforcing support to the FSCs.

Area Support Platoon. The Area Support Platoon is comprised of a Platoon Headquarters Section, a Recovery Section, and a Mechanical Maintenance Section, the Area Support Platoon provides mechanical, automotive, and track field maintenance for the BSB and limited reinforcing maintenance to the FSCs. Each section of the Area Support Platoon is responsible for the following functions:

- Platoon Headquarters Section – Provides command and control of assigned and attached personnel and supervision for the administrative functions of the other sections. Through direction from higher headquarters, it coordinates all training activities for assigned personnel.

- Recovery Section – Provides welding and recovery/lift support to the BSB and other units operating within the LSA/FOB. A limited equipment density of recovery vehicles dictates the extent to which the Recovery Section can perform its mission. Self-recovery and like-vehicle recovery are emphasized as the primary means of recovery across the brigade. Maintenance Collection Points (MCP) are established throughout the brigade AOR in the event that distance recovery by the FSCs to the Field Maintenance Company is too far. After an FSC has recovered a vehicle to the UMCP, assets from the Recovery Section transport the vehicle the remaining distance to the BSA.
- Mechanical Maintenance Section – Provides automotive and track field maintenance for the BSB. As directed by the MCS, this section also provides maintenance on an area support basis to other units residing in the BSA and reinforcing maintenance to the FSCs. Area support maintenance includes reinforcing maintenance support to the BSTB Maintenance Section.

Base Support Platoon. The Base Support Platoon performs consolidated maintenance on low-density equipment for the brigade, to include the BEB, Brigade Headquarters, and FSCs. It is comprised of four sections that perform distinct key functions, as follows:

- Platoon Headquarters Section – Provides command and control of assigned and attached personnel and supervision for the administrative functions of the other sections. Through direction from higher headquarters, it coordinates all training activities for assigned personnel.
- Missile/Electronics Repair Section – Provides missile, electronic equipment, and weapon systems field maintenance

for those units within the brigade that do not have the capability embedded in their supporting FSCs. This section conducts float management of communications and electronic equipment to the FSCs; float management entails 'floating' a piece of mission-capable equipment to an FSC as a temporary replacement for a non-mission capable piece of equipment. This program maintains the combat power of a line company by limiting the duration of time a unit is without a piece of equipment.

- Ground Support Equipment (GSE) Repair Section – Provides field maintenance on non-vehicular environmental control, power generation, water purification, petroleum, CBRN, and engineer equipment for the BSB, BEB, and Brigade Headquarters and on an area basis for brigade LSA/FOB tenant units.

- Armament Section – Provides field maintenance for weapons assigned to the BSB, BEB, and Brigade Headquarters and on an area basis for brigade LSA/FOB tenant units. This section further provides consolidated low density equipment armament support to the brigade as required.

Brigade FMC Maintenance Concept of Support. (*Figure 2-10*) All requests for BSB maintenance support flow through the Maintenance Control Section (MCS). The maintenance message flow begins when the MCS receives a call for support (CFS) message from a supported unit other than an FSC – requests for support from the FSCs must first go through the BSB Support Operations Section. The MCS forwards a Logistic Task Order (LTO) to the appropriate maintenance section via FBCB2. The section responds to the LTO with an acknowledgement message, which is then forwarded to the requesting crew/operator. When the LTO is accepted, the section NCOIC coordinates support with the requesting unit and dispatches a mechanic to the location identified. The mechanic will diagnose the problem and determine if the required combat spares are on-hand to complete the repair. If the parts are not on-hand, he will send a message via FBCB2 to the MCS requesting the required repair parts. When the parts are readily available, the mechanic replaces the part forward at the breakdown site or at the Maintenance Collection Point (MCP). When required parts are not on-hand, the MCS orders required parts through GCSS-A; if the Class IX Section of the Distribution Company does not have the parts available or the part has a long order ship time from the vendor, either the unit of the Recovery Section recovers the vehicle to the BSA. As necessary, the MCS coordinates with the Support Operations Section to evacuate the system to a Sustainment Brigade maintenance unit for repair.

MAINTENANCE
CONCEPT OF SUPPORT

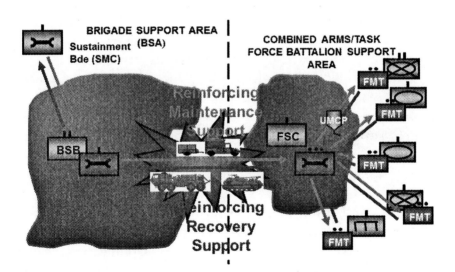

Figure 2-10 Maintenance "Concept of Support"

* Brigade Support Medical Company (BSMC) (BCTs only).
The overall mission of the Brigade Support Medical Company

(BSMC) is to provide Level II FHP to all BCT units operating within the BCT area of operations (AO). This includes ground ambulance evacuation, dental services, Class VIII resupply and medical equipment maintenance support, limited medical laboratory and radiology diagnostic services, limited patient holding, preventive medicine consultation and support, combat and operational stress control support, mass casualty triage and management, and patient decontamination. The company also provides Level I FHP on an area basis to BCT units that do not have organic medical assets. This includes sick call services and emergency medical treatment for wounded and non-battle injury patients.

The organizational structure and mission of the BSMC is fundamentally the same despite the composition of the BCT to which it is assigned. The medical company assigned to the SBCT is equipped with one Treatment Section consisting of three treatment teams rather than the Treatment Squad found in the ABCT and has five evacuation squads, like the ABCT. Additionally, the BMSO is located within the Company Headquarters Section as opposed to serving as its own section.

As mentioned prior, the Field Artillery Brigade, Combat Aviation Brigade, and the Maneuver Enhancement Brigade do not have an organic medical company and should coordinate for FHP support from the FHP units force pooled managed by the theater Medical Deployable Support Command (MDSC) via their command HQ's to obtain level II FHP.

The BSMC locates and establishes its company headquarters in the BSA and establishes a Level II Medical Treatment Facility (MTF). The company is organized into a Company Headquarters Section, a Preventative Medicine Section, a Behavioral Health Section, a Treatment Platoon, an Evacuation Platoon, and a Brigade Medical Supply Office.

The **Company HQ' Section** is organized into a command element, a supply element, and an operations and communications element. The Company Headquarters Section provides command and control for assigned and attached units. It also provides unit-level administration, general and Class VIII logistics supply/re-supply and medical maintenance (SBTC only), arms maintenance, CBRN operations, and communications/ electronics support to organic and attached units. For communications, the Company Headquarters Section employs AM and FM tactical radios, unit level computers, FBCB2, MC4, and a manual switchboard.

The command element is responsible for providing billeting, security, training, administration, and discipline for assigned personnel.

The operations and communications element sets up communications equipment and establishes the net control station (NCS) for the company. This element also establishes the internal wire communications net and establishes contact with battalion headquarters and with supporting and supported units.

The supply element establishes both the unit and Class VIII supply distribution points. They ensure all supplies are secured, properly stored, and protected from the environment. The supply element also establishes the unit fuel and water points and supports the company during establishment with additional items such as sandbags, tent pegs, and other standard equipment associated with establishment.

The **Preventative Medicine Section** is OPCON to the Brigade Surgeon Section although assigned to the BSMC. This section provides advice and consultation in the areas of food, water, and arthropod-borne diseases, non-battle injuries (NBI), environmental sanitation, epidemiology, and entomology, as well as conducts occupational and environmental health (OEH) surveillance and medical surveillance. This section also provides limited sanitary engineering services and pest management.

The **Behavioral Health Section** is comprised of a behavioral science officer and a behavioral health specialist this Section provides training and advice in the control of stressors, the promotion of positive combat stress behaviors, and the early identification, handling, and management of misconduct stress behavior and battle fatigue. This section also surveys social and psychological data and counsels personnel with personal, behavioral, or psychological problems.

The Behavioral Health Section utilizes the BSMC Level II Medical Treatment Facility (MTF) as the hub of its operations but may travel to supported units as required. The section's priority functions are to promote positive stress behaviors, prevent unnecessary evacuations, and coordinate return to duty (RTD), not treat cases.

The **Treatment Platoon** is responsible for operating the Level II Medical Treatment Facility (MTF). This platoon provides professional services in the areas of sick call service, emergency medical treatment, advance trauma management, and operational dental care. In addition, the platoon provides basic diagnostic laboratory and radiological services and patient holding support. The Treatment Platoon is organized around a Platoon Headquarters, Medical Treatment Squad, Area Support Squad, Area Treatment Squad, and Patient Holding Squad.

The Platoon Headquarters directs, coordinates, and supervises platoon operations, including overseeing platoon operations, OPSEC, communications, administration, organizational training, supply transportation, patient accountability, and statistical reporting functions. This section also directs the activities of the company's Level II MTF and monitors Class VIII supplies, blood usage, and inventory levels. Additionally, the Platoon Headquarters coordinates with the Support Operations Section for patient evacuation.

The Medical Treatment Squad within the BCT, which is comprised of two treatment teams, and the Medical Treatment Section within the SBCT, which is comprised of three treatment teams, provides emergency and routine sick call to soldiers assigned or attached to supported units. This squad can perform its functions while located in the company area, or can operate independently of the BSMC for limited periods of time. The

Medical Treatment Squad/Section has the capability to split and operate as separate treatment teams for limited periods of time. While operating as separate elements, both teams may operate separate treatment stations.

The Area Support Squad includes the dental and diagnostic support elements of the Level II MTF. Typically staffed with a dental officer, a dental specialist, a medical laboratory sergeant and specialist, and an x-ray sergeant and specialist, the Area Support Squad is organized into three elements with each performing specific functions:

- Dental Element – Provides operational dental care, to include emergency treatment.
- Medical Laboratory Element – Performs clinical laboratory and blood banking procedures to aid physicians and physician's assistants (PA) in the diagnostics, treatment, and prevention of diseases. This element is responsible for storing and issuing blood, performing urinalysis and occult blood procedures, collecting and processing clinical specimens for shipment, and maintaining the blood inventory status.
- Radiology Element – Performs routine clinical x-ray procedures to aid physicians and physician's assistants in the diagnosis of patients. Specific functions performed by this element include operating and maintaining fixed and portable x-ray equipment, taking x-rays of the extremities, chest, trunk, and skull, and performing manual and automatic radiographic film processing.

The Area Treatment Squad is the base medical treatment element of a Level II MTF. It provides sick call services and initial resuscitative treatment (advanced trauma management and emergency medical treatment) for supported units. This squad does not deploy from the BSMC nor reinforce/reconstitute other medical units.

The Patient-Holding Squad operates the patient-holding facility of the BSMC Level II MTF. Its primary mission is to hold patients awaiting evacuation out of the brigade AO; a secondary mission is to hold patients, who are expected to return to duty within 72 hours, and is staffed and equipped to provide care for up to 20 patients.

The **Evacuation Platoon** performs ground evacuation and en route patient care for supported units. The platoon consists of a Platoon Headquarters, three Evacuation Squads (Forward), and two Evacuations Squads (Area).

The Platoon HQs directs and coordinates ground evacuation of patients, supervises the platoon, and plans for its employment. It maintains communications to direct ground evacuation, provides ground ambulance evacuation support for the maneuver battalions of the BCT, and provides ground evacuation support to other units receiving area medical support from the BSMC.

The Evacuation Squads provide ground ambulance evacuation of patients from forward areas to the BSMC Level II MTF. Evacuation personnel perform emergency medical treatment (EMT), evacuate patients, and provide for their continued care en route. Each team carries an on-board medical equipment set (MES) designed for medical emergencies and en route patient care. Evacuation personnel obtain appropriate dispatch and road clearances and establish ambulance exchange points (AXP) as required by mission. Ambulances are usually positioned forward with the aid stations of maneuver battalions. Forward ambulances normally evacuate patients from the aid stations to AXPs where patients are placed in a ground or air ambulance for evacuation to the BSMC.

The mission of the **Brigade Medical Supply Office** is to provide Class VIII/blood resupply and unit-level medical equipment maintenance and repair. Personnel assigned to this section plan, coordinate, and manage a variety of functional areas pertaining to technical materiel, equipment, and services used in support of the FHP mission.

The BSMC possesses limited Class VIII/blood management capability. During deployment, lodgment, and early buildup phases, medical units operate from planned, prescribed loads and from existing pre-positioned stocks identified in applicable contingency plans. Initially, the Class VIII resupply effort will be via pre-configured Class VIII packages tailored to meet the needs of the BCT. These medical logistics (MEDLOG) packages are scheduled based on projected casualty estimates and are adjusted based on requirements identified by the Brigade Surgeon Section (BSS). MEDLOG packs will continue until line item requisitioning can be established. All BCT medical units will deploy with supplies to support a 72-hour self-sustainment mission within the AO.

Brigade Medical Evacuation Concept of Support. (*Figure 2-11*) At the point a soldier is injured, treatment is first rendered at the unit level. Depending upon the extent of the injury, the soldier may treat himself (self-aid), be treated by a fellow soldier (buddy-aid), or receive more advanced first aid by a soldier trained at the unit-level as a combat lifesaver. In the event that emergency resuscitative care or advanced trauma management is required, the soldier is first taken to the maneuver battalion aid station.

Due to OPTEMPO and relative size of the battlefield, all maneuver battalions assigned or attached to the BCT are equipped with either an organic medical platoon or medical section responsible for establishing the Battalion Aid Station (BAS). Assigned to the HHC, each medical section consists of at least one trauma specialist trained to perform Level I emergency life-saving measures and stabilization of the patient for evacuation to a higher level facility. The Battalion Aide Station may be augmented by Treatment Teams from the BSMC Treatment Platoon and/or Ambulance Squads from the Evacuation Platoon for a limited period of time.

Ground ambulances from the BSMC Evacuation Platoon evacuate the injured soldier from either the BAS or designated patient collection points to the BSMC Level II MTF. As determined by METT-TC, the Evacuation Platoon may also established ambulance exchange points (AXP) – designated locations forward of the BSA where patients are exchanged from one evacuation platform to another. AXPs are utilized by the BSMC when it is unfeasible for the Evacuation Platoon to travel as far forward as the BAS or when it is unfeasible for ambulance crews from the BAS to travel as far to the rear as the BSA.

Upon arrival at the BSMC Level II MTF, the injured soldier receives further resuscitative care and diagnostic laboratory and radiological services as required. When injuries are beyond the capability of the BSMC, the soldier is evacuated to a Level III MTF, either a Combat Support Hospital (CSH) or other hospital with advanced clinical treatment capabilities. Depending upon the location of the Level III MTF, the patient may be evacuated by ground or air. The injured soldier can be placed in the patient-holding facility while awaiting evacuation to the next level of care.

COMBAT HEALTH SUPPORT
CONCEPT OF SUPPORT

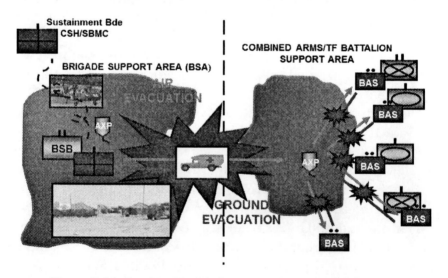

Figure 2-11 Combat Health Support "Concept of Support"

The FHP concept of support is greatly enhanced by the use of the Medical Communications for Combat Casualty Care (MC⁴) digitized communications system. MC⁴ integrates medical information systems with contingency support to warfighters across all levels of healthcare by providing timely medical information to support mission command, situational understanding, and Class VIII management. It is capable of sharing data with other emerging digitized systems including Army Battle Command System (ABCS), Global Combat Support System–Army (GCSS-A), and Battle Command Sustainment Support System (BCS³). MC⁴ links commanders with health care providers to track casualties throughout the battlefield in order to focus FHP where it is most needed. Of the many benefits it offers, maximizing the use of limited medical assets, minimizing and focusing patient evacuation, linking health care providers in theater with the sustaining bases, and increasing the span of control of medical units are most significant.

d. The Forward Support Company (FSC). In Chapter 1, one of the structural components to come out of the *Force XXI* concept was the inception of the Forward Support Company. The Forward Support Company (FSC) are assigned to a BSB in order to provides field maintenance, distribution-based re-supply of Classes I through VII and IX, and subsistence support for all organic and attached units of a maneuver battalion. FSCs are assigned to Brigade Support Battalions supporting Armored, Infantry, Stryker, and Airborne Brigade Combat Teams (BCTs), Field Artillery Brigades (FABs), Combat Aviation Brigades (CABs), and Maneuver Enhancement Brigade (MEBs). (See Figure 2-12). FSCs are not found in the following battalion-size organizations: Military Police, Civil Affairs, Chemical, ADA, and Special Forces Battalions. It should be noted that this discussion on the FSC is only an overview.

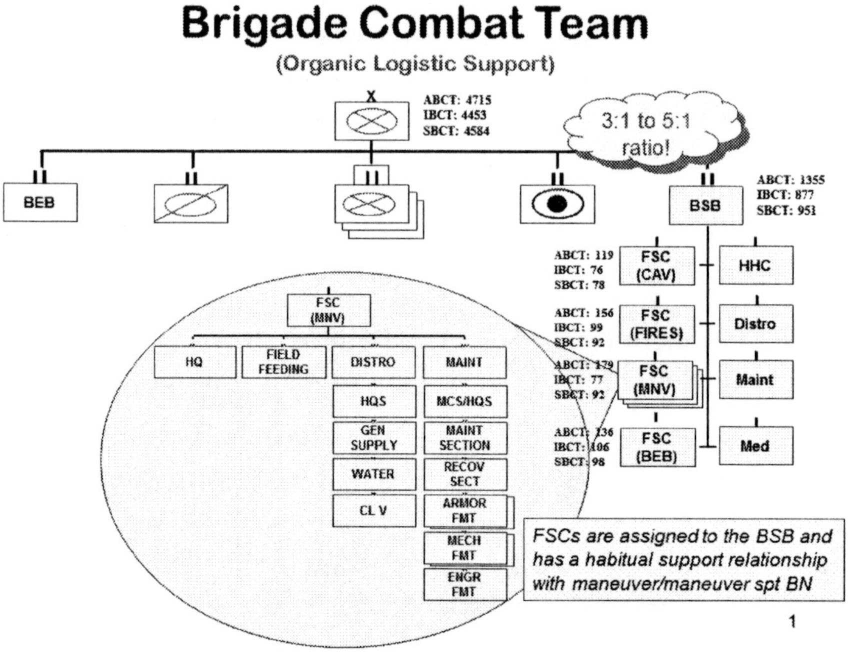

Brigade Combat Team

(Organic Logistic Support)

Figure 2-12 FSC Composition and Disposition, Brigade Combat Team

There is much discussing in the field today as to whether FSCs can be assigned or attached to maneuver battalions. Unit Commander's will direct whatever command relationship is necessary to facilitate a successful operation, but bear in mind that officially, FSCs cannot be assigned or attached to the maneuver battalions since the FSC Direct Combat Probability (DCP) Code is 2 which allows females inside such organizations, but not within combat (i.e. DCP Code 1) units. Attaching/assigning FSCs to the maneuver battalions limits the flexibility of the BSB Bn Cdr to surge capability within the BCT, such as moving a Company Repair Team (CRT) from one battalion to another to quickly improve the unit OR.

In Support Brigades (i.e. Combat Aviation, Field Artillery or Maneuver Enhancement) the relationship between the BSB, FSC, and battalion is not as clear cut as found within the Brigade

Combat Teams, especially within the Reserve Component where each piece may be located over several states. Here, FSCs have a more direct support relationship with its supported battalion than with the BSB, which has the possibility of creating problems, especially in delineating reporting responsibilities and requirements. Ultimately, it is the Brigade Commander who directs the command and reporting relationship between the FSC, the supported battalion, and the BSB.

The FSC is comprised of three core elements – a Headquarters Platoon with a Field Feeding Section, a Distribution Platoon, and a Maintenance Platoon. The organizational structure of an FSC may be augmented or reduced as necessary to meet the mission requirements of the supported maneuver battalion. In particular, the Maintenance Platoon is tailored to reflect the equipment density of the supported maneuver battalion. Maintenance sections are reorganized and equipped with mechanics and tools specific to the equipment utilized by each maneuver battalion. This modular construct allows an FSC to be self-sustaining and provides the maneuver battalion commander the flexibility to stage FSC assets far forward of the Combined Arms Battalion/ Task Force Support Area.

    * **FSC Company Headquarters**. The role and organization of the Company Headquarters is similar throughout each variation of the FSC. The Company Headquarters is comprised of a Company Commander, Company Executive Officer, First Sergeant, Supply Sergeant, CBRN Specialist, Armorer, and various support personnel.

The Field Feeding Section provides food service support to the maneuver battalion and all personnel assigned or attached to the FSC. The Field Feeding Section is equipped with one or two Containerized Kitchens (CK). Each CK interfaces with the company level kitchens located either forward with the line company to which they are assigned or in the TF/CABSA with the FSC. Key functions of the Field Feeding Section include food distribution to maneuver units forward of the TF/CAB Support

Area and preparation of both heat-and-serve meals and cook-prepared (A or B) meals. The Field Feeding Section has the capability to prepare one heat-and-serve meal and one cook-prepared (A or B) meal per day.

* **Distribution Platoon**. The Distribution Platoon is comprised of four sections – Platoon Headquarters, Class III/Water, Class V, and General Supply – the Distribution Platoon provides Class I (rations), II, III (P and B), IV, V, VI, and VII support to the maneuver battalion.

Aside from providing C2 and administration support to the Distribution Platoon, the Platoon Headquarters Section manages the distribution of supplies coming from or passing through the FSC in support of the maneuver battalion. Co-located with the Platoon Headquarters Section is the Stock Control Section; utilizing SARSS or GCSS-A, the Stock Control Section facilitates on-site item management. Key functions of this section include operating SARSS or GCSS-A for ordering and receiving; maintaining a current listing for all on-hand commodities; processing receipts, issues, and turn-ins; establishing a limited storage, receipt, and issue facility for all supported commodities; and delivering issued assets (LOGPAC) and picking-up retrograde (turn-ins to maintenance and/or for disposal).

The Class III/Water Section provides fuel and water support to the maneuver battalion through SRO and CRO. During SRO, bulk fuel is received from the Distribution Company of the BSB and stored in HEMTT tankers located in the FSC AO. The fuel is then distributed to maneuver units located forward of the TF/CAB Support Area via LOGPAC through CRO.

Within a BCT, water purification, storage, and distribution occurs within the Distribution Company of a BSB. The BSB delivers water forward to an FSC during SRO; an FSC in turn delivers water to maneuver units located forward of the CABSA via LOGPAC during CRO. It is important to note that bulk water purification is not conducted forward of the BSB.

The Class V Section provides ammunition re-supply support to the maneuver battalion through SRO and CRO. The General Supply Section transports Class I, II, III (P), IV, and VII to maneuver units located forward of the CABSA through SRO and CRO.

* **Maintenance Platoon**. The Maintenance Platoon is comprised of a headquarters section, maintenance control section, recovery section, maintenance service section, and field maintenance teams (FMT) specific to the equipment density of the supported unit. The platoon's mission is to provide field maintenance (organizational and DS level) to both the maneuver battalion and all equipment assigned or attached to the FSC.

The Headquarters Section provides C2 and administrative support to the Maintenance Platoon. Co-located with the Headquarters Section, the Supply Section possesses the capability of providing Class IX support (combat spares) to each maneuver company, the engineer company, and the HHC. The Supply Section also maintains the FSC's combat spares (PLL, shop and bench stock) and provides exchange of repairable items.

The Maintenance Control Section (MCS) is the primary manager for all field maintenance in both the FSC and the supported maneuver battalion, and establishes the maintenance platoon's priorities based on command guidance. The MCS performs all TAMMS functions and dispatching operations and tracks scheduled services using the Standard Army Maintenance System – Enhanced (SAMS-E) for the maneuver battalion and the FSC. Although services are not a responsibility of the HBCT, they are still recorded in order to ensure compliance with service schedules. All maneuver company SAMS-E boxes are consolidated at the MCS and it is the responsibility of the MCS to supervise all SAMS-E operators.

The Recovery Section provides direct recovery support to elements of the FSC and limited reinforcing recovery support to the FMTs. Reinforcing recovery support becomes necessary when a vehicle cannot be repaired on-site and the FMT does not have the required assets to transport the vehicle to the Maintenance Collection Point (MCP).

The Maintenance Section provides field maintenance to the FSC and maneuver battalion HHC. Field maintenance is the combination of organizational maintenance and direct-support maintenance. Mechanics assigned to the FSC have the capability to perform both organizational and direct-support repairs. This capability enhances the flexibility of the maneuver battalion in that vehicles requiring direct-support repairs do not have to be evacuated to the BSB. This section also provides maintenance support to elements attached to the battalion and reinforcing maintenance to the FMTs.

The Maintenance Section is also responsible for assisting with organizational services on selected pieces of equipment organic to the FSC and the maneuver battalion HHC, and assists the FMTs in completing services for the maneuver companies. Services, however, are not performed by the FSC on its vehicles. This requirement is supported by the sustainment brigade through its maintenance units or through contracted services.

The maneuver battalion's first level of support is provided by the Field Maintenance Teams (FMTs). The FMTs are organized to provide field maintenance for all combat platforms organic to maneuver companies/troops/batteries. The type of maneuver battalion supported by the FSC determines the number and composition of FMTs.

The scope and level of repairs completed by the FMTs are METT-TC dependent. Repairs are performed as far forward as possible in order to limit the duration of time a piece of equipment is removed from the battle. During combat, FMTs will perform battle damage assessment and repair (BDAR), diagnostics, and on-system replacement of line replaceable units. Emphasis is placed on trouble-shooting, diagnosing malfunctions and fixing the equipment by component replacement. If the tactical situation permits, FMTs focus on completing jobs on site. The

FMTs carry limited Class IX repair parts; if inoperable equipment is not repairable due either to METT-TC or a lack of repair parts, the team uses recovery assets to assist the maneuver company and may, as necessary, recover inoperable equipment to the UMCP or designated linkup point.

3. Summary and Conclusion.

How do these newly transformed structures work together in achieving material and service distribution across the operating environment? An overview of the roles and responsibilities between the above sustainment organizations is depicted in Figure 2-13 below.

Outside the TSC and ESC, Sustainment Brigades command all CSSBs and all other sustainment forces inside their task organization. The Sustainment Brigade issues distribution directives to the CSSBs, which in turn issue orders to transportation companies for execution. The Sustainment Brigade needs to attend the various Logistics Distribution Boards to understand the overall theater situation.

To maintain situational awareness of the operating environment distribution network, Sustainment Brigades collect and analyzes In-Transit Visibility (ITV) distribution information to monitor routes and provide location of its convoys. This assists in movement control for convoy force protection through a unit's battlespace. Sustainment Brigades also uses ITV to establish delivery schedules to its CSSBs in support of the TSC and/or its supported command's priority of supply and effort.

The Sustainment Brigade and subordinate CSSBs track and maintain visibility of its assets (known as Total Asset Visibility or "TAV" – ground and aerial platforms) that are available for distribution. The CSSB maintains visibility of its capacity to store commodities as another aspect of physical distribution.

Sustainment Brigade and Brigade Support Battalion Distribution Operations Roles

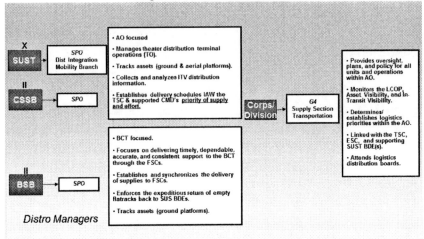

Figure 2-13 Distribution Operations Roles

The Brigade Support Battalion (BSB) is not under the command of the TSC but rather is its respective brigade customer. The BSB commands the FSCs and the Distribution Company. The BSB SPO issues distribution directives to the Distribution Company to replenish the FSCs.

The BSB focuses on delivering timely, dependable, accurate, and consistent support to the BCT through the FSCs. It monitors and tracks inbound Sustainment Brigade convoys to synchronize force protection plans. The SPO synchronizes and establishes delivery schedules to the FSCs through its Distribution Company.

The BSB's role for physical distribution is to enforce the expeditious return of empty flatracks back to Sustainment Brigades. Like the CSSB, it tracks its capability to distribute commodities to FSCs in addition to maintaining visibility of its ability to store various commodities.

The Forward Support Company does not have a distribution management mission but rather a distribution *execution mission*. This unit provides habitual support to a designated battalion.

Distribution operations in the modular force are more dynamic than in the past. The competition for scarce resources and the reduction of large piles of commodities have forced the Army to go to a distribution system. With current enablers such as RFID, BCS3, MTS, and eventually GCSS-A, distribution managers are now able to track commodities as they traverse the battlefield.

Blast from the Past

"I don't know what this *logistics* stuff is, all I know is I want some"

Admiral William "Bull" Halsey, 1941

CHAPTER 3

THE SUSTAINERS MILITARY DECISION MAKING PROCESS (MDMP)

✮ ✮ ✮

*"A good staff has the advantage of being more lasting
than the genius of a single man"*
- Baron Henry De Jomini, The Art of War, 1862

1. Background. The most fundamental planning activity a Sustainment unit must achieve is how it organizes itself to fulfill its portion of the overall Theater Supply Chain management and accomplish distribution operations in an effective and cost efficient manner without endangering the very soldiers its supports. This is the process of Sustainment MDMP, the process of which is covered in greater detail in the Chapter 4 – 18 of this guide.

At this point, I should comment that it is not the intent of this Battlestaff Guide to supplant any prior published commercial MDMP guides, Chapter 9, FM 6-0 (Commander and Staff Organizations and Operations Guide), or Appendix B, FM 5-0 (C1) (The Operations Process), but rather to supplement and provide guidance from a Sustainment operations perspective. Far too many times, Sustainment (aka *"Combat Service Support"* or *"CSS"*) soldiers are trained in the Military Decision Making Process from the maneuver (*combat arms*) stand point, completely missing those critical aspects sustainers need to identify and plan for outside what *"the trigger pullers"* look for.

The Military Decision Making Process is not new. The applied process of solving tactical situations and problems can be traced back at least 2,000 years, but began to gain prominence in the early 19th century post-Napoleonic Europe. Following the writings Baron Henri De Jomini, the Prussians took the lead with the creation of a *"Generalstab"* or General Staff under the direction of General Helmuth von Moltke. Using the process of "staff studies" (the forerunner of the MDMP), the German General Staff was able to create various operations (then known as "War") plans in the event of general war within Europe, most notably the infamous *"Von Schlieffen Plan"*[18] of World War I fame. By the turn of the century, this process was adapted by the world's leading powers to include the United States. Throughout the First and Second World War, the process slowly evolved. It was in the late 1980's and early 90's that the decision process used today by Army staffs from battalion to Army level took shape.

2. The Process Itself. Per Appendix B, FM 5-0 (C1, 18 Mar 2011), the Military Decision Making Process is defined as:

> *'An iterative planning methodology that integrates the activities of the commander, staff, subordinate headquarters, and other partners to understand the situation and mission; develop and compare courses of action; decide on a course of action that best accomplishes the mission; and produce an operation plan or order for execution.'*

In concept, MDMP is a blending of the Commander's guidance, intuition, experience, (coined as an understanding of *"The Art of War"*) coupled with the Staff's knowledge of doctrine, tactics,

---

18 Contrary to popular brief, the *"Von Schliefflen Plan"* was less a warplan and more an operational "concept". The plan, as designed in 1905, theorized a massive offensive operation into France based on a projected force structure that was anticipated to be in place within five – ten years of the plan's development. Unfortunately for the German Army, the Reichstag (Parliament) never allocated funding for their creation – instead diverting money to the Kaiser's pet project – creation of the Imperial German Navy.

techniques, and methodology (otherwise known as "*The Science of War*") (See Figure 3-1). Strong Commander's can compensate for weak staffs by articulating clear planning guidance and establishing definitive course of action criteria. Conversely, strong staffs can accommodate weak commanders but only up to a point. Balancing this process is the all encompassing factor of "*time*" availability. The less time available, the greater the direct command involvement in the process (See Figure 3-2 – The Planning Continuum). Ultimately, it is the organizational commander who must assume responsibility for what the unit does or fails to accomplish.

As stated in FM 5-0 and FM 6-0[19], the strength of the MDMP process is that it is "*an established and proven analytical planning process.*" The total process consists of seven major steps, from receipt of mission to orders production, with over 40 substeps involved. The MDMP entails deliberate planning and development of multiple courses of action in order to determine the best course of action for a given situation or circumstance.

CONCEPTUAL FRAMEWORK

THE ART & SCIENCE OF WAR

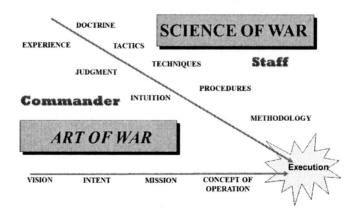

Figure 3-1 The MDMP Conceptual Framework

---

19   For this guide, FM 6-0, The Commander and Staff Organizations and Operations used is dated 5 May 2014.

MDMP's Advantages: The main advantages to using the MDMP process is that it analyzes and compares multiple friendly and enemy Course of Action (COA) in order to identify the most effective possible friendly COA. The process also allows for extensive coordination and synchronization in plans and orders. With total staff involvement in the process, it minimizes the chance of overlooking critical aspects of the operation. Finally, it helps identify possible contingencies for branch and sequel development.

MDMP's Weakness. The MDMP's greatest weakness is the large amount of time required to conduct a detailed mission analysis. Time is usually the one asset there is never enough of, making a complete MDMP ineffective. Whether in the training environment of NTC/JTRC or the present world COE, unit commanders often do not have sufficient time to conduct deliberate planning because of the rapidly changing situation and mission.

Although Para 9-196 through 9-199 (pg 9-43) of FM 6–0 provide guidelines for conducting planning in a time-constrained environment, it still focuses on a very structured decision making process. Current operations often cannot support a structured decision making process that takes a significant amount of time to conduct.

3. Sustainment MDMP Focus and Overview.

The focus of any MDMP planning process is to quickly develop a flexible, tactically sound, fully integrated, synchronized and effective distribution plan that: compliments the existing theater distribution plan, and increases the likelihood of the customer's mission success with the fewest casualties possible.

The MDMP is a sound and proven process that required modification with slightly different techniques to ensure effectiveness when time is limited. Although there is still only one process, omitting steps of the MDMP is not the solution. Anticipation, organization, and prior preparation are the keys to success in a time-constrained environment.

The commander decides how to shorten the process (See Figure 3-2 The Planning Continuum). There are four primary techniques to save time.

The first is for the commander to limit the number of COAs developed and war gamed. This is normal for Sustainment units since the number of different COAs (FLE, CSC, CRSP, etc) is generally smaller than for maneuver/maneuver support units.

The second is to increase the unit commander's involvement, allowing him to make decisions during the process without waiting for a detailed briefing after each step.

The third is for the commander to become more directive in his guidance and limiting options. This focuses the staff on what the commander feels is the most important.

The fourth is maximizing parallel planning. Some portions of the planning sequence can be conducted at the same time or carried out in more detail to assist later in the process (i.e. identifying tasks for subordinate units for use in the OPORD while in the COA process). Any involvement by either the unit's organic/ attached organizations (and in the case of the BSB: FSCs) will greatly facilitate this action.

While the steps used in a time-constrained environment are the same, many of them may be done mentally by the commander or with less staff involvement than during the full process. The products developed when the process is abbreviated may be the same as those developed for the full process; however, they may be much less detailed or some omitted altogether. This is entirely the unit commander's or XO's call.

For Sustainment Brigades and CSSBs, the SPO & S-3 are the key players in the MDMP process. For a BSB, the SPO, S-3 and BSMO are key players in the Brigade Combat Team MDMP process. In all three organizations, the SPO is the most critical part of the unit's mission analysis and COA steps. In BSB's, the BSMO will stay with the Brigade planners throughout the MDMP process.

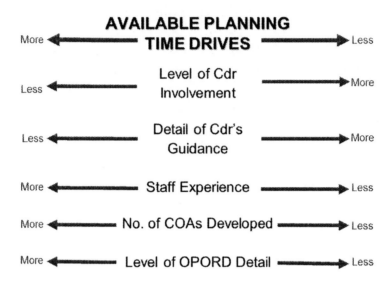

Figure 3-2 The MDMP Planning Continuum

4. Sustainment MDMP and Design.

Recent changes to FM 5-0 introduced staffs to the concept of 'Design' and its applicability to the overall MDMP process. Without the need of going into intricate detail, the first question a sustainer needs to ask: "Is this a complex problem or situation?" If not, then Design is not required (but a problem statement still is). Overall, all sustainment operations (and thus the Unit's problem statement) needs to focus on "*How to efficiently and effectively conduct distribution operations to my customers*" (i.e. – the tactical supported units)

Of a personal note, not only do I believe that design is applicable at the tactical level of sustainment; I believe that most sustainers should incorporate Design into MDMP for planning. Commanders, or staff, should organize their thoughts along functional lines focused to location or customer. Of course, the "steps" remain the same: identify the current situation, describe the end state, identify the problem(s) (or difference between the current situation and desired end state), then define the tasks required to address the problem. The end product, matrixed against time, is essentially a Gantt Chart. For the CSSB or BSB commander/ staff, a sample of this matrix is depicted in Figure 3-3 below.

Customer or Location:			
Functional Area (Lines of Effort)	**What is the current sustainment situation?**	**What is the desired objective?**	**What is the real issue(s)?**
Automation			
Contracting			
Distribution			
Human Resources			
Material Readiness			
Mobility			
Munitions			
Supply & Services			

Figure 3-3 Functional areas shown equate to the SPO branches, but others are just as applicable: fixing, fueling, manning, arming, sustaining; or simply: sustainment, distribution, Human Resource (HR), and contracting

Once the commander or staff has identified what the issues are in each functional area, then the staff identifies tasks, or courses of action, required to address each issue. A COA that addresses multiple issues or functional areas, or addresses the same functional area for multiple customers would be a high-payoff task. Developed COAs are then laid out in a synchronization matrix type format (Pert Chart).

I believe that using design in conjunction with MDMP would be more appealing to sustainers is due to the number of times I have observed sustainers complain that *'there is only one way to accomplish the commander's desired endstate for sustainment so we can only develop one COA and there is nothing to wargame'*. Design assists the SPO in looking at the sustainment situation from a different angle and possibly seeing multiple COAs. If they still only see one COA, it also helps analyze the single course of action by laying the multiple tasks on a single time chart and determining how to complete each.

5. Sustainment MDMP Steps. (See Figure 3-4 below) As mentioned prior, the MDMP consists of seven (7) steps along with the appropriate chapter each step (inputs and outputs) is addressed in detail:

1. **Receive warning order from higher (Chapter 4)**
    *   Alert the Staff and other Key Participants
    *   Gather the tools and other documents related to the mission
    *   Begin Intelligence Preparation of the Battlefield (IPB)
    *   Situation update briefings by staff
    *   Commander provides initial guidance
    *   Issue Warning Order #1 (Identify change of mission and initial guidance to commanders)
    *   Update staff (running) estimates/Commander's Estimate

Receive OPORD from higher (followed by confirmation brief to higher)

2. Mission Analysis (Chapter 5)

Mission Analysis Brief (Chapter 14)
- Commander's guidance and intent
- Issue Warning Order #2 (Refined guidance and approved mission statement)

3. Course of Action Development—criteria approved for course of action comparison **(Chapter 6, with Briefing format found in Chapter 15)**

4. Course of Action analysis and "wargaming" (Chapter 7)
- Initial wargame
- Course of action analysis
- Update staff estimates

5. Course of Action comparison (Chapter 8)

6. Decision brief to commander (Chapter 16)
- Commander decision
- Issue Warning Order #3 (Scheme of Support, Scheme of Defense)

Gather tools
- Detailed graphics
- Detailed concept (support and defense)

Finalize plan—detailed support matrix

7. Order Preparation & Production (Chapter 9)
- Order approved for issue
- Rehearse operations order brief

Issue operation order (followed by confirmation brief or 'back brief')

Key inputs	Steps	Key outputs
• Higher headquarters' plan or order or a new mission anticipated by the commander	**Step 1:** **Receipt of Mission**	• Commander's initial guidance • Initial allocation of time
	Warning order	
• Higher headquarters' plan or order • Higher headquarters' knowledge and intelligence products • Knowledge products from other organizations • Design concept (if developed)	**Step 2:** **Mission Analysis**	• Problem statement • Mission statement • Initial commander's intent • Initial planning guidance • Initial CCIRs and EEFIs • Updated IPB and running estimates • Assumptions
	Warning order	
• Mission statement • Initial commander's intent, planning guidance, CCIRs, and EEFIs • Updated IPB and running estimates • Assumptions	**Step 3:** **Course of Action (COA) Development**	• COA statements and sketches - Tentative task organization - Broad concept of operations • Revised planning guidance • Updated assumptions
• Updated running estimates • Revised planning guidance • COA statements and sketches • Updated assumptions	**Step 4:** **COA Analysis (War Game)**	• Refined COAs • Potential decision points • War-game results • Initial assessment measures • Updated assumptions
• Updated running estimates • Refined COAs • Evaluation criteria • War-game results • Updated assumptions	**Step 5:** **COA Comparison**	• Evaluated COAs • Recommended COAs • Updated running estimates • Updated assumptions
• Updated running estimates • Evaluated COAs • Recommended COA • Updated assumptions	**Step 6:** **COA Approval**	• Commander-selected COA and any modifications • Refined commander's intent, CCIRs, and EEFIs • Updated assumptions
	Warning order	
• Commander-selected COA with any modifications • Refined commander's intent, CCIRs, and EEFIs • Updated assumptions	**Step 7:** **Orders Production**	• Approved operation plan or order
CCIR commander's critical information requirement COA course of action		EEFI essential element of friendly information IPB intelligence preparation of the battlefield

Figure 3-4 The steps of the MDMP as depicted in FM 6-0

Blast from the Past

"No battle plan survives first contact with the enemy."

Field Marshal Helmuth Von Moltke, Chief of the Prussian General Staff

CHAPTER 4

(RECEIPT OF MISSION)

✯✯✯

RECEIPT OF MISSION

The MDMP always begin with the receipt of a mission, whether that is in the form of a hard copy or digital OPORD/OPLAN, Warning Order (WARNORD), or Fragmentary Order (FRAGORD). Commanders are expected to make informed decisions based on the best and most thorough information at hand. This decision-making process can be deliberate, using an extended period of time prior to execution; or it can be constrained by time or circumstances; or in anticipation of a new mission and conducted under combat conditions.

ACTIONS UPON RECEIPT OF MISSION

1. S-3 issues a warning order to staff alerting them of the pending planning process.

2. One order is broken into the basic order and annexes, which are distributed to the necessary staff sections for immediate reading. Ten (10) copies of the basic order must be produced along with Annex A (TASKO) and should be given immediately to CDR, XO, S-1, S-4, S-2, S-3, OPS NCOIC, S-6, and the SPO (Spt Ops Off). The Plans Officer also receives a copy (Sus Bde/CSSB). See Chapter 20 for specific Orders Breakdown.

3. S-2/3 & SPO meet with the CDR and XO to receive initial guidance. Planning guidance considerations (See Chapter 12).

4. The XO calls the staff (or applicable Plans Cell/Work Group) together for initiation of the MDMP. Other staff officers can be present for planning as needed.

5. A current situation update is called for, as necessary, from the OPS NCOIC. An S-2 section rep briefs the staff on current enemy situation, based on the new mission.

6. The following tools are gathered: OPORDS, appropriate maps, standard drops, graphics overlays, own and higher SOPs, appropriate FMs/ADPs/ATPs, and any existing staff (henceforth known as 'running') estimates. A COP (Common Operating Picture) workstation is set aside for any graphics requirements. SPOs should also obtain a copy of the HHQ's and supported customer unit Concept of Support. Refer to Figure 4-1 for a listing of various MDMP 'tools'.

7. The XO, based on current time and execution time, establishes planning guidance and timeline for planning milestones based on a 1/3 - 2/3 time analysis (See Chapter 10).

8. The S-6 off posts an updated POC listing with key personnel and phone numbers

   a. For the Sus Bde, key personnel are ESC Cdr/SPO, Supported Corps/Div S-4s, attached CSSB Cdrs/SPOs.
   b. For CSSBs, key personnel are the HHQs Sus Bde Cdr, S-3, SPO, habitual supported BCT/Spt Bde S-4's, BSB SPOs, and CSSB Co Cdrs/1SGs.
   c. For BSBs, key personnel are the supporting Sus Bde Cdr/ SPO, habitual supporting CSSB Cdr/SPO, BCT/Bn S-4s, and FSC Co Cdrs.

9. Staff members read the mission and intent statement one and two levels up and begin their mission analysis and staff estimates. Staff estimate guidelines are found in Chapter 12.

10. Staff Officers should develop a generic list of requirements for particular types of missions (See Para 4.1, Chapter 4).

11. The S-3 issues Warning Order #1 to all subordinate units.

12. At the Sustainment Bde level ICW Cdrs guidance, XO dispatches LNOs to the supported Div G-4 or other critical supported organization (if not co-located) and co-ordinates with respective CSSB LNOs for integration with Sustainment Bde Plans Staff. BSBs may opt to dispatch LNOs to supporting Sus Bde/CSSBs (either or).

13. Staff members return at a given time to review their estimates and begin the process of gathering information for the Mission Analysis Briefing (See Chapter 14). As a TTP – if it takes longer than 15 minutes to update a staff estimate, it is not considered a current 'running' estimate.

14. The S-3 (or designated Plans Off) completes a current Situation Template prior to Mission Analysis.

15. At the Sustainment Bde level, the SPO receives any (available) Div or supported BDE Spt Concept overlays from the Div G-4/BDE SPO per suspense in WO #1.

Tool	Who Gathers	For What MDMP Activity	Timeline (Gather when)
Large scale map of the area of operations, 1:25,000 or larger	S3 OPS NCO	Mission Analysis	Mission Receipt
Higher echelon orders, INTSUMs, INTREPs, and graphics of the AO	S3 OPS NCO	Mission Analysis	Mission Receipt
Cartoon sketch or representation of the AO depicting prominent terrain features, both topographic and man-made	S3 OPS NCO	Mission Analysis	Mission Receipt
Formatted mission analysis worksheets	S3 OPS NCO	Mission Analysis	Mission Receipt
Blown-up, laminated mission analysis briefing boards	S3 OPS NCO	Mission Analysis	Mission Receipt
Enlarged, blank timeline with space for light data, enemy & friendly actions	S3 OPS NCO	Mission Analysis	Mission Receipt
Examples of previous products used & approved by the CDR	Staff NCOs	Mission Analysis	Mission Receipt
CDR's guidance checklist	S3 OPS NCO	Mission Analysis	Mission Receipt
Wargaming staff input checklist	S3 OPS NCO	Wargaming	COA Development
Mission Analysis nesting diagram	S3 OPS NCO	Wargaming	COA Development
Synchronization matrix	S3 OPS NCO	Wargaming	COA Development
COA statements and sketch boards with decision graphics	Staff NCOs	Wargaming	COA Development
CDR's guidance	S3	Wargaming	COA Development
Battle staff estimates	Staff	Wargaming	COA Development
Operational graphic overlays	S3 OPS NCO	Wargaming	COA Development
List of friendly forces available	S3 OPS NCO	Wargaming	COA Development
Enemy SITEMPs and EVENTEMPs	S2 NCO	Wargaming	COA Development
List of possible enemy reinforcements	S2 NCO	Wargaming	COA Development
List of known higher / friendly & enemy critical events	S2, S3	Wargaming	COA Development
List of known higher / friendly & enemy decision points	S3 OPS NCO	Wargaming	COA Development
Friendly and enemy ICONs	S3 & S2 NCOs	Wargaming	COA Development
Supplies (paper, markers, acetate, etc.)	S3 OPS NCO	Wargaming	COA Development
Imagery (if available or applicable), TERRABASE II products	S3 & S2 NCOs	Wargaming	COA Development
Task organization chart	S3 OPS NCO	Wargaming	COA Development
Reference library (CD or paper)	Staff NCOs	Throughout MDMP	Mission Receipt

Figure 4-1 MDMP Product Tools

4.1 RECEIPT OF A MISSION CHECKLIST & DRILL

STEP 1 ALERT THE BATTLE STAFF

TASK DESCRIPTION	PERSONNEL
Upon receipt of the mission (or WARNORD), alert & assemble the Staff	OPS NCOIC
Prepare initial planning timeline – post time schedules	CDR, XO

STEP 2 RECEIVE OPLAN/OPORD

TASK DESCRIPTION	PERSONNEL
Acknowledge receipt of OPLAN/OPORD	S3/OPS NCOIC
Inventory/Confirm components of OPLAN/OPORD/record list of TBPs	S3/OPS NCOIC
Reproduce OPLAN/OPORD, ANNEXES and appropriate OVERLAYs	OPS NCOIC
Distribute OPLAN/OPORD	OPS NCOIC
Receive Situational Update Brief	CDR, STAFF, APPROPRIATE UNIT PSNL

STEP 3 PREPARE PLANS, AREAS, AND SYSTEMS

TASK DESCRIPTION	PERSONNEL
Establish/Open Request for Information (RFI) Log	OPS NCOIC
Set up the Command Post (CP)/Plans Area for mission analysis	S-3/Plans Off, OPS NCOIC
Determine map boxes for 1:50,000, 1:100,000 and 1:250,000 scale maps. Set appropriate MCS system raster map series as required	S-2, S-3, OPS NCOIC
Prepare map boards (1: 50,000, 1:100,000 and 1:250,000 scale maps). Post any doctrinal templates on appropriate (digital) map/COP. Post appropriate Div/Bde Opns and Sustainment graphics.	Plans Off, S-2 & OPS NCOIC
Determine naming & numbering conventions for this mission/operation	S-3/Plans Off
Update Subordinate Unit Status (Personnel, Intelligence, Sustainment, SPT Opns, Staff Estimates)	STAFF

STEP 4 ISSUE WARNING ORDER #1

TASK DESCRIPTION	PERSONNEL
Receive initial Cdr's planning guidance	STAFF
Prepare Warning Order #1 (Current/Future/Plans Ops)	S-3/Plans Off
S-3 reviews warning order	S-3
CDR signs warning order	CDR
Issue Warning Order #1 to all subordinate and supporting units	S-3, OPS NCOIC
Confirm receipt by all addressees	OPS NCOIC

4.2 WARNING ORDER #1 CHECKLIST

1. Reproduce the following parts of higher order for inclusion in WO #1:

   a. All heading data including classification, issuing HQ data, order number and code name, references and time zone data.
   b. Situation, including enemy, friendly attachments/detachments and assumptions (if OPLAN). Attach ANNEX A (TASK ORGANIZATION) and ANNEX B (INTELLIGENCE) if available.
   c. Mission of higher commands one and two levels up.
   d. Execution, including concept of operations, tasks to subordinate units and coordinating instructions.
   e. Sustainment paragraph (Paragraph 4).
   f. Command and Signal (Paragraph 5).
   g. All overlays.
   h. Other ANNEXES as appropriate.

2. Cover sheet specifying:

   a. Type of Operation
   b. Location of operations
   c. Initial planning guidance of CDR including planning timeline.
   d. Subordinates movement requirements.
   e. LNO dispatch instructions.
   f. *Suspense for submission of initial BDE Spt Concept overlays from BDE Spt Ops Off's to Sustainment Bde Spt Ops.*
   g. Requirement for submission of updated PERSTAT/ LOGSTAT and other required status reports by subordinate units within one (1) hours of WO #1 receipt.
   h. Distribution to all staff elements and all subordinate and supporting units.

4.3 WARNING ORDER (WARNORD) FORMAT.

_____
(Classification)
(Change from oral orders, if any) (Optional)

Copy ____ of ____ copies
300th CSSB
(Place of issue)
(Date-time-group of signature)
(Message reference number)

WARNING ORDER _____ (EX: WARNING ORDER #4)

(U) References: (Refer to higher headquarters OPLAN/ OPORD, and identify map sheet for operation).

(U) Time Zone Used Throughout the OPLAN/OPORD: (Optional)

(U) Task Organization: (Optional)

1. **(U)** <u>Situation</u>.
   a. (U) <u>Area of Interest (AI).</u>
   b. (U) <u>Area of Operation (AO)</u>
   c. (U) <u>Enemy Forces.</u>
   d. (U) <u>Friendly Forces</u>.
   e. (U) <u>Interagency, Intergovernmental, and Nongovernmental Organizations</u>.
   f. (U) <u>Civil Considerations</u>.
   g. (U) <u>Attachments and Detachments</u>. (*Provide initial task organization*)
   h. (U) <u>Assumptions</u>. (*List any significant assumptions for OPORD development*)

2. (U) <u>Mission</u>. (S-3, XO) (*State the issuing headquarters mission*)

3. (U) <u>Execution</u>.
    a. (U) <u>Initial Cdrs Intent</u>. (Cdr) (*Provide a brief commander's intent statement*)
    b. (U) <u>Concept of Operations/Support</u>. (SPO) (*This may be 'To Be Determined' in the initial WARNORD*)
    c. (U) <u>Tasks to Subordinate Units</u>. (S-3)
    d. (U) <u>Coordinating instructions</u> (S-3).
        (1) (U) CCIR.
        (2) (U) Risk guidance.
        (3) (U) Time line.
        (4) (U) Guidance of orders and rehearsals.
        (5) (U) Orders group meeting (attendees, location, and time).
        (6) (U) Earliest movement time and degree of notice.

4. (U) <u>Sustainment</u>. (S-1/S-4) (Optional)
    a. (U) <u>Special equipment</u>. (Identify requirements and coordinate transfers)
    b. (U) <u>Logistics and Transportation</u>. (Identify requirements and coordination for pre-position of assets)
    c. (U) <u>Personnel or Human Resource</u>. (Identify requirements and coordination for pre-position of assets)
    d. (U) <u>Health Service Support</u> ((Identify requirements and coordination for pre-position of assets).

5. (U) <u>Command and Signal</u>. (XO / S-3) (Optional)
    a. (U) <u>Command</u>. (XO)
        (1) (U) Location of the Commander (State where the Commander plans to locate him/herself. If the operation is phased, state the location of the commander by phase).
        (2) (U) Succession of command (State the succession of command if different from unit SOP).

    (3) (U) Special Instructions for XOs (Specify respon-sibilities of XOs and associated CPs, by phase if necessary).

b. (U) <u>Control</u>. (XO/S-3)

    (1) (U) Scheme of CP employment (State the scheme of CP employment, including each CP location and how the CP is used. State which CP is the primary controlling CP for the operation). *(Note – a Forward Logistics Element (FLE) or CRSP must have a C2 (mission command) node system for effective operations).*

    (2) (U) Special Instructions for CPs (State tasks or additional instructions for each CP not detailed elsewhere. This might include movement of key staff officers between CPs and movement of functional cells. List by phase if necessary).

    (3) (U) Liaison requirements (Provide instruction for liaison to higher, lower, and adjacent commands).

c. (U) <u>Signal</u>. (S-3)

    (1) (U) Network operations (Include network con-trol procedures for network administration and management).

    (2) (U) Signal Operating Instructions (Identify cur-rent SOI edition in effect).

    (3) (U) Recognition and identification instructions (Special instructions not included in the SOP, friendly recognition signals, vehicle markings, etc).

ACKNOWLEDGE:

MENTER
LTC

OFFICIAL:

POND
S3

ANNEXES: *(List annexes by letter and title)*

DISTRIBUTION: *(List recipients)*

(Classification)

4.4 CDR's INITIAL GUIDANCE CHECKLIST

1. Upon initial review of a new mission, the CDR will issue initial guidance to the XO, SPO, and S-3 to guide the planning process. Periodic review and update of this guidance is done by the CDR as planning progresses.

2. CDR's guidance will focus on the CDR's purpose, method and desired end state of any event.

3. CDRs estimate will review available data including:

    a. CDR's assessment of staff experience, cohesiveness and level of rest or stress.
    b. Weather and light requirements for customer (i.e. supported unit), planning, rehearsals and movement.
    c. Presence or absence of needed staff estimates.
    d. Time requirements, specifically time available for mission receipt to mission execution, time requirements to plan, coordinate, issue OPORD, and prepare/execute mission.

4. Initial CDR's guidance will contain the following as a minimum:

    a. Whether to use Design Methodology, or whether full/abbreviated MDMP is conducted.
    b. Abbreviations to the MDMP, if any.
    c. Scope of IPB to be prepared.
    d. Guidance on timeline for planning, preparation and execution of mission.
    e. CCIR guidance, especially FFIR instructions.
    f. Special LNO instructions and whether to dispatch.
    g. Initial recon to begin.
    h. Any authorized movement required

    i. Any additional tasks.

    j. Any Decision Points (DPs).

As a minimum, basic Sustainment Commander's Guidance should include:

1. Does the distribution mission involve long hauls? (Preference for Line Haul or Local Haul distribution operations). If Line Haul, is a FLE, CRSP or CSC required? Have the commander define his/her 'operational reach'.

2. For Sustainment Brigade: Use of a Ring Route or 'Hub and Spoke' distribution operation or the creation of Logistical Task Forces (LTF) using Trailer Transfer Point detachments.

3. For Sus Bde/CSSBs: Cross leveling of transportation units to create a 'multi-functional' transportation capability.

4. Guidance on the unit of Host Nation trucking or 'White' contractor assets.

5. Guidance on 'Red Line' (i.e. when available assets dip below a particular level of availability of 'Red Line'. Example: M1075 PLS availability dips below 50%).

4.5 COMMANDER'S GUIDANCE WORKSHEET.

Commander's Guidance Worksheet

OPORD #	Unit HQs	DTG	Cdr's Signature

1. **Commander's Intent**
   a. **Broader purpose**

   b. **Key tasks**

   c. **Endstate**

2. **Decisive points/ actions:**

3. **COAs to consider (where/ when/ how to mass to accomplish mission and intent)**
   a. **Friendly**

   b. **Enemy**

4. How we must posture for next phase (logistically/ geographically)

5. Intelligence Collection (formerly ISR) guidance

6. Deception guidance

7. Priorities for:
    a. Man

    b. Arm

    c. Fuel

    d. Fix

    e. Move

    f. Sustain

  g. Force protection/ security measures to be implemented

  h. Intelligence

8. Risk (areas acceptable)

9. CCIR
  a. PIR

  b. FFIR

  c. EEFI

10. Decisions I see myself making:

11. Time plan (confirm/ readjust proposed timeline)

12. Type order

13. Type Rehearsal

Para 4.6 REQUEST FOR INFORMATION (RFI) LOG

Request for Information (RFI) Log   Page ____ of ____

FROM	TO	SUBJECT	ACTION TAKEN	DATE/ TIME	REC BY

NOTE: The S-3 NCO maintains a copy of this log in the CP during the planning and execution of an operation. During planning, each staff section develops RFI's for the assigned units or Sus Bde/CSSB /Div/BCT which are recorded here and updated at each briefing. Sample RFI format is found in Para 4.7. The following codes are used to identify staff sections, followed by a number/and DTG. Example S14/110900 is from Support Opns, #14, on 110900. P = S-1, I = S-2, O = S-3, L = S-4, X = XO, S = SPO, M = CSM, C = BC

Para 4.7 REQUEST FOR INFORMATION (RFI) FORMAT

XYZ[th] BSB Request For Information (RFI)

123rd BSB, 99th HBCT			
Request for Information (RFI) Worksheet			
Classification (circle one):	TOP SECRET CONFIDENTIAL		SECRET UNCLASSIFIED
RFI #:	Urgency:		FLASH IMMEDIATE
DTG:			PRIORITY ROUTINE
Info needed by:			
LTIOV:			
Subject:		From:	
POC:	PH#:	FAX#:	Call Sign:
To:		Unit:	
Question:			
Resources Consulted:			
Response to:		From:	
To:		DTG:	

Answer:				
Method Received:	FM	FAX	HARD COPY	Other:
Control #	Received by:	Staff Section:	Forwarded to:	Date forwarded:

CHAPTER 5

MISSION ANALYSIS

✮✮✮

Of all the steps in the Military Decision Making Process, Mission Analysis is the most. Overall, the Sustainment unit must determine whether it has the capability to provide support to its customer (usually a tactical maneuver unit). Determination of supported unit requirements is a fairly straight forward process obtain through a variety of means (historical data, use of the Logistics Estimate Worksheet, OPLOG Planner, etc), but determination of a sustainment units 'capabilities' is the challenge for staff planners during Mission Analysis. While time and time management are critical, XO's should consider allocating upwards of 40-50% of available time towards Mission Analysis.

MISSION ANALYSIS STEPS

1. Analyze the higher HQ's plan or order.
2. Perform initial Intelligence Preparation of the Battlefield (IPB)/Logistics Preparation of the Battlefield (LPB) (Terrain analysis focusing on road networks, weather analysis, enemy OB, and threat integration).
3. Determine specified, implied and essential tasks.
4. Review available assets and identify resource shortfalls.
5. Determine constraints. (Note – restraints and constraints are now considered one. *Additionally, Constraints must be stated, but may be constrictive or prescriptive*).
6. Identify critical facts and develop assumptions.
7. Begin Risk Management.

8. Determine initial Commander's Critical Information Requirements (CCIR) and EEFIs.
9. Develop the initial information collection plan.
10. Update plan for use of available time.
11. Develop initial themes and messages.
12. Development of a proposed Problem Statement
13. Develop a proposed Mission Statement.
14. Present the Mission Analysis briefing.
15. Develop and issue initial commander's Intent.
16. Develop and issue initial planning guidance.
17. Develop Course of Action evaluation criteria
18. Issue Warning Order #2 to all subordinate and supporting units.

MISSION ANALYSIS PROCESS

1. XO ensures that the designated staff members work sequentially through the tasks set forth in the "Mission Analysis Checklist", Para 5.2 (Mission Analysis Checklist).

2. The S-3 and S-2 Off/NCO, (with input from all staff), prepares the IPB/LPB products (MCOO, Intel Estimate, Enemy SITEMP's) based on the considerations contained in Para 5.4 (IPB/LPB Considerations in the Sustainment Planning Process). Remember that Sustainment IPB/LPB focuses on the major road networks, how terrain interacts (i.e. – bridges, passes, towns and cities), and the impact/influence of forces considered hostile towards the sustainment unit conducting distribution operations.

3. Each Staff Section prepares a "Mission Analysis Work Sheet" (Para 5.6 - Mission Analysis Worksheets) for review by the S – 3 and SPO. Use the generic considerations found in Para 5.3 (Mission Analysis Guidelines) and the Sustainment Functions based considerations found in Para 5.5 (Sustainment Mission Analysis Initial Worksheet).

4. The CDR prepares his own Mission Analysis (called the *Commander's Estimate*) in parallel with the staff. He issues his initial intent and guidance following the Mission Analysis Briefing. The CDR's initial intent is based on the considerations initially addressed in Para 5.1 (Mission Analysis Products) as well as thoughts derived from his/her Commander's Estimate. The CDR's guidance is based on the considerations at that criteria identified in Chapter 12 (Commander's Guidance Guidelines). Finally, the CDR approves the restated mission at the end of the Mission Analysis Briefing.

5. Final result is the products listed in Para 5.1 (Mission Analysis Products).

5.1 MISSION ANALYSIS PRODUCTS

MISSION ANALYSIS PRODUCTS

1. Staff Estimates. (Most critical: Intel, Logistics (Sustainment), and Personnel)

2. List of Specified, Implied, and Essential Tasks.

3. List of Facts and Planning Assumptions necessary to continue planning. **(Test for an assumption: "Would the result change if the assumption wasn't made?")**

4. MCOO, SITEMP's and Event Templates. Another good tool to develop is a time/distance matrix or template.

5. Enemy "most likely COA" and "most dangerous COA."

6. Enemy/COE operations template down to squad level, Ground Avenue of Approach Overlay down to company level, Air Avenue of Approach Overlay and artillery range fans for all templated indirect fire systems.

7. Priorities for each sustainment function (human resources, supply, maintenance, transportation, field service, Health Service Support (HSS), EOD, Finance Management Spt, Legal, and Religious)

8. Commander's Planning Guidance used to develop COAs. Key to COA development is how to efficiently and effectively lengthen the '*Operational Reach*' and distance to the customer.

9. Commander's Intent.

   a. The Commander's Intent is a clear concise statement of what the sustainment force must do to succeed with respect to the conduct of distribution to the sustainment unit's customer's factoring in terrain (the existing distribution network), weather, enemy and the desired end state. It provides a link between the mission and the concept of the operation by stating key tasks that, along with the mission, are the basis for the subordinates to exercise initiative when unanticipated opportunities arise or when the original concept of the operation no longer applies. Intent is normally expressed in four to five sentences and is mandatory for all orders. The mission and the commander's intent must be understood two echelons down.

   b. Key tasks are those that must be performed by the unit, or conditions that must be met, to achieve the stated purpose of the operation (para 2 of the OPLAN/OPORD). The operation's tempo, duration, and effect on the enemy, and terrain that must be controlled, are examples of key tasks. Remember –

all key tasks provided by the commander must be applicable to all COAs directed by the commander.

c. The commander's intent does not include the "method" by which the force will get from its current state to the end state. The method is the concept of the operation. End state is the conditions that, when achieved, accomplish the mission. The conditions to attain are the "aims" set for within the operation. (FM 5-0, *Operations*). It is not another "checklist" of events or circumstances.

d. The **commander personally prepares his intent statement (time permitting)**.

10. Approved Restated Mission.

11. Warning Order #2.

12. Time and Location for Course of Action Brief.

5.2 MISSION ANALYSIS CHECKLIST & DRILL

STEP 1.1 DETERMINE HIGHER COMMANDER'S INTENT

TASK DESCRIPTION	PERSONNEL
Review Commander's Intent (higher and next higher)	ALL
Extract Intents and load into Briefs (MA, COA DB, and OPLAN/OPORD)	S-3, *Plans Off*
Post Commander's Intents	Clerk
Determine any "language" or doctrinal terminology conflicts between Intents	S-3, *Plans Off*

STEP 1.2 DETERMINE HIGHER HEADQUARTERS' MISSION

TASK DESCRIPTION	PERSONNEL
Review Mission Statements (higher and next higher)	ALL
Extract Mission Statements and load into briefs (MA, COA DB and OPLAN/OPORD)	S-3, *Plans Off*
Post Mission Statements	Clerk
Review AO – check operational graphics to verify and ID Area of Interest	ALL
Analyze concept of operation and the higher/customer concepts of support	ALL
Develop standard area of operation sketch for COA development	S-3, *Plans Off*
Determine any "language" conflicts between missions	S-3, *Plans Off*
Provide staff with Mission Analysis Worksheets, Asset Availability Worksheets, and RFI forms.	S-3/OPS NCO

STEP 2 CONDUCT INTELLIGENCE/LOGISTICAL PREP OF THE BATTLEFIELD

TASK DESCRIPTION	PERSONNEL
Complete/Brief weather effects chart	S-2/NCO
Complete/Brief terrain effects to include the distribution networks within the AO/AOR (MSRs and ASRs)	S-2/NCO
Complete/Brief situational templates	S-2/NCO
Review AO/AOR-check operational graphics to verify and ID Area of Interest	ALL
Analyze concept of operation and the higher/customer concepts of support	ALL
Develop standard area of operation sketch for COA development	S-3, *Plans Off*
Determine any "language" conflicts between missions	S-3, *Plans Off*

STEP 3.1 IDENTIFY SPECIFIED AND IMPLIED TASKS

TASK DESCRIPTION	PERSONNEL
Identify specified (OPORD paragraphs 2, 3, coordinating instructions and annexes) tasks (Mission Analysis Worksheet – Para 5.3)	ALL
Load specified tasks in Mission Analysis brief	S-3, *Plans Off*
Identify implied tasks (Mission Analysis Worksheet – Para 5.3)	ALL
Load implied tasks in Mission Analysis brief	S-3, *Plans Off*

STEP 3.2 IDENTIFY ESSENTIAL TASKS

TASK DESCRIPTION	PERSONNEL
Identify essential tasks (Mission Analysis Worksheet – Para 5.3)	ALL
Determine final list of essential tasks	S-3, *Plans Off*
Load final list of essential tasks in mission analysis brief	S-3, *Plans Off,* Clerk
Complete/brief Draft Operational Timeline	SPO, S-3

STEP 4 REVIEW AVAILABLE ASSETS (CUSTOMER AND SUPPORTING) & ID SHORTAGES

TASK DESCRIPTION	PERSONNEL
Review all higher forces available	ALL
Determine all Sus Bde/CSSB/BSB forces and sustainment related assets available	ALL
Complete/Brief Unit Task Organization	S-3, *Plans Off*
Review Customer forces available list	ALL
Load supporting (i.e. Sustainment) & supported unit (i.e. customer) forces and assets available for mission analysis brief	S-3, *Plans Off*, Clerk

STEP 5 DETERMINE CONSTRAINTS

TASK DESCRIPTION	PERSONNEL
Determine constraints (must do) (Mission Analysis Worksheet – Para 5.3)	ALL
Determine restrictions (can't do) (Mission Analysis Worksheet – Para 5.3)	ALL
Determine external support mission	SPO
Load constraints in mission analysis briefing	S-3, *Plans Off*, Clerk

STEP 6 DETERMINE CRITICAL FACTS AND DEVELOP ASSUMPTIONS

TASK DESCRIPTION	PERSONNEL
Identify critical facts (Mission Analysis Worksheet, Para 5.3)	ALL
Identify assumptions (Mission Analysis Worksheet, Para 5.3)	ALL
Load facts and assumptions info for mission analysis brief	S-3, *Plans Off*,

STEP 7 BEGIN RISK MANAGEMENT

TASK DESCRIPTION	PERSONNEL
Determine higher guidance on risk	S-3, S-1, *Plans Off*
Risk-What fails to accomplish the mission	ALL
Risk-What achieves the mission, but fails to achieve the desired results	ALL
Risk-What achieves the mission, but at too great a cost	ALL
Prepare risk information for mission analysis brief. Fill in CRM Matrix	S-3, S-1, *Plans Off*, Clerk

STEP 8 DETERMINE INITIAL CCIR (PIR, FFIR) AND EEFI'S

TASK DESCRIPTION	PERSONNEL
Determine Priority Intelligence Requirements (PIR) (Note – All PIRs should be tied to either a decision required of the Commander or the execution of a Battle Drill)	ALL
Determine Friendly Forces Intelligence Requirements (FFIR)	ALL
Determine Essential Elements of Friendly Information (EEFI)	ALL

STEP 9 DEVELOP INITIAL INTELLIGENCE COLLECTION (IC) PLAN

TASK DESCRIPTION	PERSONNEL
Identify requirements and intelligence gaps	S-2/S-3
Evaluate available assets (int/ext) to collect information	S-2/S-3
Recommend IC assets controlled by organization to collect on IRs	S-2/S-3
Submit requests for information (RFIs) to adjacent/ higher collection support	S-3
Begin assembling the IC Sync Matrix	S-3

STEP 10 UPDATE PLAN FOR THE USE OF AVAILABLE TIME

TASK DESCRIPTION	PERSONNEL
Review time available for mission execution	XO
Review time available for collaborative planning sessions and the medium (Adobe Chat, face-to-face, teleconference, etc) over which they will take place	XO
Prepare time analysis info for MA brief and WARNO #2	XO
Review total time from receipt of mission to execution	XO
Review use of 1/3 of total time as planning time	XO
Complete detailed planning timeline-alert battle staff	XO

STEP 11 DEVELOP INITIAL THEMES AND MESSAGES

TASK DESCRIPTION	PERSONNEL
ID 'Actors' (Individuals, Organizations, Public) connected with the planned operation	XO, S-3, S-2, S-7 (if avail)
Develop 'Information Themes' that support the points the Commander desires to get across to the public at large about their operation. (Note – Ensure that themes tie objectives, Lines of Effort (LOE), and End State conditions).	XO, S-3, S-7 (if avail)
Develop 'Messages' to support appropriate Information Theme (Note – A message is verbal, written, or electronic communication that supports an Information Theme focused on a specific actor, or public. It must be in support of a specific action or task.	XO, S-3, S-7 (if avail)

STEP 12 DEVELOP A PROPOSED PROBLEM STATEMENT

TASK DESCRIPTION	PERSONNEL
Compare current situation with the desired end state	ALL
Brainstorm and list issues that impede the unit from achieving the desired end state. (Note – In developing the Problem Statement for Sustainment units, the problem inevitably becomes one of establishing the most *efficient* and *effective* means to conduct distribution to the unit's customers within the assigned AO/AOR.	ALL

STEP 13 DEVELOP A PROPOSED MISSION STATEMENT

TASK DESCRIPTION	PERSONNEL
Develop proposed mission statement - load in MA Brief and WARNO #2. As a minimum, the Mission Statement must contain **'WHO'**, **'WHAT'**, **'WHERE'**, **'WHEN'** (either On Order O/O, or with a Date/Time/Group – DTG), **'WHERE'**, and **'WHY'**. A Mission Statement may also contain more than one essential task.	S-3, *Plans Off & Clerk*
Review proposed mission statement	ALL
Write/Brief proposed CCIR	XO, S-3, S-2

STEP 13.1 COMPLETE MISSION ANALYSIS WORKSHEETS

TASK DESCRIPTION	PERSONNEL
Review base plan and all appropriate annexes	ALL
Identify and record critical tasks and assumptions	ALL
Identify and record forces available	ALL
Identify and record specified and implied tasks	ALL
Identify and record essential tasks	ALL
Identify and record draft CCIR	ALL
Complete header information on worksheet and turn in to XO or (S-3)	ALL

STEP 13.2 STAFF ESTIMATE EXCHANGE

TASK DESCRIPTION	PERSONNEL
Update staff estimate for exchange of information with staff	ALL
Present critical information to staff	ALL
Receive terrain analysis from S-2/Intel NCOIC	ALL
Complete/Brief commo-logistics automation support and charts	S-6, SASMO

STEP 14 PRESENT THE MISSION ANALYSIS BRIEF

TASK DESCRIPTION	PERSONNEL
Provide MA information input to S-3 (Annotate Mission Analysis Worksheet, Para 5.3)	ALL incl LNO's
Review forces available information	ALL (as necessary)
Site setup for briefing	S-3 Section
Prepare slides and handouts	OPS NCOs
Rehearse briefing	ALL
Conduct briefing	ALL
Receive & Post Cdr's guidance	ALL
Update/Brief RFI status	OPS NCOIC

STEP 15 DEVELOP AND ISSUE INITIAL COMMANDER'S INTENT

TASK DESCRIPTION	PERSONNEL
Develop and review the purpose of the mission	CDR, XO, S-3
Develop and review key tasks the unit needs to accomplish in order for the mission to be successful. These are not a regurgitation of the Units 'Specified' Task. An example of a key task might be the establishment of a CRSP, or FLE, or might require the unit's OR rate must remain above 75% operational.	CDR, XO, S-3, SPO
Develop what constitutes the 'End State' of the mission and/or criteria of success.	CDR, XO, S-3, SPO

STEP 16 DEVELOP AND ISSUE INITIAL PLANNING GUIDANCE

TASK DESCRIPTION	PERSONNEL
Cdr provides planning guidance obtained through his/her CDR's Estimate.	CDR
Number of Courses of Action for staff consideration are identified	CDR
Unit cross attachments if any/LNO dispatch locations	CDR

Mission Cmd Control Nodes/CPs/Echelonment of Forces (if any)	CDR, XO, S-3, S-6
Modifications to time available	CDR, XO

STEP 17 DEVELOP COURSE OF ACTION EVALUATION CRITERIA

TASK DESCRIPTION	PERSONNEL
Determine proposed criteria with weights based on the assessment of its relative importance and CDR's guidance.	XO
Criteria reviewed and presented at the MA Briefing for CDR approval	XO, STAFF

STEP 18 ISSUE WO#2

TASK DESCRIPTION	PERSONNEL
Provide input for WO#2	ALL
Prepare WO#2	S-3, SPO
S-3 review and CDR sign	S-3, CDR
Issue Warning Order #2 to all subordinate and supporting units	XO, S-3

5.3 MISSION ANALYSIS SUSTAINMENT STAFF OFFICER GUIDELINES

All Staff Officers:
1. Specified and implied tasks (Note – if an implied task is found within a unit TACSOP, do not list)
2. Mission essential tasks
3. Constraints & Restraints
4. Time considerations
5. Recommended CCIR

S-1:
1. Personnel status of organic and attached units.
2. Forecasted personnel status out 72 to 96 hours.
3. Civilian and military medical assets available (including Class VIII supply status).

S-4:
1. Maintenance status
2. Forecasted vehicle, weapons and equipment status
3. Supply status of Classes I, II, III, IV, V, VII and IX supplies for internal support
4. Transportation assets available
5. Availability and status of services for internal organizational support
6. Host nation and foreign nation support

S2 & S2 NCO
1. Initial IPB, including the following:
   (a) Define battlefield environment
   (b) Define battlefield effects
   (c) Evaluate the threat, to include:
      (1) Enemy combat power
      (2) Enemy vulnerabilities
      (3) Threat COAs (arranged in order of probability of adoption)
   (d) Determine assets available

2. COE and local criminal elements - capabilities and trend analysis.
3. Cultural, religious, historical, and high-density civilian population areas

S-3 & S-3 NCO:
1. Current situation of subordinate units and activities
2. Status of task organization
3. Assets available
4. Mission and intent two levels up
5. Engineer assets available in the area of operations.
6. Capabilities of available engineer assets (for example: MSR/ASR maintenance & repair, number of survivability emplacements for CL III and V facilities)

S-6 Signal:
1. Communications maintenance status and connectivity (JNN, VSAT, FM, MSE, etc)
2. Network Signal Company status and deployment
3. Higher headquarters' signal plan

CBRN:
1. Assets available, to include reconnaissance, decontamination, smoke, and constraints
2. MOPP status
3. CBRN threat status
4. Troop safety criteria

SPT OPS:
1. Displaced civilian movement, routes, and assembly areas
2. Host nation and foreign nation support
3. Non-government and private volunteer organizations; independent organizations operating
4. Status of CL I, II, III, IV, V, VI, VII and IX for external support.
5. Customer (supported units) maintenance status

BSB Co C (Med)/BSMO (Note: Sus Bde must coordinate med support for subordinate CSSBs and Trans Bns via nearest Medical Brigade)
1. Brigade medical asset capabilities
2. CL VIII status
3. Causality density and location estimates by critical event
4. Ability of host nation to care for civilians

Aviation Planner/LNO (if available)
1. Coordination of airspace requirements.
2. Fixed and rotary wing lift assets.
3. LZ's, FLS's, FARP's and other air infrastructure.
4. Threat and friendly ADA review.

5.4 IPB CONSIDERATIONS

IPB CONSIDERATION IN THE SUSTAINMENT PLANNING PROCESS

TERRAIN IMPLICATIONS:

- Can the terrain support sustainment operations?
  - Are host nation (HN) assets available for logistics operations?
  - Any existing structures/built-up areas present?
  - Any usable medical facilities
  - Is there any overhead storage/work areas?

- What are the ground and air avenues of approach (AA) that could interfere with sustainment operations? Offensive operations could produce by-passed or stay behind enemy elements that must be recognized and averted by sustainment assets to be able to maintain continuous support.

- Where are the infiltration lanes that could be used by the enemy?
  - Identify and locate the routes the enemy could use to move insurgents, light infantry and/or unconventional warfare units into the organization's AOR.
  - Is there any area in the organization's AOR that could provide concealed positioned to these enemy units?

- Identify possible AAs, LZs, DZs, and MSR ambush locations in the organization/Sus Bde AO.

WEATHER IMPLICATIONS:

- What will be the effect on the entire road network (hard surfaced and unimproved road surfaces) as a result of different types of precipitation (rain, snow, fog/mist, ice) and temperature?
    - Will a rain soaked unimproved dirt road in a tree line support the weight of fuel HEMTTs or 5K – 7.5K tankers? How about an M1070 HET loaded with a M1A2 weighing 138.5 tons?
    - How will an iced over hard surface MSR effect LOGPAC operations?
    - Will an unplowed, snowed over MSR affect replenishment operations (RO) travel time?

- Will the temperature have any effect on:
    - Friendly forces TA-50 (hot and cold weather)
    - Classes of supply
    - Storage of CL I, bottled water, and VIII
    - Consumption of CL III (Bulk & Packaged) or IX (filters, tire chains, batteries, starters)?
    - Production of potable water (frozen pipes, iced over ponds, creeks, etc)?

- How would poor visibility/illumination affect:
    - Enemy infiltration
    - Force Protection
    - Driving/resupply activities (slower convoy speeds, accidents)

OTHER IMPLICATIONS:

- Security:
    - Does the area offer adequate cover/concealment?

- Do we have observation/overwatch positions along possible AAs / LZs?
- Can we disperse our assets to reduce possible collateral damage?
- Can we minimize our unit's signature?
- MSR/ASR security. Are there chokepoints or possible ambush sites?

- General:
  - Does the area afford good commo? Can the maneuver unit talk to the FSC and the BSB LOC (20-30 km away)? Can the task organized FLE OIC communicate with the BSB/CSSB?
  - Is the road network adequate and trafficable? Can the turf support and allow good movement within the AO for the vehicles that will occupy it?
  - Is the AO in proximity to the MSR, not on the MSR but near it? By doing so it reduces unit signature and might take the unit off an AA.
  - Potable water/raw water source location (available, frozen over)
  - Access to MEDEVAC LZ?
  - Existing bridges capable of handling full HEMTTS, 5K tankers and HETS evacuating M1s (140 tons)? What is the height clearance for overhead bridges?
  - Any water/rail capability? Although not normally used at Sus Bde level, these assets may be available.
  - Are there airfields located nearby for emergency use?

SUSTAINMENT CONSIDERATIONS IN DEVELOPING THE MCOO

- Does the terrain offer an area suitable for sustainment operations? (Remember, M1070 HETS do not function well in highly sandy off road areas)

- Is it away from possible AAs and mobility corridors?
- Is this area close to a useable road network?
- Does the MSR travel through primary or secondary engagement areas?
- Are there any obstacles that could restrict/divert sustainment/replenishment operations such as bridge restrictions (classification and overhead clearance), choke points, road surface/trafficability concerns?

5.5 IPB to ORDERS PROCESS COMPARISON

STAFF ACTION	IPB TASKS
BCT (BSB)/SUS BDE (CSSB) WARNING ORDER	Define the operational environment
	Begin weather and terrain analysis
	Develop doctrinal template
RECEIVE OPORD	Begin S-2 Mission Analysis
	Develop MCOO
	Evaluate the threat, situational template
	Determine threat capabilities
MISSION ANALYSIS BRIEF	Current weather situation
	Current enemy situation
	Terrain (Road network) analysis
	Situation Template Overlay
COMMANDER'S GUIDANCE	Guidance on CCIR (PIR, FFIR) & EEFI
COA DEVELOPMENT	Develop event template for each COA
	Develop IC collection matrix for each COA
SYNCHRONIZATION	Collection Plan for approved COA
	Begin intelligence portion of OPORD
	Refine IC collection matrix
OPORD PRODUCTION	Complete Annex B, Intelligence IC Plan
	Disseminate and save all intelligence updates

IPB Products

STAFF PHASE	PRODUCT
RECEIVE MISSION	Define the Operational Environment
	Doctrinal Template (Order of Battle and Timeline)
MISSION ANALYSIS	Key Terrain/MSR/ASRs
	Situation Template
WARGAMING	Identify enemy actions
SYNCHRONIZATION	Sketch in enemy time line phases when applicable
OPORD DEVELOPMENT	Complete Annex B for OPORD

5.6 SUSTAINMENT MISSION ANALYSIS INITIAL WORKSHEET

1. Each key staff member should use this initial worksheet as an internal "scratch sheet" to gather data for updating their Staff Estimates and for transfer to the final Mission Analysis Worksheet to be turned in to the S-3 (Para 5.7, Sustainment Mission Analysis Worksheet)

2. Consider all Sustainment Functions (HR, Supply, Maintenance, Field Services, Transportation, HSS, EOD, Religious/Fin Svc) as it relates to each Plans Staff's area of concern.

3. Coordinate your information with the other planners.

4. Retain these worksheets within the staff section and update as new information is developed.

SUSTAINMENT MISSION ANALYSIS INITIAL WORKSHEET

1. <u>HUMAN RESOURCES SUPPORT (formerly "MANNING")</u>

A. Any specified, implied or essential tasks:

B. Any Constraints

C. Facts

(1) Status of units

HUMAN RESOURCES SUPPORT (Cont)

(2) Critical MOS's/Shortages

(3) Expected replacements:

(4) Other

D. Assumptions:

(1) Casualty rates:

(2) EPW, Refugee, HNS requirements

(3) Projected losses:

(4) Other

E. Conclusions:

(1) Projected Status on D-Day:

F. Shortfalls:

G. Risk Assessment

H.   Any CCIR

I.   Analysis:

J.   Recommendations

2. SUPPLY - ARMING

A.   Any specified, implied or essential tasks:

B.   Any Constraints

C.   Facts

(1)   Class V Status in Days of Mission Support

(2)   Distribution System

(3)   Restrictions:

(4)   Critical Shortfalls

SUPPLY - ARMING (Cont)

   D.   Assumptions:

       (1)   Resupply rates:

       (2)   Host Nation Support

       (3)   Other

   E.   Conclusions:

       (1)   Projected Status on D-Day:

   F.   Shortfalls:

   G.   Risk Assessment

   H.   Any CCIR

   I.   Analysis:

   J.   Recommendations

3. <u>SUPPLY - FUELING</u>

    A.   Any specified, implied or essential tasks:

    B.   Any Constraints

    C.   Facts

        (1)   Class III(B) Status in Days of Mission Support

        (2)   Distribution System

        (3)   Restrictions:

        (4)   Critical Shortages

    D.   Assumptions:

        (1)   Resupply rates:

        (2)   Host Nation Support

        (3)   Other

SUPPLY - FUELING (Cont)

E.   Conclusions:

   (1)   Projected Status on D-Day:

   (2)   Projected Distribution System

F.   Shortfalls:

G.   Risk Assessment

H.   Any CCIR

I.   Analysis:

J.   Recommendations

4. MAINTENANCE (formerly "FIXING")

A.   Any specified, implied or essential tasks:

B.   Any Constraints

C.   Facts

    (1)   Maintenance Status:

    (2)   Class IX Status (Critical Items):

    (3)   Critical Shortages:

    (4)   Class VII Status

D.   Assumptions:

    (1)   Host Nation Support:

    (2)   Other

E.   Conclusions:

    (1)   Projected Status on D-Day:

F.   Shortfalls:

G.   Risk Assessment

H.   Any CCIR

MAINTENANCE (Cont)

I. Analysis:

J. Recommendations

5. TRANSPORTATION (formerly "MOVING")

A. Any specified, implied or essential tasks:

B. Any Constraints

C. Facts

    (1) Status of Transportation Assets:

    (2) Critical LOC and MSR/ASR Status:

    (3) HET Lines/Limits AND CROP/Flatrack Collection Points

    (4) Critical Shortages:

D. Assumptions:

    (1) Host Nation Support

    (2) Other

E. Conclusions:

    (1) Projected Status on D-Day:

    (2) Transportation Priorities

F. Shortfalls:

G. Risk Assessment

H. Any CCIR

I. Analysis:

J. Recommendations

6. FIELD SERVICES (FS), HEALTH SERVICE SUPPORT (HSS) SUSTAINMENT

A.   Any specified, implied or essential tasks:

B.   Any Constraints

C.   Facts

    (1)   Patient-holding capacity, evacuation policy and available evacuation assets

        a.   Level I (BAS):
        b.   Level II (BSMC/SBMC):
        c.   Level III (CSH):

    (2)   Shower, Laundry, Clothing, Repair (SLCR) Loc/ Status and Availability:

    (3)   Mortuary Affairs Evacuation Point (MACP) Loc, Status, and Availability

    (4)   EOD Status and Availability:

    (5)   Financial Management Support Status and Availability:

    (6)   Religious, Legal and Band Support Status and Availability:

    (7)   Status of Overall Field Services

(8) Critical Shortages

D. Assumptions:

(1) Casualty rates:

(2) Projected Losses:

(3) Other

E. Conclusions:

F. Shortfalls:

G. Risk Assessment

H. Any CCIR

I. Analysis:

J. Recommendations

5.7 SUSTAINMENT MISSION ANALYSIS ABBREVIATED TASK WORKSHEET

MISSION ANALYSIS WORKSHEET

Section: **DTG:**

Officer:

1. Specified Tasks	Reference
2. Implied Tasks	

3. Constraints	
4. Assumptions	
5. Facts	**Reference**

6. Concerns	
7. Requests	

Note: Identify mission essential tasks with a *.

Note: Ensure classification is printed on document as a header and footer.

5.8 CONSIDERATIONS UNDER EACH SUSTAINMENT FUNCTION

The areas of consideration listed below *are not intended as an all-encompassing checklist and may not always be applicable.* Rather, they are intended as a point of departure for Sustainment planners developing a support concept. Although the items are considered, they are not necessarily addressed in the support concept unless they are critical, non-SOP, or unusual.

1. Items for overall consideration:

    a. Support boundaries, support areas, and support relationships.

    b. Priorities of routes/events (timing).

    c. Support of attached or detached forces, (Cavalry, light infantry, SOF, out-of-sector support, heavy/light mixes, etc – if required)

    d. Sustainment MSO actions in the assembly area (AA), staging areas, and attack positions (if any) and any MRO.

    e. Programmed locations and projected displacements of sustainment support units and areas.

    f. Support provide by/to higher or adjacent units or other unusual support arrangements; e.g. refuel on the move (ROM), FARP Opns, caches, Special Operations Forces unique requirements, etc.

    g. Sustainment actions that support security and/or deception plans and/or operations.

h. Foreign nation support and /or host nation support arrangements.

i. Sustainment organization task organization (Sustainment unit's capability versus supported units' requirements)

j. Unusual and /or critical impact of weather, terrain, and security on sustainment operations.

k. Major Replenishment Operations (MRO) that support unit refit & reset.

l. Special considerations for joint (Air Force, Navy, USMC0 or combined (Allied) sustainment operations.

2. Items to consider in each phase of the operation:

a. **Maintenance**: Maintenance priorities (air, ground). Anticipated workload (battle damage and maintenance failure rates/projections). Battle damage assessment and repair (BDAR) procedures. Maintenance repair time lines. Controlled substitution or cannibalization procedures. FMT/CRT employment, locations/displacement of maintenance/repair part supply units. Support from other sources. Distribution methods for classes VII and IX. Evacuation procedures may include recovery procedures. Location and placement of M1070 HETs within AOR. Significant risks involved with recovery.

b. Transportation: Transportation requirements (logistic versus tactical). Movement and route use priorities (units and/or commodities). Traffic control requirements. Transportation unit/asset displacements. Throughput operations. Trailer Transfer Point arrangements (TTPs) or cargo transfer/terminal operations. Alternate modes of transportation; e.g. rail, foreign/host nation support. Lines of communication (LOC) and MSR security, supply routes, route maintenance requirements (effects of weather, enemy, and engineer support). Mode selection heavy-equipment transport (HET) priorities and backhaul priorities. Movement Control Team (MCT) availability. Support from joint services. Significant risks involved.

c. Supply: Day of Supply Availability and O/H. Classes of supply I, II, III, III(P), IV, V, VI, VII, and IX (less VIII). Supply point or unit distribution methods. Support from other sources. Refugees. Quality of life of the soldier and their family. Current status (in vehicles and bulkcarriers/storage). Bulk refueling procedures. Refuel-on-the-move (ROM activities. FARP operations. Reful assets and system capabilities, fuel allocations. Displacement of fuel/refueling assets. Basic and operational load status. Required Supply Rate (RSR) versus Controlled Supply Rate (CSR) for Class V & VIII. Forecasted requirements and ammunition prestocking arrangements. CSR sub allocation. ATHP, ASA and ASP locations (only general locations, grids on the LCOP overlay). Distribution methods, Combat/Mission-configured load (CCLs/MCLs). Emergency resupply procedures. Expenditure restrictions (e.g. no more than what percent of the CSR may be expended to support the covering force?) Monitoring and reporting requirements. Field storage requirements and missile maintenance.

d. Health Service Support: Projected casualties and their effect on combat readiness. Establishing or adjusting personnel and medical support priorities. Locations of medical treatment facilities. Evacuation procedures for killed in action (KIA)/wounded in action (WIA).

e. Field Services: Location of Sus Bde Field Service units and capabilities. Location of mortuary affairs personnel, collection points. Location of aerial delivery units, clothing exchange, laundry, showers, textile repair, and food services.

f. Explosive Ordnance Disposal: Location of EOD units and capabilities. Identifying procedures for neutralizing domestic or foreign conventional, chemical, and biological munitions and devices that present a threat to military operations and civilian facilities.

g. Human Resource Support: Personnel services, EPW procedures, Friendly confinement requirements/procedures. Identifying personnel support to service members, their families, DA, civilians, and contractors. Location of personnel accounting activities, casualty management, postal operations, and moral, welfare, and recreation (MWR) facilities and equipment.

h. Financial Management Operations: Location of financial services and resource management services.

i. Religious, Legal, and Band Support: Location of religious support operations, legal operations, and band support.

5.9 CONSIDERATIONS FOR SUPPORTING OFFENSIVE OPERATIONS.

1. If offensive momentum is not maintained, the enemy may recover from the shock of the first assault, gain the initiative, and mount a successful counterattack. Therefore, the sustainment priority must be to maintain the momentum of the attack.

2. A successful attack may develop into an exploitation or pursuit, and the sustainment planner must be flexible enough to support either type of operation. The following techniques and considerations apply to sustainment offensive planning:

   • Position essential sustainment assets, such as ammunition, petroleum, oils, and lubricants (POL), and maintenance, in advance within the FSC, and ensure that basic loads remain replenished.

   • Establish maintenance priorities based on the commander's guidance or intent and the factors of mission, enemy, terrain, troops, time, and civilian considerations (METT-TC). Priorities may change as different phases of an operation are completed.

   • Recover damaged vehicles only to the main supply route for further recovery by TF assets.

   • Plan for increased consumption of POL, especially with M1A2 Abrams tank centric units.

   • Push planned and pre-configured logistics packages of essential sustainment items.

- Plan for increased vehicular maintenance, especially over rough terrain.

- Make maximum use of forward maintenance teams (FMTs) with supported IN TF/CABs.

- Request unit distribution at forward locations.

- Increased use of meals-ready-to-eat (MRE) and bottled water.

- Use of captured enemy supplies and equipment, particularly support vehicles and POL. Before use, test for contamination.

- Suspend most field service functions except airdrop and mortuary affairs.

- Prepare for increased casualties and additional evacuation and mortuary affairs requirements. Plan replacement operations based on known and projected losses.

- Select supply routes, logistics release points, and subsequent FSC Support Area locations based on map reconnaissance.

- Plan and coordinate enemy prisoner of war (EPW) operations; expect more EPWs.

- Consider the increasing distances and longer travel times to ammunition supply areas (ASAs) and ammunition transfer holding points (ATHPs)

- Ensure that sustainment Major Staging Operations (MSO) preparations for the attack do not compromise tactical plans.

3. These considerations apply to some degree to all offensive operations. The change from one type of operation to another, such as from a hasty attack to a pursuit, does not require a major shift in sustainment plans and procedures. However, the priorities and requirements for support may change. The Brigade Combat Team Executive Officer (XO), assisted primarily by the S-4 and in conjunction with the BSB Cdr, organizes the BCT/task force's sustainment assets to permit uninterrupted support. The main purpose of sustainment in the offense is to maintain the momentum of the attack.

5.10 CONSIDERATIONS FOR SUPPORTING THE DEFENSE.

1. The immediate purpose of the defense is to cause an enemy attack to fail, or in contrast to offensive operations, to break the momentum of the attack.

2. As in offensive operations, perhaps the most critical time in the defense is the preparation stage. General considerations in preparing for defensive operations include the following:

   - Pre-position limited amounts of ammunition, POL, and barrier material in centrally located battle positions in forward areas. Make plans to destroy those stocks if necessary.

   - Resupply during limited visibility to reduce the chance of enemy interference.

   - Plan to reorganize to reconstitute/regenerate lost sustainment capability. Identify personnel from the field to train as potential replacements to reestablish lost capability.

   - Use maintenance support teams in the MCP to reduce the need to recover equipment to the Brigade Support Area (BSA). Consider pre-positioning of M1070 HETs as far forward as possible.

   - Consider the additional transportation requirements for the movement of Class IV barrier material, mines, and pre-positioned ammunition, plus the sustainment requirements of additional engineer units assigned for preparation of the defense.

   - In defensive operations, pre-position ammunition on occupied and prepared positions. However, plans must be made for the control of this ammunition.

5.11 PREPARATION FOR MISSION ANALYSIS BRIEFING

PREPARATION FOR MISSION ANALYSIS BRIEFING

1. The S-2/S-2 NCO prepares the MCOO, enemy Situation Template overlays (SITTEMP's), (enemy intent & objectives, COAs, and terrain analysis) and Event Templates. The S-2 briefs as if he is the enemy commander (i.e., " I intend to..." "I will..." "My objective is to...").

2. The S-2/S-2 NCO develops (1) the enemy's most likely COA based on doctrine and situation, and (2) the enemy's most dangerous course of action, if he employed it, against the brigade/division. In many cases, the most likely is the most dangerous but not always. These enemy COAs will later form the basis for friendly COA development; we should develop at least three friendly COAs against the "most likely" and the "most dangerous."

3. The S-3 prepares friendly OPS overlays. Spt Ops Off prepares the Support Concept overlay. Include on the OPS overlay: Brigade, Division AO/AI, (*Corps AO for Sus Bde*), concept 1 and 2 levels higher, and friendly COA's currently under consideration by Division Plans Staff. Build the Support Concept overlay from the initial Support Concept overlays received from the Div G-4 (in the case of Sus Bde and CSSBs) or from the Bde S-4 (in the case of BSBs) following WO #1.

4. **Select for briefing only those bullets of information gathered during mission analysis that are of primary importance to the CDR.** The XO/S-3 keeps the entire list for future information and refinement.

5. Complete relative combat power for friendly and enemy as it is at this time.

6. Conduct analysis of relative support requirements based on requirements of supported units' verses capabilities of supporting units.

7. When considering shortfalls or "War stoppers", capture solutions, recommendations and additional assets required from other sustainment units that could resolve or eliminate the shortfalls and war stoppers.

8. Prepare proposed mission statement for CDR's approval.

9. Have "Sequence of Command and Staff Actions" chart and "arrow sticker" for use during the briefing.

10. Conduct a rehearsal of the mission analysis briefing for the Executive Officer.

11. Appoint two scribes to take notes and annotate overlays throughout the rehearsal and the briefing and to document commander's intent and guidance.

5.12 AFTER MISSION ANALYSIS BRIEFING

<u>AFTER MISSION ANALYSIS BRIEFING</u>

1. Prepare chart with elements of Commander's Guidance from mission analysis briefing. As a minimum Commander's Guidance should address:

   a. Specific courses of action to consider or not to consider, both friendly and enemy, and the priority for addressing them.

   b. The CCIR.

   c. Levels of acceptable risk.

   d. The Intelligence Collection (IC) guidance.

   e. Deception guidance (if applicable).

   f. Fire support and any Effects Based Operations (EBO) guidance.

   g. Security measures to be implemented.

   h. Specific priorities for each Sustainment Function (MAFFMS).

   i. Any revisions or modifications to the time plan.

   j. The type of order to issue.

   k. The type of rehearsal to conduct.

2. Consolidate a request for additional assets desired from the next sustainment organization (Sus Bde/CSSBs).

3. Prepare and issue Warning Order #2. (should contain at a minimum)

   a. The restated mission.

   b. The commander's intent.

   c. The unit's AO (a sketch, overlay, or some other description).

   d. The CCIR.

   e. Risk Guidance.

   f. Reconnaissance to be initiated by subordinate units.

   g. Security measures.

   h. Deception guidance (if applicable)

   i. Specific priorities for each Sustainment Function.

   j. The time plan for each remaining step of the planning and preparation for the operation.

   k. Guidance on rehearsals.

4. Revisit Facts and Planning Assumptions and revise essential tasks and restated mission as necessary.

Blast from the Past
Commander's Guidance

"I do not propose to lay down for you a plan of campaign ... but simply to lay down the work it is desirable to have done and leave you free to execute it in your own way."

General Ulysses S Grant to Gen William T. Sherman, April 1864

CHAPTER 6

COURSE OF ACTION DEVELOPMENT

★★★

COURSES OF ACTION (COAs). COAs are stated as alternative concepts of operation or support – developed after task analysis is complete, objectives are stated, and constraints identified. Recommended COAs should be based on current *Staff and Commander's Estimate* and COA criteria analysis. The adopted COA is the basis for the concept of operation (Para 3a) in the order/plan.

Two (2) systems for Course of Action Development are available for this step.

1. Commander Directed Single Course of Action
2. Full Staff Multiple Course of Action Development

1. **Commander Directed Single Course of Action** is conducted at the discretion of the commander. The commander provides a single Course of Action to the staff. The staff then moves directly to Course of Action Evaluation (Wargaming). This process is used primarily in time constrained situations and in other situations selected by the commander. The commander will, at a minimum, consider the steps shown below for the Full Staff Multiple Course of Action Development. The commander must remain ready to modify or change the directed Course of Action if Wargaming reveals it to be unsuitable, unfeasible, unacceptable or incomplete.

2. **Full Staff Multiple Course of Action Development** is the formal process used when selected by the commander. The process is detailed below.

FULL STAFF MULTIPLE COURSE OF ACTION DEVELOPMENT

1. Prepare generic unit symbols (stickies) for friendly units (supported, supporting) at BN level (S-3) and for enemy forces (maneuver, FA, ADA, AHB's) at BN level (S-2/NCO). Show enemy operations forces down to platoon level if at all possible. These are used to array forces for COA development. Symbols MUST show relative combat power for each.

2. The S-2/S-2 NCO reviews Friendly and Enemy Relative Combat Power and complete the Event Template.

3. The SPO reviews "Relative Support Load" for each supporting unit. "Relative Support Load" is an analysis of the support demands (requirements) placed on each support unit (capabilities) as developed in the Spt Opns cell prepared logistics estimates of requirements, capabilities, shortfalls and recommended solutions.

4. XO lists and disseminates CDR's guidance for determining validity of COAs.

5. S-3 develops tactical COAs against "enemy most like COA" and "enemy most dangerous COA" for templated threats to the sustainment organization and the customer (i.e. the supported unit).

6. Spt Ops Off develops support COAs for support of each friendly maneuver COA currently under consideration by the supported unit.

7. Each COA will have a sketch and concept of operation paragraph using the battlefield framework of Decisive (DO), Shaping (SO) and Sustaining Operations. Other planners can assist in COA development as needed. These COAs must be flexible to accommodate "most likely" and "most dangerous" enemy and friendly COAs, they must meet the guidance and intent of the commander, and they must be significantly different from one another. S-3 and SPO coordinate their tactical and support COA's. **The goal is** *"how does the sustainment organization synchronize and execute effective and efficient distribution down to the soldier level."*

8. Other planners return to their work areas for continued planning and information gathering while COAs are being developed. All planners return at the appropriate time to review COAs. All planners get an initial shot at the COAs to screen for validity, soundness, and general content. All planners have to understand the COAs before presenting them to the XO for review. Each COA must meet criteria of suitability, feasibility, acceptability, distinguishability, and completeness

9. Upon review and approval by XO, sketches and concept of operations paragraphs are prepared for briefing.

10. Other charts and overheads are prepared in accordance with the COA Briefing Format at Chapter 15.

11. Prepare relative combat power for each COA down to regiment/brigade and battalion level. Prepare any overheads, charts, and standard drops for briefing.

GUIDANCE GIVEN TO EACH PLANNER

1. Determine decisive points and times to focus the main effort.

2. ID purpose to be achieved by the main and supporting efforts.

3. Determine essential tasks to subordinates (ensure all tasks from higher order are addressed, assigned or delegated to some unit). Assign assets to sub units (Task Organization).

4. Assign control measures (minimum necessary to achieve synchronization of operation) and phases.

5. Prepare COA statement and sketches:
   a. Restated mission.
   b. Restate/Expansion of commander's intent.
   c. Designation of decisive point/main effort, supporting efforts and purpose of each.
   d. Array tactical and support forces within the supported units' form of maneuver.
   e. Critical factors/elements underlying the plan.
   f. Phases of operation.
   g. Idea on timelines for each event and decision point.
   h. Idea on branches and sequels.

STEPS IN COURSE OF ACTION DEVELOPMENT

1. Analyze Relative Combat (i.e. 'Sustainment') Power and Relative Support Load. **(S-3 & SPO). Sustainment power is:** *How many pallets (or TEUs), and gallons can I receive, store, issue? What is my distribution capability? How much water can I produce and distribute? How fast can I recover, repair and issue damaged vehicles? What Field Services can I provide and when?*

2. Generate options. **(ALL)**
   a. A good COA should be capable of executing all distribution operations while defeating all feasible enemy COAs and supporting all supported units' COAs.
   b. COA options should focus on distribution techniques that circumvent enemy COAs while supporting friendly

maneuver/sustaining COA's, each arranged in order of probable adoption.

c. Staff determines the decisive points where the unit will focus the support effort relative to terrain, enemy and time to enable the supported units to achieve their purpose.

3. Array initial forces of Sustainment units. This includes location, composition, task, and purpose for each sustainment element (i.e. BSA, LSA/FOB, CRSP, CSC, FLE, AXP, UMCP, EPW Holding area). **(S-3 & SPO)**

4. Develop concept of support. **(S-3 & SPO)**
   a. The purpose of the operation.
   b. A statement of where the commander will accept tactical and logistical risk.
   c. Identification of critical friendly events and phases of the operation (if phased).
   d. Designation of the main effort, along with its task and purpose.
   e. Designation of supporting efforts, tasks and purposes, linked to support the main effort.
   f. Support to the reserve, to include location, composition, task, and purpose.
   g. Support to deep, close, and rear operations.
   h. R&S operations of Sus Bde/CSSB/BSB units.
   i. An outline of the movements of the Divisional forces and SUSTAINMENT BRIGADE unit movements.
   j. Identification of support options that may develop during the operation.
   k. Location of attack objectives and counterattack objectives.
   l. Responsibilities for area of operations.
   m. Concept of fires (if applicable).
   n. Prescribed formations or dispositions when necessary.

o. Priorities for each Maneuver Support (MS) and Sustainment element by tactical logistics function. (Internal & external)

p. Consideration of the effects of enemy weapons of mass destruction (WMD) on the force.

5. Assign headquarters. **(S-3)**

6. Prepare Course of Action statements and sketches. **(S-3 & SPO)**
   a. How to accomplish the mission and explain the concept of support.
   b. As a minimum, it will include:
      (1) Array of supported and supporting forces and logistics facilities.
      (2) Planning unit and subordinate unit boundaries that establish the AO.
      (3) The FEBA or LD/LC, control measures and subsequent phase lines.
      (4) Reconnaissance and Surveillance (R&S) graphics.
      (5) Ground and air axes of advance, MSR's.
      (6) Assembly areas, battle positions, strong points, engagement areas, and objectives.
      (7) Designation of the main and supporting efforts.
      (8) Enemy known or templated locations with FA range fans.

SUSTAINMENT CONSIDERATIONS IN COA DEVELOPMENT

Sustainment Planners should focus on logistical factors that constrain the tactical operations

- Key is to identify and eliminate any COA that is not supportable.

- Identify limitations that planners must be concerned with (CL IV availability for barrier plans, CL V CSR vs RSR, vehicle/driver availability)

- Identify the cost or risk in terms of resources for each COA

- Update logistics and personnel estimates as additional information becomes available

Key questions for the Sustainment planners are:

- How will the Sustainer achieve distribution operations in an effective and efficient

- Will sustainment support require relocation (BSB) or echelon (Sus Bde/CSSB) during the operation?

- MSR and ASR traffic ability?

- Are the line haul or local haul distance factors exceeded?

Specific items to focus on for COA development

- BSA/LSA/TF-CAB Support Area, CSC and CRSP locations, Level II and III medical facilities.

- MSR plan for the conduct of replenishment operations (RO) of the units

- Use of logistics release points (LRPs)

- Medical and maintenance recovery along MSRs

- SECFOR availability for convoy security. Availability and employment of IED defeating electronic warfare (EW) systems.

- Will the BSB need to relocate to support the COA?

- Will the Sustainment Brigade need to echelon/establish a CSC, TTPs, Mini-mart, or CRSPs?

- Are any Forward Logistics Elements (FLEs) or larger Logistics Task Forces (LTF) required?

QUALITIES OF COA'S

1. **Suitability:** It must accomplish the mission and comply with the commander's guidance.

2. **Feasibility:** The unit must have the capability to accomplish the mission in terms of available time, space and resources.

3. **Acceptability:** The tactical or operational advantage gained by executing the COA must justify the cost in resources, especially casualties.

4. **Distinguishability:** Each COA must differ significantly from any others. Significant differences may result from use of reserves, different task organizations, day or night operations, or a different scheme of maneuver.

5. **Completeness:** It must be a complete mission statement to include who, what, when, where, and why.

PREPARATION FOR COA BRIEFING

1. Rehearse briefing. One person briefs while another planner points. (Chapter 14)

2. Be prepared to display all friendly COAs side-by-side for final review by CDR.

3. Address concept of logistics/sustainment for all COAs.

4. Show end state disposition of friendly forces in COA sketches.

5. Identify a time line (red timelines for enemy movement against our defense) (blue timelines for friendly movement against enemy defense) for each COA.

6. Ensure the following are visually displayed for briefing:
   - Map showing AOR, friendly and enemy units on 1:50,000 (*1:250,000 at Sus Bde*)
   - Mission statement and Intent 1 and 2 levels up.
   - Narrative for each enemy COA.
   - Division restated mission.
   - Task Organization (highlight any additional assets added from higher since last brief).

7. Display relative combat power for friendly and enemy (at battalion or brigade/regiment level) for viewing with each COA.

PRODUCTS FROM COA BRIEFING

1. Additional commander's guidance on selected COAs for war gaming.

2. Time and Location for COA Decision Briefing.

3. COA statements and sketches

6.1 COURSE OF ACTION DEVELOPMENT CHECKLIST

STEP 1 REVIEW COMMANDERS MISSION ANALYSIS GUIDANCE

TASK DESCRIPTION	PERSONNEL
Extract and publish Commanders Guidance	ALL/Clerk
Update Restated Mission	XO, S-3
Update/Brief Subordinate Unit Status	STAFF
Update/Brief RFIs received	OPS NCO

STEP 2 DEVELOP COURSES OF ACTION

TASK DESCRIPTION	PERSONNEL
Analyze force ratios	S-3
Array initial forces	S-3
Draft Commanders Intent	XO, S-3
Develop Scheme of Maneuver per COA	ALL
Determine Mission Command means and maneuver control measures	S-3
Prepare COA statements and Operational Sketches	S-3, ANY APPLICABLE STAFF

STEP 3 ANALYZE AND COMPARE COURSES OF ACTION

TASK DESCRIPTION	PERSONNEL
Extract and publish Commanders Guidance	S-3 Clerk
Refine proposed CCIR	ALL
Conduct initial wargame each COA. The focus of the Battle Staff is more on the entire sector than on each battle. The purpose of the initial wargame is to allow each Battle Staff Section to gather enough insight on a COA to make a recommendation to the commander	ALL
Determine decision criteria and assign weighting values to criteria	ALL
Make recommendation	ALL

STEP 4 PREPARE AND CONDUCT COA DECISION BRIEF

TASK DESCRIPTION	PERSONNEL
Provide COA decision brief input to the XO or S-3 NCOIC	ALL
Review COA decision criteria and COA comparisons	ALL (as necessary)
Site setup for briefing	S-2/3 NCOs
Prepare slides and handouts	S-2/3 NCOs
Rehearse briefing to XO	ALL Briefers
Conduct briefing	ALL
Receive Guidance	ALL

6.2 BSA and FORWARD LOGISTICS ELEMENT (FLE) SELECTION CRITERIA (BSB Only)

1. **Approval Authority.** In concert with the BSB Bn Cdr, the BSB S-3 will designate the general location of the primary and alternate BSAs and/or FLEs. The S-3 determines the exact location based on input and guidance from the Battalion Commander, Battalion XO, Battalion SPO and the Brigade S-4.

2. **Size.** Minimum size of the Brigade Support Area depends on factors of METT-T (Mission, Enemy. Terrain, Time Available, Troops Available, and civilian considerations) and it normally requires 2-3 square kilometers. Minimum size of the FLE is based on the support role it is required to perform.

3. **Criteria.** Primary considerations in the selection of the BSA (or FLE location) are: survivability and defendability (out of artillery range and good overhead concealment), mobility, accessibility and responsiveness. In selecting a BSA/FLE site, the following criteria will be considered:

   00 Log Spt Responsiveness to Tactical Requirements
      o CL I-IX. Svcs
      o Must consider time / distance factors for all supported units
   00 Sufficiency of AO
      o Access to Ground LOCs
      o Ease of Gnd Mvt/Traffic Plan
      o Drop Zones (DZs)
      o Landing Zones (LZs)
      o Helicopter Landing Zones (HLZs)
      o Air/Sea Ports
      o Water source for ROWPU teams, access to a water source
      o Size/Dispersion

  o Hardstand
  o Supply routes / dirty routes
 00 Command. Control, Communications
 00 Risk
  o Security
   - OCOKA (Observation. Cover & Concealment. Obstacles,
   - Key/Decisive Terrain, and Avenues of Approach)
   - Fields of Fire
  o Distance from Enemy Indirect Fire
  o Safety
 00 Supports Sus Bde planned MRO/MSOs

Items to consider:
Expandability of area (e.g. what if we get more assets prior to the battle?)

4. **Forward Logistics Element/Base Criteria**. If deployment of a FLE is in consideration as a COA, as a minimum, the following five (5) criteria must be addressed.

 * **Mission**. What is the mission of the FLE (Who, What, Where, When, Why – Task & Purpose)
 * **Duration**. FLEs are not indefinite structures that can be sent out for long period of time.
 * **Mission Command.** Who is in charge (by name) and how does the unit communicate with the FLE (by communications device)?
 * **Security**. How does the FLE provide its own security or how is it tied in to other unit's security plan?
 * **Composition**. What specific elements and equipment make up the FLE? Required equipment and elements become a tasking to subordinate units in the final OPORD preparation.

6.3 BSA/FLE DISPLACEMENT CRITERIA

- BSA & FLE Displacement criteria occur when:

    ✓ Ordered to do so by higher HQ

    ✓ Required to maintain signal support

    ✓ Boundary changes forward or rearward

    ✓ Within tube Artillery or insurgent mortar/rocket range

    ✓ MSR interdicted or closed over 24 hours

    ✓ Enemy eyes on confined

    ✓ LOCs become extended by time and/or distance, making ft to difficult to maintain continuous support to maneuver units

6.4 BSA/FLE Positioning Criteria

This chart may be useful for reconnaissance as well as decision making. Weights may be assigned to each dependant upon **Mission, Enemy, Terrain, Time, Troops, and Civilian Consideration (METT-TC) Available**.

CRITERIA	POSSIBLE SITES					
	WT	1	2	3	4	5

LOG SPT RESPONSIVENESS TO TACTICAL SITUATION
* Supply
* Maintenance
* Medical
* Services
* Transportation
* Ground LOC Distance & Condition

SUFFICIENCY OF BRIGADE SUPPORT AREA
* Trafficability
* Water Source
* Road Network
* Helicopter LZs
* Air/Sea Ports
* Hardstand
* Drainage

COMMAND, CONTROL, COMMUNICATIONS RISK
* Security – OCOKA (Observation and fields of fire, Cover and concealment, Obstacles, Key/Decisive terrain, and Enemy Avenues of Approach)
* NBC Effetcs

* Distance from Enemy Indirect Fire
* Support Deception
* Safety

LOCATION SUPPORTS REORGANIZATION

CONCLUSION: SITE ___ IS THE BEST COA

6.5 THE SUSTAINMENT OVERLAY (AKA "THE LOGISTICS COMMON OPERATING PICTURE or "LCOP")

1. The sustainment overlay (or LCOP in digital mission command Main CP) is a graphic representation of the tactical allay of support areas and units. Ideally, it accompanies copies of the OPLAN and/or OPORD distributed to subordinate HQ and is used as a graphic backdrop to the support concept briefing. The list below is a representative example of elements that could be expected to locate in the BSA and key logistical resources areas that will occur within the units' area of operation. This overlay must be synchronized with the operations overlays.

   - Command Posts: Sus Bde, CSSB, BSB and local Division TOC
   - Alternate/Proposed BSA, TF/CAB SA, and FLE Locations
   - MSRs, from the TD Sus Bde to the BSA including FDRPs and TCPs
   - SRs and Dirty Routes within the sector
   - LRPs and LZs
   - Boundaries for Sustainment Unit responsibilities.
   - BSB Distribution Company CP
   - Class I point & Water point
   - Class II, III, IV, and VII (if applicable) point
   - ASA (Sus Bde) and/or ATHPs active/planned within AOR
   - Salvage collection point
   - Mortuary Affairs Collection Point (MACP)
   - BSB Forward Maintenance Company CP
   - Class IX point
   - Support Maintenance Company shops
   - Maint Collection Points (MCPs)
   - BSB Medical Company/Support Brigade Medical Company CP/Class VIII Point

- Battalion Aid Stations (BAS)
- Smoke Platoon
- Decontamination Point
- Reconnaissance Squad
- Military Police Platoon
- EPW Collection Point
- Military Intelligence Team
- ADA Battery (-)
- Network Support/Signal Units within AOR
- Aviation Elements

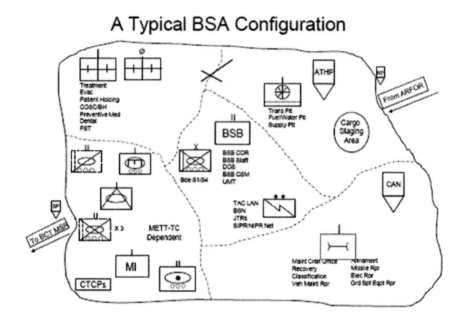

Figure 6-1 Typical BSA Layout and Configuration

6.6 SUSTAINMENT UNIT LOCATION GUIDELINES

1. Position CP's near the center of the FOB/LSA/BSA Perimeter for MC and security reasons.

2. Balance the advantages of dispersion (reduced destruction from a single enemy rocket/mortar strike) with the disadvantages (MC constraints and extended perimeter).

3. Make supply points accessible to both customers and re-supply vehicles and helicopters.

4. Keep Class III points away from other supplies to prevent contamination. They should also be located at least 100 ft from water supplies.

5. Locate the ATHP at least 180 meters from other supplies and 620 meters from the nearest inhabited tent.

6. Position MACP and salvage points near the MSR possibly near the ATHP to maximize back- haul mission of vehicles used for ammunition re-supply.

7. Locate the Class I point near the water point whenever water sources allow.

8. Locate the clearing station away for likely target areas (ATHP, Class III points, bridges, road junction) but near evacuation routes and open area for landing air ambulances.

9. Locate maintenance sites to be accessible to customers, including recovery/evacuation vehicles.

10. Ensure maintenance shops, along with parking and equipment holding sites are on firm ground.

11. Position Network Support/Signal assets and any attached MP platoon HQ near the BDE/BSB CP to enhance support and security.

12. Position the ATHP near the rear of the BSA and near but off the MSR so that the large number of PLS systems and trailers bringing ammo into the area do not clog up the MSR with in the BSA. The ATHP requires sufficient area to perform transload operations without interfering with BSA traffic.

13. Position units with the heaviest fire-power, such as the FSC maintenance platoon, along the most threatening avenue of approach.

6.7 BSB MOVEMENT TECHNIQUES

Primary goal is to provide continuous support to the BDE while displacing the BSB

1. <u>MOVEMENT OF THE BSB WITHIN THE BDE FORMATION</u>

- Enemy contact not expected
- Long road march to Tactical Assembly Area (TAA)
- Requires BDE to resupply prior to movement to allow the BSB to pack up
- MSTs should move with TFs, BSA moves as a unit
- Relies heavily on theater/corps support
- "Tailgate" support should be available

<u>— Maintenance</u>
* MST and maj assy w/ TF
* 30 min repair limits
* Recovery plan
* O/O MCPs identified
*Drag NMC Veh w/ short repair times

<u>— Medical</u>
* Transport "delayed casualties.
* MEDEVAC
* Some Ambulances w/ BSA
* Air Evac coordinated

<u>- Bulk Refuel</u>
* SRO by Sus Bde (TD/CSSB
* Alternate refuel plan

<u>- Mortuary Affairs</u>
* Collection Plan
* Transportation Plan

2. <u>ATTACHMENT OF CRITICAL SUSTAINMENT ASSETS TO BCT</u>
"TUCK UP PACKAGES"
Advantages

- Most responsive method
- Combat essential CL III, V, medical and water sent w/ each TF
- Supply point distribution for all other customers

- Primarily used during Offensive Operations
  - Operational distances are great
  - Secure LOCs are uncertain
  - Log turnaround time too long to support the TFs

Disadvantages

- High risk to scarce resources (eg 5K Tankers ambulances etc)
- Results in longer resupply times for BSB assets or requires CSSB to push far fwd,
- Limits support for other customers in the BSA
- Limited capability to transport Class V forward

3. SUPPORT FROM THE BSB: DISPLACE AS AN ENTITY

- Best used when BCT is operating with clearly defined phases with identifiable windows b/w operations (e.g. river crossings)
- Supply point distribution from the BSB
- BSB jumps partly or in whole during time provided by window
- Sustainment black out for BCT for 12-24 hours as BSB re-establishes
- May be used ICW tuck up packages to minimize support disruption
- BSA must be resupplied by the Sus Bde (MSO) prior to jump in order to re-establish sustainment ops at new site
- Close out times, start up times and new locations must be coordinated w/the Sustainment Brigade, the BCT and (time permitting) the Div G-4.
- Consider jumping the BSB ahead of the BCT if new BSA is secure. Jump when least detrimental to BCT.

4. BSB DISPLACEMENT BY ECHELONS

- Used when continuous support is required
- Supply point distribution at both ends
- Critical CSS assets are split, displace by bounds
- Sections that can be easily split
  - BSB TOC
  - Water (FAWPSS or SMFT)
  - Class III tankers
  - Major assembles
  - MSTs (displace with TFs MCPs)
  - Medical (ambulances, treatment squads)
- Sections that cannot be easily split
  - Water production
  - Class I
  - Class II/IV
  - Mortuary Affairs
- ATHP has limited capability to split operations
- Critical Class V may be pushed fwd using organic tractors
- SPO deploys w/ forward element
- BSB TOC remains in rear until BCT Sustainment Cell (S-1/4) CP assumes control
- Asst SPO remains with TOC to coordinate sustainment at old site
- Support Ops provides BCT, Div G-4, and Sus Bde SPO with shut down and start up times and grids for new locations once established

CHAPTER 7

COA ANALYSIS (WAR-GAMING)

★ ★ ★

WAR-GAMING

After the COA briefing, select staff gathers in the Plans area to begin war-gaming the COAs that survived the COA briefing. War-gaming is a disciplined process with rules and steps that attempt to visualize the flow of the operation – in this case the conduct of distribution operations. Planners take necessary time to return to their staff sections to develop further information, gather additional tools, etc. and return at the appointed time.

PURPOSE OF WAR-GAMING

1. Determine how to maximize '*sustainment*' combat power.
2. Provides identical vision of the battle.
3. Anticipate battlefield events.
4. Determine conditions and resources for success.
5. Decide how to apply support capabilities.
6. Focus IPB on enemy strengths/weaknesses, center of gravity, desired end state and decisive points in both the shaping and decisive efforts, with focus on the main and supporting efforts.
7. ID coordination necessary to synchronize results.
8. Determine most flexible COA.

WAR-GAMING PROCESS

1. Considers friendly disposition, strengths and weaknesses.
2. Considers enemy assets and probable COAs.
3. Based on characteristics of AO.
4. Focuses the staff on each phase of operation in a logical sequence.
5. Iterative process of action, reaction and counteraction.

WAR-GAME RESPONSIBILITIES

1. **XO**: Responsible for coordinating actions of the staff during the war game.
2. **S-1**: Analyze potential battle losses and personnel support.
3. **S-2/Intel NCO**: Role play enemy commander; develops enemy decision points, reaction to friendly actions, enemy losses. Participates in the Security (Rear) Battle Targeting meeting and identifies High Value Targets for Security Battle. Be sure to also reflect any MSR/ASR inhibitors that could potentially interfere with distribution operations.
4. **S-3**: ID information requirements, refines event template to include NAIs, refines sustainment unit Sustainment Sync matrix with DPs, TAIs, HVTs; refines situation template, ID area of interest. Selects the war gaming method. Maintain Sustainment synch matrix/ sketch notes.
5. **S-4**: Analyze internal sustainment unit internal logistics and effects on ability to support sustainment operations to the customer.
6. **SPO**: Critical requirements for each sustainment function, assesses status of all sustainment functions; ID potential shortfalls and recommends actions to eliminate; assesses movement times and assets to support each COA.
7. **All Staff Members**: Determine force requirements for external support, risks, and each COAs strengths and weaknesses.

WAR-GAMING STEPS

Gather the necessary tools: current coordinating staff estimates, event templates, recording method, completed COAs to include maneuver and Intel Collection (IC) graphics, means to post enemy and friendly unit symbols, map of AO (blank synch matrices, butcher paper, blank overlays to record DST during war gaming, etc.).

1. List all friendly forces.
2. List assumptions (Review previous assumptions for continued validity and necessity).
3. List known critical events and decision points.
4. Determine evaluation criteria.
5. Select the war game method (Revisit the war gaming procedure as necessary).
6. Select a method to record and display results (Identify a scribe to post all notes from war gaming onto the synch matrix and a planner to record the DST).
7. War game the battle and assess results (Establish timelines for war gaming and post on a blank overlay the enemy or friendly timelines for movement. Begin a list of additional assets to be requested from Corps as a result of war gaming.

EVALUATION CRITERIA

1. This portion of the sustainment planning process will allow you to determine which customer COA can best be supported from a sustainment perspective. In order to do this, screening and evaluation criteria must be defined. Screening criteria screens out unsatisfactory and unfeasible COAs. Evaluation criteria, is evaluated further for suitability, feasibility, and acceptability.

2. The following list contains examples of evaluation criteria:

    a. Mission Command: provides unity of command
    b. Commander's intent; best supports to objectives of the commander
    c. Location: provides suitable location to support sustainment/CHS operations.
    d. Routes: provides the most responsive and safest means for moving supplies and personnel.
    e. Risk: requires minimal risk to unit/personnel
    f. Security: provides best security posture for sustainment/HSS assets
    g. Re-supply operations: promotes ease of re-supply in an expedient manner
    h. Medical evacuation: best use of medical and non-standard evacuation assets that will maintain a continuous flow of rapid casualty evacuation.

WAR-GAMING SEQUENCE (See 7.1)
DURING WAR-GAMING

1. <u>Develop additional planning assumptions</u>, as necessary.
2. <u>Capture PIR/IRs</u> during each war gaming turn from PIR/IRs developed during Mission Analysis.
3. <u>List additional assets</u> to be requested from other Sustainment Brigades or ESC.
4. **TIP**: Keep the war-gaming moving and on track. Scribe doesn't have to write everything down. Each planner should be keeping notes, by WFF, of the significant elements of the war gaming that apply to him.
5. The S-2/Intel NCO plays the part of the enemy commander and fights the battle from two perspectives: the enemy's "most likely course of action" and the enemy's "most dangerous course of action." If there are two distinct enemy COAs, then each friendly COA must be considered against them.

Again, do not forget to factor in possible (but realistic) factors into MSR/ASR status that could potentially effect distribution operations.

6. At the end of each "war-gaming iteration," <u>assess friendly and enemy loss percentages</u> and present combat power and support capabilities.

ITEMS THE COMMANDER AND STAFF SHOULD IDENTIFY, REFINE, DEVELOP OR FINALIZE AS A RESULT OF WAR-GAMING COAs

1. Refining or modifying the COA, to include identifying branches and sequels that become on-order or be prepared missions.
2. Refining locations and timing of the decisive points.
3. Identifying key or decisive terrain and determining how to use it.
4. Refining the enemy event template.
5. Refining task organizations, to include forces retained in GS of the command.
6. Identifying tasks the unit must retain & tasks to be assigned to subordinate commanders.
7. Allocating maneuver, maneuver support, and sustainment assets to subordinate commanders to accomplish their missions.
8. Developing a Sustainment Synchronization Matrix and Decision Support Template.
9. Estimating the duration of each critical event as well as of the entire operation.
10. Projecting the percentage of total enemy forces defeated in each critical event, and overall.
11. Identifying likely times and areas for enemy use of WMD and friendly CBRN defense requirements.
12. Identifying the location and commitment of the reserves.
13. Identifying the most dangerous enemy COA.

14. Identifying the location of the commander and unit command posts.
15. Identifying additional critical events.
16. Identifying additional requirements for maneuver support and sustainment support.
17. Determining requirements for deception and surprise.
18. Refining C2 requirements, to include control measures and updated graphics.
19. Finalizing CCIR and FFIR with the latest time information is of value (LTIOV) or latest event information is of value (LRIOV).
20. Finalizing the R&S plan and graphics for the basis for the collection plan.
21. Refining CCIR and incorporating them into the IC plan and graphics.
22. Developing Fires, Protection, and sustainment plan and graphics.
23. Identifying or confirming the locations of decision points, NAIs, and TAIs, and the information needed to support the decision points.
24. Determining the timing of force concentrations.
25. Developing the intelligence collection and dissemination plan.
26. Determining movement times and tables.
27. Identifying, analyzing, and evaluating strengths and weaknesses of the COA.
28. Integrating the targeting process, to include identifying or confirming high pay-off targets and determining attack guidance.
29. Synchronizing Class III (fog oil) ISO smoke operations.
30. Identifying additional hazards, assessing their risk, developing control measures to reduce risk from all identified hazards, and determining residual risk.

WAR GAMING OUTPUT

1. War game results. Which COA best supports both efficient and effective distribution operations.
2. Task Organization. (It's OK to cross level pure companies such as Truck Companies into multifunction transportation units, such as cross attaching a HET Platoon from a HET Company with a PLS Platoon from a Medium Truck company possessing PLS systems.
3. Mission to subordinate units. Remember – if you opt to create a Forward Logistics Element, one unit needs to pick up the C2 portion.
4. CCIR. These should change from those initially developed in Mission Analysis.

PRODUCTS FROM WAR GAMING

1. Refined Courses of Action
2. Synch Matrix for each war game.
3. Decision Support Template/DSM for each war game.
4. Potential branches and sequels – contingency planning if required
5. List of areas of concern to be engaged during shaping and decisive operations.
6. Sustainment combat power at the end of the war game for friendly and enemy and support capabilities for friendly forces.
7. Updated running estimates and assumptions.

7.1 The Wargaming Sequence.

Wargaming Sequence

1. Visualize the operation.
2. Considerations in developing COA's based upon METT-T
   a. Movement planning (air, ground).
   b. Task organization
   c. FOB/LSA/CRSP/TTP/CSC/Base cluster locations
   d. Availability of addition support (MP, SECFOR, EN, ADA, higher headquarters, etc.)
   e. Security /Force Protection measures
      (1) Entry to AO
      (2) Convoy operations
      (3) Critical equipment sites [Example: ROWPU, FSSP, FARE, FAWPSS].
3. List advantages and disadvantages (remain unbiased).
4. Assess feasibility of COA.
5. Avoid comparing COA's until comparison phase.
6. Avoid premature conclusions.

THOUGHTS ON WAR-GAMING

"When he looked at a map, Zhukov did not just reproduce the picture of the past engagement; he could foresee the nature of the future encounter and in a matter of minutes play out as it were, the various scenarios first for himself and then for the enemy. He could put himself in the enemy's place for a while so that when he became himself again he could evaluate the intentions of the enemy."

FROM; A. CHAKOVSKLY, THE BLOCKADE IN FUNDAMENTALS OF TACTICAL COMMAND AND CONTROL, BY D.A. IVANOV ET AL. (MOSCOW, 1977), P.203

15

CHAPTER 8

COURSE OF ACTION COMPARISON

★★★

1. After war gaming, the staff prepares to do comparison of the courses of action. The course of action comparison starts with each staff officer analyzing and evaluating the advantages and disadvantages of each COA from their perspective. The planners return to their work areas, as time permits, to begin their individual COA comparison. Each planner must take the comparison criteria and individually apply them to each COA, paying particular attention to developing rationale to support his decision about which COA is **best** supported by his/her War Fighting Functional Area. When the planners reconvene, each staff member presents his/her findings for the others' consideration. Using the evaluation criteria developed earlier, the staff then outlines each COA, highlighting its advantages and disadvantages with respect to each other. Planners have the opportunity to make points pro and con about each COA.

2. The staff compares feasible courses of action to identify the one that has the highest probability of success against the most likely enemy course of action and the most dangerous course of action. The selected COA should also:

   a. Pose the minimum risk to the soldiers, equipment, and mission accomplishment.
   b. Best position the force for future operations.

    c.   Provide the best flexibility to meet "unknowns" during execution.

    d.   Provide maximum latitude for initiative by subordinates.

3.   The actual comparison of COAs is critical. The staff may use any technique that facilitates reaching the best recommendation and the commander making the best decision. The most common technique is the Decision Matrix (FM 6-0, Table 9-7, pg 9-39). Each staff officer may use his/her own matrix, using same evaluative criteria, for comparison in his/her own field of interest. Decision matrixes cannot alone provide decision solutions. The matrix should use the evaluation criteria developed earlier. The XO normally determines the weight of each criterion based on its relative importance. The staff officer responsible for a functional area scores each COA using those criteria. Multiply the score by the weight yields the criterion's value. Comparing a COA by category is more accurate than attempting to aggregate a total score for each COA.

COA Comparison (the Leavenworth "School Solution"): Let's assume there are three COAs to the compared. The criteria is established and agreed to. For the each criteria, the COA that is best supported gets a "3". The next in order of supportability gets a "2" and the last COA gets a "1". If one sees little or no difference in the last two COAs (for supportability), then each COA gets a "1.5" (the average of the sum of 2+1). Using the same thought process, if all COAs are deemed to be equally supportable against a particular criteria, then they would all get a "2" (average of the sum of 3+2+1). If there were 4 COAs to be compared, then the most supportable would get a "4" and so on. None of the criteria is weighted, initially. If at the end of the comparison and the totaling of the numbers given to each COA against the criteria there is not a clear cut "winner", then the planners should go back to the commander's guidance, pick the one or two most important points and assign a weight to those criteria, do the multiplication and addition again, and see if one COA comes out ahead. This is the comparison method that is taught in ILE (formerly CGSC), and SAMS.

4.   Output from the COA Comparison is the Decision Matrix.

8.1 COMPARISON CRITERIA – A METHOD

1. COA's for Sustainment units are limited in the number and extent of available options due to the assigned missions, available task organization, and METT-T of the situation. As a result, Sustainment C2 units should spend their available time comparing missions to available assets to insure that resources are available to ensure success. Distance, terrain, weather, personnel strength, mission requirements, potential enemy action, and equipment loss all must be taken into consideration. Ultimately, the best COA is the one that conducts effective and efficient "end-to-end" distribution management with little/no loss of life and equipment. Typical COAs are:

    a. For Sus Brigades/CSSBs: Echelonment of a FLE/FLB or Logistics Task Force (LTF) Establish a Centralized Receiving and Shipping Pt (CRSP) Establish a Trailer Transfer Point (TTP) Establish a Convoy Support Center (CSC) or "Mini-Mart"

    b. For BSBs: Echelonment of FLE/FLB Split the BSB into two equal elements, capable of independent operations.

2. All task organization unit assets and capabilities must be recorded and tracked by both the S-4 (internal unit readiness) and Support Operations (external support operations) staff sections due to the multiple capabilities of many pieces of equipment, primarily transportation assets which are the key to any operation.

3. All COA's must place the battalion and its task organization in a position to support follow-on missions.

CONCEPT OF SUPPORT

8.2 SCHEME OF SUPPORT FOR COURSE OF ACTION DEVELOPMENT

General Instructions

In the course of COA development, the staff takes the *input* and completes the development process to create the *output* which becomes the Scheme of Support.

Input
    Restated Mission
    Commander's Guidance
    Intelligence Estimate

Process
    Analyze support requirements and unit capabilities
    Match capabilities with mission tasks
    Determine mission requirements
    Complete Personnel, Intelligence, Sus, and Support
        Operations Estimates
    Determine C2 requirements

Output
    Course of action statements
    Intelligence update
    Recommended course of action for analysis

8.3 SCHEME OF SUPPORT COA DEVELOPMENT WORKSHEET

1. Identify tasks that require both equipment and material. Make assumptions for consumables (Class III and IX) as necessary.
2. Identify if shared resources are used for a task (i.e. one tractor for two or more trailers).

Unit	Tasks	Equipment	Shortfalls/ Issues

8.4 SCHEME OF SUPPORT COURSE OF ACTION SKETCH

Annex C to 123 BSB OPORD

CONCEPT OF SUPPORT	Phase I: Prep/ Counter-recon	Phase IIA & B: Motorized IN, Mech Armor Fight	Phase III: Consolidation and Reorganization
CONCEPT OF SUPPORT: 123 BSB conducts GAC and LOGAIR missions to provide uninterrupted CSS to the 30 HBCT as they defend in sector. Priority of supplies is Class IV, V, III(B), and water. BPT push out LOGPACs and FLEs to rearm and refit the 30HBCT as they transition into offensive operations.	T: A Co move 1-120 CAB and 1-150 CAV into sector P: Allow units to establish defense T: A Co BPT move 1-252 CAB fwd into sector P: Allow unit to prepare for defense in the event no air is available T: A Co move CL IV & V into sector P: IOT est. Brigade defense	T: A Co BPT push emergency resupply of CL I, III, IV, V, VIII, IX, and water fwd by air or ground P: Allow units to continue the fight T: A Co BPT refuel BDE reserves P: Allow the reserve to remain flexible	T: A Co BPT push emergency resupply of CL I, III, IV, V, VIII, IX and water fwd by air or ground P: Allow units to continue the fight T: A Co O/O push necessary classes of supply forward P: Allow the 30 HBCT to transition into the offense
See Appendix 1 to Annex F to 123rd OPORD			Priority of Support: Priority of support is 1-120, 1-150 CAV/ 1-252 and 1-113 FA Pr. of Troop movement from TAA to def position: Air moves 1-150 CAV 210600-UTC: A/1-120, C/1-120 No air avail: 210600-UTC: 1-252, B/1-120, D/1-120

Priority of Maintenance:
- Priority of ground maintenance is M1, M3, Q36, M198, M119, Avenger, Stinger, ROWPU, MHE
- Priority of air maintenance is AH64, OH58D, UH60, CH47

Routes:
- All MSRs need to remain open until 23 1800 JUL
- MSRs need to be closed NLT 23 1800 JUL
- At the conclusion of the defense, o/o open MSRs in their AOs to allow for resupply to move forward

CL IV Movement Assets pushed fwd:
1-120: 3 x 4K FL, entire operation
1-252: 1 x 10K FL 211800-212400
1-150: 1 x 10K FL 211800-212400

RSR—CSR except the following:

A. 155MM

HE APICM DPICM HC RAP WP ILL RAAMS ADAM CLGP

25 3 50 6 2 6 3 2 1 2

B. 105MM

HE APICM APERS HC RAP WP ILL HEP-T

40 40 1 3 6 6 2 1

C. 81MM

HP WP ILL

114 12 6

D. 60MM

HE WP ILL

60 15 15

E. AT4

F. Mines

20 per company per day

M21 VOLCANOES MOPM

3000 2 10

Class I:
- Primary source for water resupply is ROWPU
- Iodine tablets are authorized for use first 15 days
- All surface water is non-potable

Class III (B):
- Pushed out daily w/ LOGPAC
- 1 HEMTT fueler stays with Cav troop, 2 pushed out w/ LOGPAC
- 23 1500 Jul LOGPAC, 3 fuelers pushed out to Cav, 1 add stays fwd (2 total)

Class IV:
- A Co BPT push 1st CL IV push NLT 21 1800 JUL
- Primary means for CL IV movement is air, then ground

Class VII:
- Pushed FWD with LOGPACs or as required

Class IX:
- Pushed out daily with unit LOGPACs

LOGPAC:
- Pushed daily at 0600 and 1700
- Last LOGPAC at 23 1500

Class VIII
- Pushed out daily with unit LOGPACs or utilizing ambulance back haul

8.5 COURSE OF ACTION COMPARISON MATRIX

Courses of Action -	Advantages
	Disadvantages

(Copy as many times as needed for each COA)

PREPARATION FOR DECISION BRIEFING

1. S-2/S-2 Intel NCO is prepared to discuss the enemy situation and enemy COAs to refresh those being briefed.

2. S-3 briefs all friendly COAs. Another planner points, as the concept of operation paragraph is read. He then indicates the comparison criteria chart to the CDR and briefly elaborates on the selected criteria.

3. Each tasked staff COA planner then is prepared to discuss in detail, by his particular Warfighting function (WFF), the comparison process he/she used to arrive at the decision that one COA was most feasible. Planners must discuss the advantages and disadvantages he considered when comparing the COAs from his/her perspective. **At no time** will a briefer state that there is *"no difference between the COAs from my perspective."* This is the kiss of death for a planner for it indicates you have little or no imagination, have not completed an in-depth analysis of the COAs, or you simply don't have the deductive thinking process necessary to make recommendations to decision-makers.

4. After each briefer elaborates on his rationale to support one COA over the others, the S-3 reveals the totals on the comparison chart and takes his seat.

COMMANDER'S DECISION BRIEFING

1. After completing its analysis and comparison, the staff identifies its preferred COA and makes a recommendation. If a decision cannot be reached, the XO decides which COA to recommend at the commander's decision brief. The decision briefing format includes: (Chapter 16)

   a. The intent of the higher HQ (higher and next higher commanders).

   b. The restated mission.

c. The status of own forces.

d. An updated IPB.

e. Own COAs, including:

    (1) Assumptions used in planning.

    (2) Results of staff estimates.

    (3) Advantages and disadvantages (including risk) of each COA (with decision matrix or table showing COA comparison).

f. The recommended COA.

PRODUCTS FROM THE DECISION BRIEFING/ COA APPROVAL

1. Approved COA. The commander's decision on which COA to complete development on and prepare an order for.
2. Refine Commander's Intent Statement (if required).
3. Level of risk the Commander is willing to accept.
4. New/approved CCIR to support execution.
5. Specified type of order.
6. Specified type of rehearsal.
7. Refine the Concept of Support (CoS) and Sustainment Sync Matrix.
8. Location and time for Orders Brief.

DECISION MATRIX
(COA Analysis)

CRITERIA	WT	COURSES OF ACTION		
		1	2	3
C2				
CDR'S INTENT				
LOCATION				
RISK				
RE-SUPPLY				
ROUTES				
RISK				
MEDEVAC				
TOTAL				
WEIGHTED TOTAL				

LOWER IS BETTER

8.6 COA COMPARISON - OFFENSE

CRITERIA:	DESCRIPTION:
SIMPLICITY	Facilitates Mission Command, Less complicated graphics, Less likelihood for fratricide
FIRE SUPPORT	Facilitates Security Area Battle fires, Simple FS measures, Org for combat, Survivability, Control of assets
MOB/PROTECTION	Maximizes engineer effort in fewer zones/avenues of approach, facilitates Class IV resupply
MASS	Concentrates combat power and support effort for the greatest effect.
INTEL	See the enemy, Disrupt the enemy, Protect the force, Do not let the enemy disrupt the replenishment operation
RISK	Which COA allows the greatest chance for enemy to disrupt our support effort or for customers to not be supported
ADA	Provides best option for use of assets by maximizing protection for friendly forces
FACILITATES END STATE	Option that supports faster defeat of enemy and maximizes the chances for commander's intent for end state of the force

DECEPTION   Best influences the enemy to our advantage, easiest to employ quickly

SUSTAINMENT   Maximized distribution over greater distances. Strive to develop more local haul operations through distro hubs versus line haul operations

8.7 COA COMPARISON - DEFENSE

CRITERIA:	**DESCRIPTION:**
SIMPLICITY	Facilitates Mission Command, Less complicated graphics, less likelihood for fratricide
FIRE SUPPORT	Facilitates Security Area battle fires, Simple FS measures, Org for combat, Survivability, Control of assets
MOB/C-MOB	Requires least amount of engineer work
MASS	Concentrates combat power and support effort
INTEL	See the enemy, Disrupt the enemy, Protect the force
RISK	Which COA gives the greatest chance for success to the enemy
ADA	Provides best option for use of assets by maximizing protection for friendly
FACILITATES END	Option that supports faster defeat of enemy and maximizes the STATE chance for commander's intent for end state of the force
DECEPTION	Best influences the enemy to our advantage, Easiest to employ quickly
SUSTAINMENT	Maximized distribution concentrating on Class IV/V. Strive to develop more local haul operations through distro hubs versus line haul operations

CHAPTER 9

ORDERS PRODUCTION

★★★

OVERVIEW

1. Plans and orders are the means by which the commander expresses to his subordinates his/her battlefield visualization, intent, and a decision, focusing on the results the commander expects to achieve – their vision of the end state of operations. This gives subordinates the maximum operational and tactical freedom to accomplish the mission which providing only the minimum restrictions and details necessary for synchronization and coordination. Plans and orders should provide the "*what*" rather than the "*how*" to encourage initiative. Plans and orders are the method the commander uses to synchronize military actions. They also help the staff synchronize the commander's decisions and concepts. The amount of detail the commander provides in a plan or order depends on the experience and competence of subordinate commanders, the cohesion and tactical experiences of subordinate units, and the complexity of the operation.

2. **Operation Plan** – (OPLAN) (Format Para 9.6) is a plan for the conduct of military operations prepared in response to actual and potential contingencies.

   a. States critical assumptions that form the basis of the plan. Assumptions must be revalidated prior to execution of the plan.

b. Becomes an Operations Order (OPORD) when the commander sets an execution time or designates an event that triggers the operation.

3. **Operations Order** – (OPORD) is a directive issued by a commander to subordinate commanders for the purpose of effecting the coordinated execution of an operation (JP 5-0). Commanders issue OPORDs to direct the execution of long term operations as well as the execution of discrete short term operations within the framework of a long-range OPORD. (Ref Para 9.6)

4. **Sustainment Order** - provides the plan for service support of operations, including administrative movements. It provides information to supported elements and serves as a basis for the orders of supporting commanders to their units. Sustainment Orders may be issued either with an OPORD, or separately when the commander expects the sustainment situation to apply to more than one operation plan or order. The G4 (S4) has primary coordinating responsibility for preparing, publishing, and distribution of the Sustainment Order. Other staff officers will provide their parts of the orders concerning their area of responsibility. (Ref Para 9.7)

5. **Movement Order** (Format Para 9.8) – The movement order is a stand-alone order that facilitates an uncommitted unit's movements. The movements are typically administrative, and troops and vehicles are arranged to expedite their movement and to conserve time and energy when no enemy interference (except by air) is anticipated. The G4 (S4) has primary responsibility coordinating staff responsibility for planning and coordinating movements with input from all other staff sections, primarily the S-3. The G4 (S4) is also responsible for preparing, publishing, and distribution of the movement order

6. **Warning Order** – (WARNORD) is a preliminary notice of an order or action that is to follow. Warning orders help subordinate units and their staffs prepare for new missions. Warning orders maximize the subordinate's planning time, provide essential details for the impending operation, and detail major time-line events that accompany mission execution. The amount of detail a warning order includes depends on the information and time available when the order is issued and the information subordinate commanders need for proper planning and preparation. The warning order clearly informs the recipient of what tasks he must do now as well as informs him of possible future tasks. However, a WARNORD does not authorize execution other than planning unless specifically stated.

7. **Fragmentary Order** – (FRAGORD) (Format Para 9.9) is an abbreviated form of operation order issued as needed after an OPORD to change or modify that order or to execute a branch or sequel to that order. Commanders may authorize members of their staff to change existing orders by issuing FRAGORDs in their name. FRAGORDs include all five OPORD paragraphs headings and differs from an OPORD only in the detail of detail provided. FRAGORDs are either verbal or written and addresses only those parts of the original OPORD that have changed. The higher headquarters issues a new OPORD when there is a complete change of the tactical situation or when many changes make the current order ineffective.

GENERAL INFORMATION – A COURSE OF ACTION IS SELECTED!

1. Based on the commander's decision and final guidance, the S-3 (with assistance of the SPO) refines the COA and completes the plan and prepares to issue the order. The plan or

order is prepared to implement the selected COA by turning it into a clear, concise concept of support and concept of operation for the decisive, shaping and sustaining battles. The COA statement will become the concept of support and operations statement. The COA sketch is the basis for the sustainment and operations overlays/LCOP. Orders and plans provide all necessary information subordinates require for execution, but without unnecessary constraints that would inhibit subordinate initiatives.

2. The concept of support is the key to the sustainment unit order. It is the commander's clear, concise statement of where, when and how he intends to concentrate the support effort to accomplish the mission IAW the higher commander's intent and to accomplish support to his customer. It includes actions within the tactical logistics functions and battlefield organization, weighting of the main effort, priorities of support, and specific command and support relationships. The relationships are then included in the Task Organization and Organization for support.

3. During orders production, the staff implements accident risk controls by coordinating and integrating them into the appropriate paragraphs and graphics of the OPORD. It is essential to communicate how controls will be put into effect, who will implement them, and how they fit into the overall operation.

4. Finally, the commander reviews and approves orders before the staff reproduces and briefs them.

PREPARATION FOR ORDERS BRIEFING

Most of the products created for the previous briefings now form the basic order.

- Intelligence Estimate becomes para 1a-c (OPLAN only) of the basic order. This information also forms the basis of ANNEX B.
- The Higher Headquarters order provides information for para 1b and 1d of the basic order.
- S-2 Mission Analysis becomes part of para 1b, 1d (OPLAN only).
- Personnel Estimate provides information for para 1g (OPLAN only) and personnel sub-paragraphs in para 4 of the basic order.
- Logistic Estimates provide information for para 1d (OPLAN only) and para 4 of the basic order.
- The Commander's Guidance and Intent provides information for Task Organization and para 3 of the basic order.
- COA statement and sketch forms the basis for para 3b of the basic order.
- War gaming products (synchronization matrix) provides information for Task Organization, para 3b through d, 3k, para 4, and para 5.

9.1 Staff Responsibility for Orders and Annexes

The following staff sections are responsible for writing (or assist with) specific portions of the OPORD and annexes. At the battalion level, only a portion of the annexes listed in FM 6-0 are needed for most operations.

Para	TITLE	PRIMARY	ASSIST	ASSIST
1	Situation	S-2		
2	Mission	XO	S-3	
3	Execution			
	Scheme of Support	SPO	BC	XO
	Scheme of Maneuver	S-2 & S-3	BC	XO
4	Sustainment			
	Concept of Support	S-4		
	Material and services	S-4		
	Personnel	S-1		
	Medical Evac and Hospitalization	S-1		
5	Command and Signal	S-3 & S-6	XO	

ANNEX	TITLE	PRIMARY	ASSIST	ASSIST
A	Task Organization	S-3	XO	SPO
B	Intelligence	S-2		
C	Operation Overlay			
	Appendix 1 – Scheme of Support	SPO	BC	XO
	Appendix 2 – Scheme of Movement & Maneuver	S-3	BC	XO
E	Protection	S-3		
F	Sustainment			
	Appendix 1 – Logistics	S-4	SPO	
	Appendix 2 – Personnel Services Support	S-1	SPO	S-4
	Appendix 3 – Health Service Support	S-1	BMSO	S-4
H	Signal	S-6	S-3	
K	Civil Affairs Operations	S-1		
L	Information Collection	S-3	S-2	
R	Reports	XO	S-3 &S-1	SPO

At the Sustainment Brigade, the flowing is a breakdown of applicable annexes.

ANNEX A	Task Organization	S-3
ANNEX B	Intelligence	S-2
ANNEX C	Operations, Synch Matrix, Graphics	S-3, SPO
ANNEX D	Fires	S-3
ANNEX E	Protection	S-3
ANNEX F	Sustainment	S-4/S-1
ANNEX G	Engineering	S-3
ANNEX H	Signal	S-6
ANNEX I	Not Used	**N/A**
ANNEX J	Public Affairs	S-1
ANNEX K	Civil Affairs Operations	S-1

ANNEX L	Information Collection	S-3 (assist by S-2)
ANNEX M	Assessment	S-3 (assist by SPO)
ANNEX N	Space Operations	**N/A**
ANNEX O	Spare	**N/A**
ANNEX P	Host Nation Support	S-1, SPO
ANNEX Q	Knowledge Management	XO, S-3, SPO
ANNEX R	Reports	S-3
ANNEX S	Special Technical Operations	S-3
ANNEX T	Spare	**N/A**
ANNEX U	Inspector General	S-1
ANNEX V	Interagency Coordination	S-3
ANNEX W	Operational Contract Support	SPO, S-1
ANNEX X, Y	Spare	**N/A**
ANNEX Z	Distribution	S-3

2. Notes regarding the preparation of OPLANs/OPORDs are at Chapter 25.

DURING THE ORDERS BRIEFING

The Orders Briefing Format is at Chapter 17. As we near the end of our 1/3 time hack we must be flexible and prepared to make any necessary corrections, additions, deletions to the order as a result of the briefing.

PRODUCTS FROM THE ORDERS BRIEFING

1. Written OPLAN/OPORD.
2. All Annexes to the OPLAN/OPORD.
3. All overlays in the necessary numbers in 1:100,000 scale.

DAILY PLANS UPDATE TO THE CDR

S-3 provides a daily update to the CDR and/or XO in the Plans area on a daily basis usually at 0900 hours. The format for this informal briefing is at Chapter 18.

BRANCHES AND SEQUELS

S-3 is responsible for continuous planning for the current operation and future operations.

Branches are contingency options built into the base plan used for changing the mission, orientation, or direction of movement of a force to aid success of the operation based on anticipated events, opportunities, or disruption caused by enemy actions and/or reactions. Branches add flexibility to plans by anticipating situations that could alter the basic plan. These plans must have as much detail as possible to them and should have gone through the MDMP (Time constrained), War gaming, and approval process. An example of such would be the deployment of a FLE to a grid location that has now become unavailable/inaccessible. An alternative (planned) site would then be utilized. (FM 6-0, Para C-17, pg C-3)

Sequels are subsequent major operations or phase based on possible outcomes (success, stalemate, or defeat) of the current major operation. For every action or major operation that does not accomplish an operational (or strategic) objective, there should be a sequel for each possible outcome, such as win, lose, or decisive win. These plans must also go through the MDMP (Time constrained), War gaming, and the approval process. An example would be the deployment of a major convoy to conduct a Major Replenishment Operation (MRO). Should the convoy be destroyed or significantly delayed, a new convoy or MRO would need to be developed, sync, and executed. (FM 6-0, Para C-18, pg C-3)

As time permits, all contingency plans must be prepared as FRAGOs with as much detail as possible and must be in the hands of those responsible for executing them. Planning is an ongoing process. The enemy will almost never act or react exactly as we might think he will, but our plans must take into consideration all the probable courses of action he might take and allow for the flexibility necessary to change our operations to meet his challenge.

9.2 DEVELOPMENTAL GUIDELINES FOR PARAGRAPH 4 (SUSTAINMENT)

1. General rules for paragraph 4.

    a. Use language that is clear, concise, and comprehensive. Avoid technical terminology.

    b. Focus on what the non-sustainment commander needs to know about how the operation is sustained. This makes paragraph 4a the logistic equivalent to the concept of the operation.

    c. Consider the sustainment functions in the context of actions by phase of an operation or, before, during, and after the operation. The operative term is '*<u>consider</u>*'. The intent is not to address each function unless it is critical or unusual. The support concept is organized into a framework based on operational phasing, or presented as before, during, and after Operations format.

    d. The *concept of sustainment* establishes priorities of support by phase or before, during, and after the operation. The commander at each level establishes these priorities in his intent statement (e.g., main effort) and in the concept of the operation (paragraph 3). This could include prioritizing such things as personnel replacements; maintenance and evacuation, by unit and by system (aviation and surface systems would be given separate priorities); fuel and/or ammunition; road network use by unit and/or commodity; and any resource subject to competing demands or constraints.

    e. Synchronize the *concept of sustainment* with the concept of the operation. Remember – your '*Concept of Operation*' should nicely dovetail into your higher headquarters *'Concept of Support'*. Refer to Figure 9-1 below.

f. Formations comprised of units that are not part of the same organization or don't have habitual relationships may not share a common TSOP and may require a more lengthy support concept. Conversely, the more comprehensive the TSOP, the briefer the support concept.

g. The more complex the operation (a multi-phased operation or operations larger formations conduct), the more critical the sustainment synchronization.

h. Routine, doctrinal, or constant information is not included in the support concept. It is incorporated into the unit TSOP.

i. Detailed and numerical data relevant to the operation, and of primary interest to unit logistic personnel, may be in another subparagraph of 4 or in the service support annex.

j. It is important to understand the next higher commander's support priorities and where your particular unit fits into those priorities.

2. Sustainment planners need to review the support concept and ensure it meets the commander's needs. There are several basic questions the Sustainment planner should ask:

a. Is the support concept easily understood, and is it comprehensive and concise?

b. Does it provide visualization (word picture) of the overall support concept?

c. Is the support concept synchronized with and does it support the concept of the operation (paragraph 3)?

d. Does it consider, and address as required, the sustainment functions by phase of an operation or in the context of before, during, and after?

e. Does it establish priorities of support by phase and do these priorities correlate with the priorities established in the commander's intent, paragraph 3, and other directives from higher?

f. Is it written for the non-sustainment commanders and their primary staffs and focused for supported units?

g. Does it address all critical, non-SOP, or unusual aspects of support?

Concept of Operations vs
Concept of Support

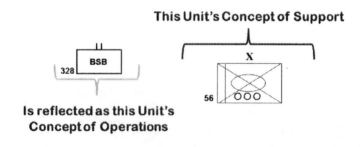

Figure 9-1 Concept of Operations vs Concept of Support

SUSTAINMENT (Paragraph 4a)
FORMAT

1. **Support Concept**. Paragraph 4 will provide all overall view of the support concept. Its intent is to provide the non-Sustainment commanders and their primary staffs an image of how the operation will be logistically supported. If the information pertains to the entire operation, or if it pertains to more than one unit, include it in the introductory portion of paragraph 4. Change it in tile ensuing subparagraphs when needed. This could include:

   - A brief synopsis of the support command mission.
   - Support command headquarters and/or support area locations, including locations of next higher logistics bases if not clearly conveyed in the sustainment overlay/ LCOP.
   - The next higher level's support priorities and where the unit fits into those priorities.
   - Priorities that remain unchanged throughout the operation.
   - Units in the next higher Sustainment organization supporting the unit.
   - Significant and/or unusual sustainment issues that might impact the overall operation.
   - The use of host nation support.
   - Any significant sustainment risks.

   a. **PHASE I** (starts with "event" and ends with "event").
      - Sustainment focus (Decisive Operation (DO), ME, and SE)
      - Priorities:
        — By unit.
        — For personnel replacements.

   — Maintenance and/or recovery and evacuation priorities (by unit and equip type)
   — Movement.
   — By class of supply.
  • Critical events or other pertinent information needed to communicate how logistics support will be conducted for the operation. Use the sustainment functions for information to include in the support concept.

b. **PHASE II** (starts with "event" and ends with "event"). If there are any differences or changes, state them in this paragraph.
  • Sustainment focus (DO, ME, and SE)
  • Priorities:
   — By unit.
   — For personnel replacements.
   — Maintenance and/or recovery and evacuation priorities (by unit and equip type).
   — Movement,
   — By class of supply.
  • Critical events or other pertinent information needed to communicate how logistics sup-port will be conducted for the operation. Use the sustainment functions for information to include in the support concept.
  • Critical decision points.

c. **PHASES III, IV and V** (starts with "event" and ends with event'). If there are any differences or changes from pre-vious phases, state them here, -
  • Sustainment focus (DO, ME and SE). Remember, your sustainment focus needs to support your higher headquarters/supported units 'Decisive Effort'.
  • Priorities:

- — By unit.
- — For personnel replacements.
- — Maintenance and/or recovery and evacuation priorities (by unit and equip type).
- — Movement.
- — By class of supply.
- Critical events or other pertinent information needed to communicate how logistics support will be conducted for the operation. Use the sustainment functions for information to include in the support concept.
- Major Resupply Operation (MRO) (referenced in the last phase).
- Preparing for future operations (last phase).

d. Paragraphs 4a through 4c are normally more detailed and are included in the service support annex. They are not part of the support concept.

e. Concept of support written before, during, and after format. Follow the same guidance as by phase.

9.3 CONCEPT OF SUSTAINMENT MATRIX (DIVISION)

SUSTAINMENT FUNCTIONS	PHASE I *(Move from TAA to ATK POS - DTG)*	PHASE IIa *(ATK to Defeat Lead Divisions)*	PHASE IIb *(Counterattack)*	PHASE III *(Hasty Defense)*
PRIORITY OF SUPPORT	52. CAB, 37 FIB, 3 BDE, 3 BDE, 1 BDE	2 BDE, 3 BDE, 52 CAB, 37 FIB, 1 BDE	3 BDE, 2 BDE, 52 CAB, 1 BDE, 37 FIB	1 BDE, 2 BDE, CAB, 3 BDE, 37 FIB
HR — HUMAN RESOURCES SUPPORT	PRI REPL: CAB, 37 FIB, 2 BDE, 3 BDE, 1 BDE	PRI REPL: 2 BDE, 3 BDE, CAB, 37 FIB, 1 BDE. SHIFT TO 1 BDE IF COMMITTED. REPL. OPS SUSPENDED UNTIL PL DESK	PRI REPL: 3 BDE, 2 BDE, CAB, 1st BDE, 37 FIB	PRI REPL: 1 BDE, 2 BDE, CAB, 3 BDE, 37 FIB. REPL OPS RESUME.
SUPPLY (CL I, II, III(p), III(B), IV, V, VI, and VII)	PRI CL III: CAB, 3 BDE, 2 BDE, 1 BDE. PRI CL V: HELLFIRE, 25MM, TANK, ATGM, 155 DPICM	PRI (LESS CL V): 2 BDE, 3 BDE, 52 CAB, 37 FIB, 1 BDE. PRI CL V: 120MM HEAT, TOW, 155 DPICM	PRI (LESS CL V): 3 BDE, 2 BDE, CAB, 1 BDE, 37 FIB. REPLENISH CL III UBLs. PRI CL V: 155 DPICM, HELLFIRE, TOW, TANK. REPLENISH UBLS	PRI ALL CLASSES: 1 BDE, 2 BDE, CAB, 3 BDE, 37 FIB.
MAINTENANCE	PRI MAINT: M109, M1, M2/3, 5K Tankers, PLS, and M88. PRI MAINT CAB: AH-64, CH-58D, and UH-60	PRI MAINT: M1, M2/3, M88, MHE. PRI CAB MAINT: UNCHANGED	PRI – NO CHANGE	PRI MAINT: M1, M109, M2/3, M88. PRI CAB MAINT: UNCHANGED
TRANSPORTATION	PRI FWD: DS 37 FIB, MONV UNITS, III, V. PRI REAR: MED, EQUIP EVAC, REFUGEES.	PRI FWD: MNV UNITS, DS 37 FIB, III, V. PRI REARWARD: MED, MAINT EVAC, EPWs, REFUGEES	PRI FWD AND REARWARD: UNCHANGED.	PRI FWD: IX, VI, III, V. PRI REARWARD: UNCHANGED
FIELD SERVICES	FS PROVIDED BY 13th CSSB IN LSA LAMP.	FS OPERATIONS SUSPENDED UNTIL PL DESK. KIA EVAC TO MA	FS – NO CHANGE	FS OPS RESUME IN SUS BDE LSA.
CHS	3456 FST & FSMT DS TO 31SD FSB, 343D FST & 1 FSMT DS TO 202D FSB, 1FSMT W/ 404th FSB, MSMT AREA COVERAGE DREAR ASMT W/ DA88	2XCH-47 AVAIL FOR MASS CAL. CSH LOCATED IN LSA BELL.	2XCH-47 AVAIL FOR MASS CAL. CSH LOCATED IN LSA BELL. 3BMC LOC IN LSA LAMP	NO CHANGE
EOD	EOD SPT AVAIL IN LSA LAMP	NO CHANGE	NO CHANGE	NO CHANGE
FINANCIAL MGT SPT	CORPS PROVIDES FINANCE SPT IN UNIT SPT AREAS	FIN OPS SUSPENDED UNTIL PL DESK	NO CHANGE	FIN OPS RESUMED
RELIGIOUS / LEGAL / AND BAND SPT	BAND SUPPORT AVAIL UPON REQUEST TO G3	DIV BAND PROVIDES FORCE PROTECTION TO DMAIN CP	NO CHANGE	NO CHANGE

9.4 BRIEFING THE CONCEPT OF SUSTAINMENT

1. The Sustainer's's role in the overall OPLAN/OPORD briefing is to brief the Concet of Support, but he/she must first understand the general concept of the operation and the commander's intent. This briefing facilitates communicating the support concept to the commander and the subordinate commanders. The support concept briefing should address the critical, non-SOP, or unusual aspects of logistic support by phase of an operation by critical sustainment functions. Doctrinal, usual, or SOP matters should not be addressed unless there is a deviation in support relationships or normal methods. The Sustainment planner briefs the support concept, working through the operation by phase. This briefing should go into greater detail than is laid out in the written support concept.

2. **Some rules of thumb for the Concept of Support briefing are:**

    a. Tell commanders what they can expect from sustainment and how many days or hours they can operate based on materiel readiness, quantities of supplies on hand, etc. Use common terms such as DOS or other terms that are meaningful to the commander. Avoid using technical terminology or SOP information.

    b. Depending of the level of sustainment, establish a common '*coin of the relm*' matrix language. For example at the FSClevel, talk in terms of *cases/packages/gallons*. At the BSB through Sustainment Bde, talk in terms of '*pallets/ gallons*'. At the Expeditionary Sustainment Command (and Sus Bdes involved with Theater Distribution/ Opening/Closing), talk in terms of '*TEUs (Twenty Foot Equivilent Units)/Containers*'.

c. Address the "culminating point" from a sustainment-logistic perspective. It is also a good idea to point out the sustainment unit's *operational reach* (distance to suppor the customer).

d. Avoid briefing the results of extensive number-crunching that is associated with the logistics estimate process.

e. The briefer should not read a written product. Rather, use the Sustainment overlay/LCOP and appropriate visual aids, such as a support concept overview matrix (see appendix H), he should show the commander how the support concept is synchronized with and supports the concept of the operation.

f. The briefing should include locations of critical sustainment (i.e. logistic) assets, headquarters, and events.

g. Address priorities, shifts in priorities, problem areas and solutions, and critical events.

h. **Bottom line: The sustainer must tell the commander what he needs to know.**

IMPORTANT: DO NOT 'FIRE HOSE' THE COMMANDER WITH LOGISTICAL 'DATA'. PROVIDE HIM WITH KNOWLEDGE!!!

Knowledge is Data (from Staff Estimates) + Analysis (from appropriate Staff person) = Informed (and Knowledgeable) Commander.

3. Concept of Sustainment/Support briefing format,

a. **Introduction** (overview of the support concept and orientation to the map, if required). Orientation to the map is not required if another briefer has done so previously. Do not assume the commander totally knows the terrain. Focus on locating critical sustainment nodes, MSRs, etc.

b. **Brief the support concept** starting with critical actions that must be accomplished in the first phase of the operation and concluding with critical actions to be accomplished in the last phase. This will prepare for future operations using the sustainment functions as a guide.

c. **Identify which units have priorities** for each critical sustainment functions (this should correlate with the commander's priorities; e.g., main effort).

d. **Identify the next higher echelon unit** providing support and/or backup support.

e. **Identify any critical shortages/problem areas** for each sustainment function and solution. For example, this can be supported, but ..., or it can be done, but not without risk in ....

f. **Identify any other sustainment problem areas**, arrangements, special requirements, or any other critical aspects addressed elsewhere in the briefing.

9.5 The Sustainment Support & Execution Matrices

Sustainment Support Matrix

ORDER #_____,   **DTG:** _____

	DATE EVENT/PL ITEM ENEMY ACTIONS				
	FRIENDLY ACTIONS				
	SUSTAINMENT DECISION POINTS				
Priority of Support	FIX				
	ARM				
	FUEL				
	SUSTAIN				
	MOVE				
	PROTECT				
	MAN				
	MSR				
	ASR				
Requirements	Class I				
	Class II				
	Class III				
	Class IV				
	Class V				
	Class VI				
	Class VII				
	Class VIII				
	Class IX				
	WATER				
	MED LOCs				
	MA CP PT				
	DC COL PT				
	EPW COL PT				

Execution Matrix

Date				
Day				
Event				
Class I				
Class I (Water)				
Class II				
Class III				
Class IV				
Class V				
Class VI				
Class VII				
Class VIII				
Class IX				
Transportation				
Showers				
Laundry				
Repair				
Maintenance/ Recovery				

Adjust table to meet requirements of assigned missions.

9.6 OPORD/OPLAN FORMAT

_____
(Classification)
(Change from oral orders, if any)

Copy ____ of ____ copies
123rd CSSB
(Place of issue)
(Date-time-group of signature)
(Message reference number)

OPERATION PLAN (ORDER) _____ **(Code name/ number)**

(U) References:

(U) Time Zone Used Throughout the Plan (Order):

(U) Task Organization:

1. **(U) Situation**
   a. (U) <u>Area of Interest</u>. (S-2)
   b. (U) <u>Area of Operations</u> (S-2)
      (1) (U) Terrain
      (2) (U) Weather
   c. (U) <u>Enemy Forces</u> (S-2)
   d. (U) <u>Friendly Forces</u> (S-3)
      (1) (U) <u>Higher HQ's Mission and Intent</u>
         (a) (U) <u>Higher HQ's Two Levels Up</u>.
            1. (U) <u>Mission</u>
            2. (U) <u>Commander's Intent</u>
         (b) (U) <u>Higher HQ's One Level Up</u>
            1. (U) <u>Mission</u>
            2. (U) <u>Commander's Intent</u>
      (2) (U) <u>Missions of Adjacent Units</u>

    e. (U)   Interagency,   Intergovernmental,   and Nongovernmental Organizations.

    f. (U) <u>Civil Considerations</u>

    g. (U) <u>Attachments and Detachments</u>

    h. (U) <u>Assumptions</u>

2. (U) Mission (S-3, XO - from analysis)

3. (U) Execution

    a. (U) <u>Commander's Intent</u>: (Cdr)

    b. (U) <u>Concept of Operations</u> (S-3)

    c. (U) <u>Scheme of Support (Maneuver & Manuever)</u> (SPO)

        (1) (U) <u>Scheme of Movement/Counter mobility</u>

        (2) (U) <u>Scheme of Battlefield Obscuration</u> (if applicable)

        (3) (U) <u>Scheme of Intelligence Collection</u> (refer to Annex L) (S-3/S-2)

    d. (U) <u>Scheme of Intelligence</u> (refer to Annex B) (S-3)

    e. (U) <u>Scheme of Fires</u> (refer to Annex D 'Fires' if applicable) (S-3)

    f. (U) <u>Scheme of Protection</u> (refer to Annex E) (S-3)

    g. (U) <u>Cyber Electromagnetic Activities</u> (refer to Appendix 12, Annex C and Annex H)

    h. (U) <u>Stability Tasks</u> (refer to Annex C 'Operations' and Annex K 'Civil Affairs') (S-3/ S-1)

    i. (U) <u>Assessment</u> (refer to Annex M 'Assessment' if applicable) (S-3)

    j. (U) <u>Tasks to Subordinate Units</u> (S-3)

        (1) (U) Sub-unit Tasks

        (2) (U) Sub-unit Tasks

    k. (U) <u>Coordinating Instructions</u>

        (1) (U) <u>Time or condition when a plan or order becomes effective</u> (XO/S-3)

        (2) (U) <u>Commanders Critical Information Requirements</u> (CCIR) (XO/S-3)

    (3) (U) <u>Essential Elements of Friendly Information</u> (EEFI) (S-3)

    (4) (U) <u>Fire Support Coordination Measures</u> (S-3)

    (5) (U) <u>Airspace Coordination Measures</u> (S-3)

    (6) (U) <u>Rules of Engagement</u> (S-3)

    (7) (U) <u>Risk Reduction Control Measures</u> (S-3/S-1)

    (8) (U) <u>Personnel Recovery Coordination Measures</u> (S-3/S-1)

    (9) (U) <u>Environmental Considerations</u> (S-3/S-4)

   (10) (U) <u>Soldeir and Leader Engagement</u> (S-3)

   (11) (U) <u>Other Coordinating Instructions</u> (As required)

4. (U) Sustainment (S-1 / S-4)

  a. (U) <u>Logistics.</u> (refer to Annex F 'Sustainment') (internal) (S-4)

  b. (U) <u>Personnel</u> (refer to Annex F 'Sustainment') (S-1)

  c. (U) <u>Health Service Support</u> (refer to Annex F 'Sustainment') (S-1)

5. (U) Command and Signal (XO/S-3/S-6)

  a. (U) <u>Command</u> (XO)

    (1) (U) <u>Location of Commander and Key Leaders</u>

    (2) (U) <u>Succession of Command</u> (see TACSOP if stated here)

    (3) (U) <u>Liaison Requirements</u>

  b. (U) <u>Control</u> (XO/S-3)

    (1) (U) <u>Command Post</u>

    (2) (U) <u>Reports</u> (refer to Annex R 'Reports')

  c. (U) <u>Signal</u> (S-6)

ACKNOWLEDGE:

                         MENTER
                         LTC

OFFICIAL:
POND
S-3

ANNEXES:

Annex A   Task Organization (S-3)
Annex B   Intelligence (S-2)
            Appendix 1 Intelligence Estimate
                Tab A Terrain Analysis (Routes, base/ base cluster)
                Tab B Weather
                Tab C Civil Considerations
                Tab D Intelligence Preparation of the Battlefield (IPB)
Annex C   Operation (S-3)
            Appendix 1 Army Design Methodolgy Products
            Appendix 2 Operations Overlay/ Graphics
            Appendix 3 Decision Support Template/Matrix
                Tab A Execution Matrix (Sustainment)
                Tab B Decision Support Template/Matrix (DST/DSM)
            Appendix 11 Rules of Engagement
            Appendix 12 Cyber Electromagnetic Activities
Annex D   Fires
            Appendix 7 Cyber/Electromagnetic Activities (S-2)
                Tab A Electronic Warfare (DUKE/WARLOCK IED Defeat Systems)
Annex E   Protection
            Appendix 9 Force Health Protection
            Appendix 11 Explosive Ordnance Disposal
            Appendix 14 Detainee and Resettlement
Annex F   Sustainment
            Appendix 1 Logistics (S-4)
                Tab A Sustainment Overlay
                Tab B Maintenance
                Tab C Transportation
                    Exhibit 1 Traffic Circulation and Control
                    Exhibit 2 Traffic Circulation Overlay

Exhibit 3 Road Movement Table
Exhibit 4 Highway Regulation
   Tab D Supply
   Tab E Field Services
   Tab F Distribution
   Tab G Contract Support Integration
   Tab H Mortuary Affairs
Appendix 2 Personnel Services Support
   Tab A Human Resource Support
   Tab B Financial Management
   Tab C Legal Support
   Tab D Religious Support
   Tab E Band Operations (N/A)
Appendix 3 Health Service Support (S-1/Unit Surgeon/Med Plt Ldr)

Annex H	Signal (S-6)
Annex J	Public Affairs (S-1)
Annex K	Civil Affairs Operations (S-1/S-3)
Annex L	Information Collection (S-2/S-3)
Annex M	Assessment (SPO/S-3)
Annex P	Host Nation Support (S-4)
Annex Q	Knowledge Management (XO/SPO/S-3)
Annex R	Reports (S-3)
Annex V	Interagency Coordination (S-3)
Annex W	Operational Contract Support (S-4)

DISTRIBUTION   _____

9.7 SUSTAINMENT ANNEX FORMAT

_____

(Classification)
(Change from oral orders, if any)

Copy ____ of ____ copies
123rd BSB
(Place of issue)
(Date-time-group of signature)
(Message reference number)

ANNEX F (SUSTAINMENT) TO OPORD/OPLAN
_____ (Code name/number)

(U) References:

    a. *List maps and charts first.*
    b. *List other references in subparagraphs labed as shown*
    c. *Doctrinal references for sustainment include ADRP 4-0, FM 3-09, ATP 4-93, etc*

(U) Time Zone Used Throughout the Plan (Order):

1. **(U) Situation**
    a. (U) <u>Area of Interest.</u> (S-2)
    b. (U) <u>Area of Operations</u> (S-2)
      (1) (U) <u>Terrain</u>
      (2) (U) <u>Weather</u>
    c. (U) <u>Enemy Forces</u> (S-2)
    d. (U) <u>Friendly Forces</u> (S-3)
    e. (U) <u>Interagency, Intergovernmental, and Nongovernmental Organizations.</u>
    f. (U) <u>Civil Considerations</u>
    g. (U) <u>Attachments and Detachments</u>
    h. (U) <u>Assumptions</u>

2. (U) Mission (S-3, XO - from analysis)

3. (U) Execution
   a. (U) <u>Scheme of Sustainment Support</u> (S-3/SPO)
   b. (U) <u>Tasks to Subordinate Units</u> (S-3)
      (1) (U) Sub-unit Tasks
      (2) (U) Sub-unit Tasks
   c. (U) <u>Coordinating Instructions</u>

4. (U) Sustainment (S-1 / S-4)
   a. (U) <u>Material and Services</u> (SPO)
      (1) (U) Maintenance
         (a) (U) <u>Ground</u>
         (b) (U) <u>Watercraft</u>
         (c) (U) <u>Aircraft</u>
         (d) (U) <u>Field Maintenance</u>
         (e) (U) <u>Sustainment Maintenance</u>
      (2) (U) <u>Transportation</u>
         (a) (U) <u>Ground</u>
         (b) <u>Sea/River/Water</u>
         (c) (U) <u>Air</u>
         (d) (U) <u>Container Management</u>
      (3) (U) <u>Supply</u>
         (a) (U) <u>Class I Rations</u>
         (b) (U) <u>Class II OCIE/Maps</u>
         (c) (U) <u>Class III Bulk (B) and Packaged (P) POL</u>
         (d) (U) Class IV Construction and Fortification Materials
         (e) (U) Class V Munitions
         (f) (U) Class VI Personal Demand Items
         (g) (U) Class VII Major End Items
         (h) (U) Class VIII Medical Supply
         (i) (U) Class IX Repair Parts
         (j) (U) <u>Class X Material for Nonmilitary/Civil Affairs Operations</u>
         (k) (U) <u>Miscellaneous</u>

(4) (U) Field Services
    (a) (U) Construction
    (b) (U) Light Textile Repair and Showers
    (c) (U) Food Preparation
    (d) (U) Water Purification
    (e) (U) Aerial Delivery
    (f) (U) Installation Services
(5) (U) Distribution
    (a) (U) Distribution Node(s) Locations
    (b) (U) Tracking Procedures
    (c) (U) Distribution Nodes
    (d) (U) Movement Request Format
    (e) (U) Container Operations
    (f) (U) Movement Control Responsibility
(6) (U) Contract Support Integration
(7) (U) Mortuary Affairs
(8) (U) Labor

b.   (U) Personnel (refer to Annex F 'Sustainment') (S-1)
    (1) (U) Human Resources Support
    (2) (U) Financial Management
    (3) (U) Legal Support
    (4) (U) Religious Support
    (5) (U) Band Operations

c.   (U) Health Service Support (refer to Annex F 'Sustainment') (S-1)
    (1) (U) Medical Evacuation
    (2) (U) Hospitalization
d.   (U) Foreign National and Host Nation Support
e.   (U) Resource Availability
f.   (U) Miscellaneous

5. (U) Command and Signal (XO/ S-3/S-6)
a.   (U) Command (XO)
    (1) (U) Location of Commander and Key Leaders

      (2) (U) <u>Succession of Command</u> (see TACSOP if stated here)

      (3) (U) <u>Liaison Requirements</u>

  b. (U) <u>Control</u> (XO/S-3)

      (1) (U) <u>Command Post</u>

      (2) (U) <u>Reports</u> (refer to Annex R 'Reports')

  c. (U) <u>Signal</u> (S-6)

ACKNOWLEDGE:

                                MENTER

                                LTC

OFFICIAL:

POND

S-3

Appendix 1 Logistics (S-4)

    Tab A Sustainment Overlay

    Tab B Maintenance

    Tab C Transportation

        Exhibit 1 Traffic Circulation and Control

        Exhibit 2 Traffic Circulation Overlay

        Exhibit 3 Road Movement Table

        Exhibit 4 Highway Regulation (Provost Marshal)

    Tab D Supply

    Tab E Field Services

    Tab F Distribution

    Tab G Contract Support Integration

    Tab H Mortuary Affairs

Appendix 2 Personnel Services Support (S-1)

    Tab A Human Resource Support

    Tab B Financial Management

    Tab C Legal Support

    Tab D Religious Support

    Tab E Band Operations (N/A)

Appendix 3 Health Service Support (S-1/Unit Surgeon/Med Plt Ldr)

9.8 MOVEMENT ORDER FORMAT

————————
(Classification)
(Change from oral orders, if any) (Optional)

Copy ____ of ____ copies
123rd BSB
(Place of issue)
(Date-time-group of signature)
(Message reference number)

MOVEMENT ORDER _____

OPERATION PLAN (ORDER) _____ **(Code name/number)**

(U) References:

(U) Time Zone Used Throughout the Plan (Order):

(U) Task Organization:

1. **(U) Situation**
   a. (U) Area of Interest. (S-2)
   b. (U) Area of Operations (S-2)
      (1) (U) Terrain
      (2) (U) Weather
   c. (U) Enemy Forces (S-2)
   d. (U) Friendly Forces (S-3)
      (1) (U) Higher HQ's Mission and Intent
         (a) (U) Higher HQ's Two Levels Up.
            1. (U) Mission
            2. (U) Intent
         (b) (U) Higher HQ's One Level Up
            1. (U) Mission
            2. (U) Intent
      (2) (U) Missions of Adjacent Units

    e. (U) Interagency, Intergovernmental, and Nongovernmental Organizations.
    f. (U) Civil Considerations
    g. (U) Attachments and Detachments
    h. (U) Assumptions

2. **(U) Mission (S-3, XO - from analysis)**

3. **(U) Execution.**
    a. (U) Concept of movement. (S-3)
    b. (U) Tasks to subordinate units. (S-3)
    c. (U) Detailed timings. (S-3)
    d. (U) Coordinating instructions. (S-3)
        (1) (U) Order of march.
        (2) (U) Routes.
        (3) (U) Density.
        (4) (U) Speed. (Include catch-up speed)
        (5) (U) Method of movement.
        (6) (U) Defense on move.
        (7) (U) Start, release, or other critical points.
        (8) (U) Convoy control.
        (9) (U) Harbor areas and/or Convoy Collection Points (CCPs).
      (10) (U) Instruction for halts – long term ('RED AIR Actions) and short term.
      (11) (U) Lighting.
      (12) (U) Air support.

4. **(U) Sustainment (S-1 / S-4)**
    a. (U) Traffic control. (Performed by MPs or coordinated Host Nation Police)
    b. (U) Recovery.
    c. (U) Medical.
    d. (U) Petroleum, oils, and lubricants.
    e. (U) Water.

5. (U) COMMAND AND SIGNAL (XO/S-3 or S-6)

    a.   (U) Command. (XO)

         (1) (U) Location of commander and chain of command.

         (2) (U) Location of key individuals or particular vehicles.

    b.   (U) Signal. (S-3 or S-6)

ACKNOWLEDGE:

                                               MENTER

                                             LTC

OFFICIAL:

POND

ANNEXES: (As required)

DISTRIBUTION:

————————————

(Classification)

9.9 FRAGMENTARY (FRAGORD) ORDER FORMAT

————————————

(Classification)
(Change from oral orders, if any) (Optional)

Copy ____ of ____ copies
123ʳᵈ Sus Bde
(Place of issue)
(Date-time-group of signature)
(Message reference number)

FRAGMENTARY ORDER _____

(U) References: (Mandatory) reference the order being modified.

(U) Time Zone Used Throughout the Order: *(Optional)*

1. **(U) Situation**. *Include any changes to the existing order or state "No Change."*

2. **(U) Mission**. *Include any changes to the existing order or state "No Change."*

3. **(U) Execution**. *Include any changes to the existing order or state "No Change."*
   a. (U) <u>Commander's Intent</u>.
   b. (U) <u>Concept of operations</u>. (SPO) (Mandatory)
   c. (U) <u>Scheme of Movement and Maneuver</u>.
   d. (U) <u>Scheme of Intelligence</u>.
   e. (U) <u>Scheme of Fires</u>.
   f. (U) <u>Scheme of Protection</u>
   g. (U) <u>Cyber Electromagnetic Activities</u>
   h. (U) <u>Stability Tasks</u>.
   i. (U) <u>Assessment</u>

j. (U) <u>Tasks to subordinate units</u>.

k. (U) <u>Coordinating instructions</u>. (Mandatory) Include statement, "Current overlay remains in effect".

4. (U) Sustainment. (S-1 /S-4) (Optional) (Include changes)

5. (U) Command and Signal. (XO/S-3) (Optional) (Include changes)

ACKNOWLEDGE: (Mandatory)

                                        MENTER
                                        COL

OFFICIAL:
POND

ANNEXES: (Optional)
DISTRIBUTION: (Optional)

                    _____
                (Classification)

CHAPTER 10

TIME ANALYSIS

★★★

1. Backwards plan the available time. Use 1/3 – 2/3 rule. XO owns the time schedule and must enforce it ruthlessly. Two versions are provided for unit use.

	DTG	H-HR
DTG MSN RECEIVED FROM HIGHER	_____	
CURRENT DTG	_____	
EXECUTE MSN NLT DTG	_____	
TIME ALLOWED FOR STAFF PREP (1/3)	_____	
TIME ALLOWED FOR SUB STAFF PREP (2/3)	_____	
INFORMATION EXCHANGED W/CDR	_____	
WARNING ORDER #1 DISSEMINATED	_____	

1/3 TIME BEGINS

MISSION ANALYSIS BRIEFING **(CDR'S PLANNING GUIDANCE)**	_____	
WARNING ORDER #2 DISSEMINATED	_____	

COURSE OF ACTION BRIEFING   _____

WAR GAMING   _____

DECISION BRIEFING   _____

WARNING ORDER #3 DISSEMINATED   _____

ORDERS BRIEFING   _____

ORDER DISSEMINATED NLT DTG   _____

1/3 TIME ENDS

STAFF CONTINUES PLANNING/COORDINATION

SUBORDINATES BACK BRIEF CDR   _____

Staff Time Schedule

EVENT	TIME	STATUS
Receive mission		
Situation update brief (mission analysis format)		
Issue Warning Order #1 (WARNORD)		

Conduct Mission Analysis
  - Prepare Cartoon of AO
  - Complete MA Worksheets / Asset
    Availability analysis
  - Complete SITEMP (MPCOA/MDCOA)
  - Draft RFI's and CCIR		

Conduct MA Worksheet scrub		
Rehearsal - mission analysis brief		
Mission analysis brief		
Receive Cdr's guidance and intent		
Issue Warning Order #2		
Develop focused course of action		
Course of action analysis		
Initial wargame		
Staff estimates (personnel, intelligence, sustainment, support operations – formats)		
(Course of action comparison) as needed		
Rehearsal – Decision brief		
Decision brief		
Issue Warning Order #3		
Wargame with Cdr		

Order preparation
  - OPORD Slides Turn in
  - OPORD Products Turn in		

Rehearsal – operation order brief		
Issue operation order		
Company commanders confirmation briefs		
Company commanders backbriefs		
Rehearsals		

10.1 ORDERS TIMELINE

EVENT	TIME	LOCATION	REMARKS
Mission Received			
Mission Analysis (MA) working group			
Battlestaff MA product turn in			
S-2 and S-3 MA initial review			
Battlestaff MA product turn in			
Battlestaff MA final product check			
S-2 and S-3 MA final review			
MA final print			
MA Rehearsal			
Mission Analysis Brief to CDR			
COA development working group			
Battlestaff COA development product turn in			
S-3 COA review			
COA brief rehearsal			
COA Briefing to CDR			
Analysis war gaming session			
Battlestaff COA Decision Brief product turn in			
S-3 COA Decision Brief initial review			
Battlestaff COA Decision final product check			
S-2, S-3, and SPO War Game final review			
COA Decision Brief final print			
COA Decision Brief rehearsal			

Decision Briefing to CDR			
Battlestaff OPLAN/OPORD product turn in			
S-3 OPLAN/OPORD initial review			
Battlestaff OPLAN product turn in			
Battlestaff OPLAN/OPORD final product check			
S-3 OPLAN/OPORD final review			
S-3 Orders Briefing review			
Orders Briefing rehearsal			
Orders Briefing to CDR			
OPLAN/OPORD change working group			
OPLAN/OPORD product review			
OPLAN/OPORD issue rehearsal			
OPLAN/OPORD issue			

10.2 OPERATIONAL TIMELINE SAMPLE FORMAT

Operational Timeline (BSB Sample)

Phase				
D-Day	**Date**			
Time	**0001-0600**	**0601-1200**	**1201-1800**	**1801-2400**
H-Hour				
Air Tasking Order				
Weather				
Enemy Activity				
BDE Activity				
BDE Resupply/RO				
BSB Resupply/RO				
Move				
Medical				
BSB Defense				
BROC/BDOC				
Mission Cmd (MC)				
Risk Management				

CHAPTER 11

BACKBRIEFS AND REHEARSALS

★★★

"An order than can be misunderstood, will be misunderstood"
Field Marshal Helmut von Moltke,
Chief of the Prussian General Staff
Battle of Sedan, September 1870

1. **Background**. The Military Decision Making Process does not come to an end at the conclusion of the OPORD/OPLAN brief as many staffs believed in the past. At the very least, the Sustainment Unit commander may require subordinate leaders to immediately provide him with a "Confirmation Brief" followed a short time later with an OPLAN /OPORD "Backbrief." Once the subordinate commander has confirmed his/her mission with the Sustainment Unit commander, a rehearsal is set to ensure in everyone's mind that the plan is well understood by all players involved and that it provides one last review of the unit's Sustainment Synchronization and Decision Support Matrix.

2. **Post OPORD/OPLAN Briefs**.

   a. **Confirmation Brief**. (Ref FM 5-0(C1), Para 4-35). Immediately after receiving the OPORD/OPLAN, subordinate leaders brief their commander on the order they just received, focusing on their understanding of the commander's intent (particularly those key tasks identified by him outside specific taskings found within Para 3b). Subordinate leaders will also go over tasks as assigned, their purposes, and the relationship of their tasks to those of other elements conducting the operation. (One example is the assembly and dispatch of a Forward Logistics Element whose creation requires more than one unit to create). They repeat any important coordinating measures specified in the order. The confirmation brief is normally used with other types of rehearsal.

b. **Backbrief**. (Ref FM 6-0, Para 12-7). **A *backbrief* is a briefing by subordinates to the commander to review how subordinates intend to accomplish their mission**. The backbrief differs from a confirmation brief in that subordinate leaders are given time to complete their plan. Backbriefs require the fewest resources and are often the only option under time-constrained conditions.

Subordinate leaders explain their actions from start to finish of the mission. Backbriefs are performed sequentially, with all leaders going over their tasks. When time is available, backbriefs may be combined with other types of rehearsals. Doing this lets all element leaders coordinate their plans before performing more elaborate drills. If possible, backbriefs are performed overlooking subordinates' AOs, after they have the chance to develop their own plans and make the necessary reconnaissance or unit taskings. A sample backbrief is provided in 11.1 below.

11.1 Sample Backbrief Format

1. Higher Unit's Purpose
2. Higher Unit's Intent
3. Constraints/Restraints/Limitations
4. Intelligence Overview
5. Specified, Implied, Essential Tasks
6. Unit's Mission Statement
7. Unit Commander's Intent (Purpose, Key Tasks, End State)
8. Task Organization for Support
9. Concept of the Operation/Concept of Support (by phase or event)
10. Rules of Engagement
11. Minimum force requirements/Convoy Security needs
12. Time Schedule
13. Critical Execution checklist items

If time does not permit for a full Back Brief, an abbreviated Back Brief may be given, consisting of the following steps:

1. Higher Unit's Commander's intent.
2. Unit's Mission Statement
3. Unit Commander's Intent (Purpose, Key Tasks, End State)
4. Concept of the Operation/Concept of Support (by phase or event)
5. Minimum force requirements/Convoy Security needs
6. Time Schedule
7. Critical Execution checklist items

11.2 Rehearsals. Per Chapter 12, FM 6-0, rehearsals are defined as:

> **.... a session in which a staff or unit practices expected actions to improve performance during execution.** *Rehearsing key combat (sustainment) actions before execution allows participants to become familiar with the operation and to translate the relatively dry recitation of the tactical plan into visual impression. This impression helps them orient themselves to their environment and other units when executing the operation. Moreover, the repetition of combat tasks during the rehearsal leaves a lasting mental picture of the sequence of key actions within the operation. This appendix contains guidelines for conducting rehearsals. It describes rehearsal types and techniques. It lists responsibilities of those involved.*

Rehearsals allow staff officers, subordinate commanders, and other leaders to practice key aspects of the concept of operations. Rehearsals are *the commander's tool* to ensure all subordinate leaders understand the plan and are "in sync" so to speak with it. Commander's use rehearsals to ensure staffs and subordinates understand their intent and the concept of operations/concept of support. Rehearsals also synchronize operations at times and places critical to successful mission accomplishment. It should be stressed that rehearsals are coordination events, not an analysis.

For units to be effective and efficient in conducting sustainment operations, unit rehearsals need to occur as a matter of habit. All commands at every level should routinely train and practice a variety of rehearsal techniques and types.

The key ingredient to conducting successful rehearsals is time. The time required for a rehearsal varies with the complexity of the task to rehearse, the type and technique of rehearsal, and the level of participation. Successful rehearsals are conducted at the lowest possible level, using the most thorough technique possible, given the time available. Under time-constrained conditions, staffs conduct reduced rehearsals. These focus on critical events determined by reverse planning.

During offensive operations, staffs address the following actions in order: the objective, passage of lines, and movement to the objective—then other phases of the operation. During defensive operations, staffs address counter reconnaissance, battle handover, and commitment of counterattack forces or the striking force—then other phases of the operation. Each unit has different critical events, based on its readiness and the unit commander's assessment.

Whenever possible, rehearsals are based on a completed operation order (OPORD). A contingency plan may be rehearsed to prepare for an anticipated deployment. The rehearsal is a coordination event, not an analysis. It is not a substitute for the war game. War games are preformed during the MDMP to analyze several COAs and determine the optimal one. Rehearsals are conducted during preparation to practice executing the COA that the commander chose at the end of the MDMP. Commanders avoid making major changes to OPORDs during rehearsals. They make only those changes essential to mission success.

11. 3 REHEARSAL TYPES

Each rehearsal type achieves a different result and has a specific place in the preparation time line. The five types of rehearsals are (in order to shortness/availability of time):

* Net Rehearsal
* Map Rehearsal
* Sketch Map Rehearsal
* Terrain Model Rehearsal
* Reduced Force Rehearsal
* Full Dress Rehearsal

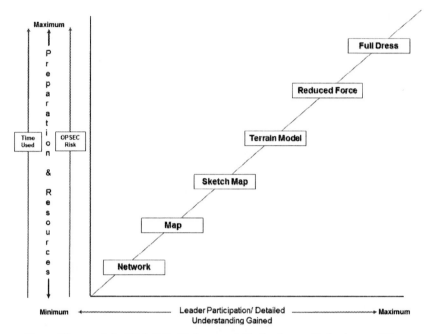

From Figure I-1, FM 5-0. Rehearsal Techniques Relative to Time, Resources OPSEC Participation, and Understanding

a. **Network**. This type of rehearsal is conducted utilizing either a unit Local Area Network (LAN) or Wide Area Network (WAN). This technique works best with units who have clear SOPs and functional/ working communications. Critical portion of the plan are talked through by Commanders and staffs using a sequence provided by the owning commander. This type of rehearsal requires all unit information systems (INFOSYS) owned by the unit as well as a copy of the OPORD/OPLAN with overlays in order to execute their portion of the plan.

b. **Map**. A map rehearsal as the name indicates, utilizes a map and appropriate overlay (either sustainment or operational) of the same used to plan the operation. Generally this technique is easiest to set up and conduct provided all units involved are operation within the same echelon and scale of map. If paper maps are unavailable, projection off an MCS or BCS[3] workstation screen will suffice.

c.   **Sketch Map**. The sketch map rehearsal technique can be used by commanders nearly anywhere regardless of daylight or weather conditions. Map sketches are drawn large enough for all participants to view and demonstrate required logistical/sustainment actions and movements using markers or "sticky" pad 'Post-it' notes.

d.   **Terrain Model**. Also known as the "sand table" rehearsal, this technique requires far less resources and time than the Reduced Force or Full Dress rehearsals. Commanders use an accurately constructed terrain model to assist subordinate leaders to visualize the terrain as well as understand the Commander's intent, vision, and the concept of the operation/support at hand. Ideally if practical, the terrain model should be placed in an area nearby that overlooks the actual terrain the unit is conducting support operations.

e.   **Reduced Force**. If mission requirements only allow for key leaders to be present, then a reduced-force rehearsal is called for, with leader involvement is usually decided by the commander. Typically, this type rehearsal is simpler, utilizing fewer resources and time that that called for in the full-dress rehearsal or used as a preparation for a full-dress rehearsal if time permits. This is generally the most popular rehearsal to conduct if time permits for the assembly of a terrain model for participates to role play.

f.   **Full Dress**. The most time consuming, detailed, yet most effective of the all the rehearsals available is the Full Dress rehearsal. Ideal for companies and below, commanders begin to trade off OPSEC and time management/availability the higher the echelon using this technique and must consider the time resource needs of their subordinates when considering this option. Traffic management and vehicular parking within the immediate area the rehearsal is conducted is also a consideration in order to maintain OPSEC. The rehearsal area must be identified, secured, and maintained prior to and throughout this option.

11.4. Rehearsal Execution.

a.   Regardless of the type of rehearsal conducted, sustainment participants should bring the following tools with them:

(1) Sus Bde/CSSB Sustainment Execution Matrix and Concept of Support for their organization and the next higher.
(2) BSB Sustainment Execution Matrix and Concept of Support for their organization and the next higher.
(3) A functional detailed plan for their part of the overall operation.
(4) An ability to "act out" their portion of the plan by phase.
(5) Confirmation of their task organization and their customer task organization. Ex: CSSB (by company/detachment) and the task organization of the customer they are tasked to support (Support Brigade or Brigade Combat Team).

b.   Order of the Brief.

For a CSSB, the following participants either speak or are on standby for questions:

SPEAKING ROLES	**INITIAL NONSPEAKERS**
BDE/BN XO	MOVEMENT CONTROL TEAM REP
BDE/BN S3	MP PLT LDR (IF AVAILABLE)
BDE/BN S2	TCF/SECFOR CDR (IF AVAILABLE)
BDE/BN S1	CSSB CO COMMANDERS
BDE/BN S4	CHAPLAIN (IF AVAILABLE)
BDE/BN S6	
BN/CO XO'S	
SPO OFFICER	
MED BDE REP/SPT BDE MED CO CDR	
COMMENTS BY CMD XO/BDE/BN COMMANDER	

 c. Speaker Roles and Responsibilities.

  (1) XO
* Appoints the scribe
* Conducts role call
* Provides Cdr's guidance for Sustainment Rehearsal

  (2) S3 Operations
* Provides overview of terrain model
* Provides boundaries and locations of friendly forces
* States Task Organization
* Friendly situation
* Mission, Concept of Operation, and Commander's Intent
* Speaks and covers each phase and events that conclude that phase
* Protection of Sustainment assets and LSA/FOB ISR
* Unit & FLE/FLB moves, CRSP and/or Trailer Transfer Points (TTPs) establishments

(3) S2 Intelligence
* Provides and overview of enemy situation
* Displays enemy symbols on terrain model
* Focuses on all enemy threats to Sustainment operations and Areas of Concern to Sustainment operators
* Portrays civilian & refugee impacts within the area of operations and their possible impact to Sustainment operations
* Reviews Commander's Critical Intelligence Requirements (CCIR)

(4) S4 Sustainment and Logistics
* Provides an overview of "*the Sustainment unit*" logistics posture
* Provides internal support unit locations
* Provides an understanding of infrastructure and alternative support (HNS)
* Identifies priorities of support
* Provides a snap shot of the Units Concept of Support (Para 4a)

(5) S1 Human Resources
* Provides personnel status by unit
* Medical support available to support sustainment operations

(6) Support Operations (SPO)
* Provide and overview of AOR logistics and Concept of Support (Annex I)
* Covers all support/sustainment actions and muscle moves for each phase (MSOs, SROs, CROs, CRSP establishment, FLE echelonment, etc)
* Priorities of support

> * Locations of all sustainment units in LSA/FOB/FLE/FLB and Unit AO
>
> * Status of on hand stocks (critical). Recommend this be done in pallets, gallons, short tons, etc. Use the term "Days of Supply" (or DOS) only if everyone has a clear understanding what this entails.
>
> * Throughtput (ATHP, CL IV, V, Fuel, CL IX) schedules

In Brigade Combat Team/Support Brigade Sustainment Rehearsals, the following is added:

> (7) BCT/BN/TF XO
> * Coverage of maneuver actions during each phase of the operation

> (8) Each Supported Unit S-4
> * Coverage of unit logistics for each phase
> * Current unit logistical assets available
> * Unit location of:
>> Battalion Aid Stations (BAS), Casualty Collection Points (CCP) and AXP
>> Unit Maintenance Collection Points (UMCP)
>> Combat Trains – Task Force/Combined Arms Support Areas and FSC locs
>> Maneuver/Maneuver Support Unit locations

> d. Conduct of the Rehearsal. Like Combined Arms Rehearsals, Sustainment rehearsals are usually conducted as a *Before, During, and After* Operations Phase.

> (1) BEFORE PHASE: Consists of all required Sustainment Bde conducted MROs, BCT/Task Force/Support Brigade movements from current locations to TAAs,

Attack Positions conducted prior to LD (or defend time). Sustainment Bde/CSSB positioning of CRSPs, FLEs, TTPs are also identified here.

(a) BCT/TF/Support Brigade XOs successfully lay out:
   - Terrain
   - Route Security and SEC FOR support utilized
   - Enroute requirements such as RO, Recovery, CASEVAC, WARLOCK employment

(b) Sustainment Brigade/CSSB/BSB Support Ops
   - Posturing
   - Pre-positioning
   - Movement of sustainment units and resulting support impact (i.e. "blackouts")

(2) DURING PHASE: This phase should reflect the same mission phases as the OPORD. Key topics of concern within this phase include water, fuel and ammunition resupply/replenishment operations (RO), casualty treatment and evacuation (via ground & air), and maintenance recovery.

(a) Unit XOs/Slice Units/BSB:
   - Layout every functional area
   - Continue to physically depict locations
   - Hasty displacement plans
   - Alternate communication, retrans plans and digital connectivity
   - Use of aerial resupply (if required)
   - Response to threats/civilian actions
   - Medical evacuation (both by ground and air)
   - Security measures employed enroute/ Warlock on/off time & locations

(b) All participates should cover the movement of critical sustainment nodes that fall within their area of concern in order to ensure full visualization of the operating environment.

For example: a Sustainment Brigade is conducting a BCT/BSB SRO.

Sus Bde SPO identifies (or confirms previous support mission tasker) BCT OCL/MCL requirements and delivery location, HNS, or contractor involvement.

MCT Rep confirms movement DTG and MSR utilized. If possible, MSR status identified/confirmed

CSSB SPO identifies distro/trans element (size, type trucks and composition) load out and PCI times.

S-3 discusses SECFOR requirements and link up sites

(c) After a particular phase or a key important movement aspect of a rehearsal is completed, the rehearsal director (usually the Unit Commander or his Deputy/XO) will require a back brief by key functional operators to confirm customer to sustainment unit linkage.

Example: Unit MEDEVAC/CASEVAC Operations. Walk through medical evacuation from the point of injury to the Battalion Aid Station and on to the Brigade Support Medical Company (or in the case of a Support Brigade, to the Support Brigade Medical Company, SBMC) – across all phases – emphasizing the connectivity of the Ambulance Exchange Point (AXP) and potential unit replenishment operations. It is vitally important that players must "*visualize*" the operation from all aspects.

One final note – all players must clearly articulate all triggers related to the movement of logistics assets across the battlefield. This is why you spend so much time developing a Sustainment Synchronization Matrix during the Wargaming Phase of the

Military Decision Making Process. Share the knowledge with everyone present.

(3) AFTER PHASE: This phase focuses on continuing to logistically shape the conduct of operation for future actions/activities. THERE ARE ALWAYS MISSIONS TO CONDUCT TOMORROW!!! ALWAYS THINK A MINIMUM OF THREE DAYS (72 HRS) IN ADVANCE.

Participants should discuss:

LOGISTICAL ACTIONS ON THE OBJECTIVE-
  – RECOVERY OF COMBAT SYSTEMS
  – CLEARING CASUALTIES
  – PRE-POSITIONING CLASS IV AND OTHER COMMODITIES

OTHER TOPICS TO ADDRESS -
  – ROUTES
  – SECURITY
  – TRAFFIC CONTROL
  – REPORTING TIMELINES

CHAPTER 12

THE 'RUNNING' ESTIMATE & STAFF ESTIMATES

✯✯✯

12.1 The 'Running' Estimate. As depicted in Chapter 8, FM 6-0, a *Running Estimate* is the continuous assessment of the current situation used to determine if the current operation is proceeding according to the commander's intent and if planned future operations are supportable (ADP 5-0). The commander and each staff section maintain a running estimate. In their running estimates, the commander and each staff section continuously consider the effects of new information and update the following:

- Facts.
- Assumptions.
- Friendly force status.
- Enemy activities and capabilities.
- Civil considerations.
- Conclusions and recommendations.

Estimates are not just for staffs. Commanders also develop a running commander's estimates to consolidate their understanding and visualization of an operation. The commander's running estimate summarizes the problem and integrates information and knowledge of the staff's and subordinate commanders' running estimates. In many regards and cases, Commander's will employ the techniques of Army Design Methodology (ADM) as the basis of their estimate.

Is a *Running Estimate* required for each staff section? The short answer is yes, especially if that section has a critical bearing on the pending operation. Overall, each staff section builds and maintains running estimates. The running estimate helps the staff to track and record pertinent information as well as to provide recommendations to commanders. Running estimates represent the analysis and expert opinion of each staff section by functional area. Staffs maintain running estimates throughout the operations process to assist commanders in the exercise of mission command.

Each staff section, command post functional cell or working group, maintains a running estimate focused on how their specific areas of expertise are postured to support future operations. Because an estimate may be needed at any time, running estimates must be developed, revised, updated, and maintained continuously while in garrison and during operations. As a rule of thumb, if it requires more than 15 minutes updating a staff estimate, it is not considered a current 'running' estimate.

12.2 Staff Estimate Make Up.

1. Mission Receipt/Analysis, facts and assumptions, and the situation analysis (of the area of operation, area of interest, and enemy, friendly, and support requirements) furnish the structure for the staff estimate. The running estimate consists of significant facts, events, and conclusions based on analyzed data. A generic running estimate is provided below in Figure 12.1. Failure to make estimates can lead to errors and omissions when developing, analyzing, and comparing COAs.

2. Essential Qualities of Running Estimates:

   a. Comprehensive estimates consider both the quantifiable and the intangible aspects of military operations.

   b. Must be as thorough as time and circumstances permit. The commander and staff must constantly collect, process, and evaluate information. Updates are made:

(1) When the commander and staff recognizes new facts.

(2) When they replace assumptions with facts or find their assumptions invalid.

(3) When they receive changes to the mission or when changes are indicated.

c. Estimates for the current operation can often provide a basis for estimates for future missions.

d. Estimates must visualize the future and support the commander's battlefield visualization.

---

1. **SITUATION AND CONSIDERATIONS.**
   a. **Area of Interest.** Identify and describe those factors of the area of interest that affect functional area considerations.
   b. **Characteristics of the Area of Operations.**
      (1) **Terrain.** State how terrain affects staff functional area's capabilities.
      (2) **Weather.** State how weather affects staff functional area's capabilities.
      (3) **Enemy Forces.** Describe enemy disposition, composition, strength, and systems within a functional area as well as enemy capabilities and possible courses of action (COAs) with respect to their effects on a functional area.
      (4) **Friendly Forces.** List current functional area resources in terms of equipment, personnel, and systems. Identify additional resources available for the functional area located at higher, adjacent, or other units. List those capabilities from other military and civilian partners that maybe available to provide support within the functional area. Compare requirements to current capabilities and suggest solutions for satisfying discrepancies.
      (5) **Civilian Considerations.** Describe civil considerations that may affect the functional area to include possible support needed by civil authorities from the functional area as well as possible interference from civil aspects.
   c. **Assumptions.** List all assumptions that affect the functional area.
2. **MISSION.** Show the restated mission resulting from mission analysis.
3. **COURSES OF ACTION.**
   a. List friendly COAs that were war-gamed.
   b. List enemy actions or COAs that were templated that impact the functional area.
   c. List the evaluation criteria identified during COA analysis. All staffs use the same criteria.
4. **ANALYSIS.** Analyze each COA using the evaluation criteria from COA analysis. Review enemy actions that impact the functional area as they relate to COAs. Identify issues, risks, and deficiencies these enemy actions may create with respect to the functional area.
5. **COMPARISON.** Compare COAs. Rank order COAs for each key consideration. Use a decision matrix to aid the comparison process.
6. **RECOMMENDATIONS AND CONCLUSIONS.**
   a. Recommend the most supportable COAs from the perspective of the functional area.
   b. Prioritize and list issues, deficiencies, and risks and make recommendations on how to mitigate

---

Figure 12.1 A 'generic' base running estimate

12.3. Types of Running Estimates:

a. **Commander's Estimate. (See 12.4)**

    (1) The commander's estimate, like the operations estimate, is an analysis of all the factors that could affect a mission.

    (2) Estimate analysis includes risk assessment, force protection, and effective utilization of all resources. The estimate also includes visualizing all reasonable COAs and how each COA would affect friendly forces.

    (3) The commander's estimate and operations estimate generally follow the same format. However, the commander's estimate deals more with assessing the intangibles of training, leadership, and morale, and it results in a decision.

b. **Operations Estimate**

    (1) The S-3 prepares the operations estimate, which considers all elements that can influence the unit's current operation and feasible future courses of action. It results in a recommendation to the commander.

    (2) To prepare the estimate, the S-3 must understand:

        (a) The commander's intent (one and two levels up).

        (b) The risk assessment.

        (c) The current task organization (two echelons below).

        (d) The unit's status, such as locations, combat capabilities, and current mission.

> (e) The availability and capabilities of higher and joint assets.
>
> (f) Other information, such as location, status, and mission of flank and supporting units.

c. **Personnel Estimate (See 12.5)**

> (1) The S-1 prepares the personnel estimate, which is an analysis of how all human resources and personnel factors impact soldier and unit effectiveness before, during, and after the mission. It includes a current overall personnel status of the organization, its subordinate units, and any attached or supporting elements. It includes assessment of the following factors:
> (a) Medical evacuation and hospitalization.
> (b) Unit strength maintenance.
> (c) Replacements.
> (d) Soldiers' readiness.
> (e) Organizational climate.
> (f) Cohesion.
> (g) Discipline, law, and order.
>
> (2) The estimate predicts losses (where and when they could occur) and when, where, and if such losses cause the culmination of an operation. It contains the recommendations and conclusions about the feasibility of supporting major operations and tactical missions.

d. **Intelligence Estimate. (See 12.6)** The S-2 or S-2 Intel NCO prepares the intelligence estimate. All examine the area of interest to identify intelligence collection needs.

e. **Sustainment (Logistics) Estimate. (See 12.7)** The SPO prepares the logistics estimate, which provides an accurate and current assessment of the CSS situation sustainment unit external support mission, its subordinate units, and any attached or supporting elements. It is an estimate of how service support factors can affect mission accomplishment. This estimate includes how the functional areas of supply, transportation, services, maintenance, labor, facilities, and construction affect various COAs. It contains any inputted S-4 recommendations and conclusions about the feasibility of supporting tactical missions.

f. **SPO Support Ops Estimates. (See 12.8)** The SPO prepares an estimate regarding the supported customer's posture within their functional area, focused on the anticipated requirements, known and projected capabilities and identified shortfalls. Estimates include recommendations for overcoming shortfalls.

g. **Signal Estimate.** The S-6 (Signal Officer) prepares the communications estimate in relation in to the situation and his functional responsibilities.

h. **Special Staff Estimates.** Each special staff officer creates his own staff estimate in relation to the situation and his functional responsibilities.

Staff Estimate Considerations Checklist

In preparing Staff (Running) Estimates, Planning Staff should review the following items to ensure all are taken into consideration under the Analysis, Comparison and Recommendation/ Conclusions paragraphs.

1. The five questions logistics planners and operators should always be able to answer are:

- **Where are we on the battlefield?**
- **Why are we here?**
- **How do we support from here?**
- **How do we get support from here?**
- **When, to where, and in what sequence do we displace to ensure continuous operations?**

2. The following Running Estimate preparation methodology is based on a requirement, capability, shortfall, analysis, and solution model. This methodology would commence after the staff received the mission and continues through redeployment. Bottom line, it is a continuous process used in each step of the MDMP and refined whenever new information is received.

3. To put this methodology into context, there must be some continuity between the tactical decision making process and the logistic planning process. Each of the model's categories (requirements, capabilities, shortfall, analysis, and solutions) must have any associated, necessary, and valid assumptions stated up front.

REQUIREMENTS

1. What method is used to determine logistics requirements? [For example: personnel density, equipment density, weather planning factors, operating tempo (OPTEMPO), combination, etc.]

2. What is the source of the requirements determination calculations? [For example: The Logistics Estimate Worksheet (LEW), Operations Logistics Planner (OPLOGPLN), The *Modular G1/G4 Battle Book*, historical data, etc.]

3. What is your customer list for this requirement? Will it change during the operation?

4. Identify implied logistics tasks based on the tactical plan. What are the ramifications of river crossings, pauses, deep attacks, etc.?

5. Is there a CBRN/WMD threat?

6. What do you need?

7. How long will you need it?

8. Where do you need it?

9. What do you need to put it there? [For example, fuel bladders/bags, rough-terrain container handlers (RTCHs), forklifts, cranes, etc.]

10. How will you get it there?

11. When do you need it there? How long will it take to get it there?

12. How soon will it be available to move there? Where is it coming from?

13. What do you need to do with it before moving it where you need it? (For example, does it have to be containerized, broken down, segregated, separated, disassembled, configured, or reconfigured before movement?)

   — How long will that take?
   — What are the requirements for that?

14. Does it have to move again after it gets there? (For example, is it a GS-GS transaction? GS-DS? DS-DS? DS-user?) Who will move it from there?

15. What are the competing demands for this requirement?

16. What is required to offload it when it gets there?

17. Does anything need to be done with it once it gets there? (For example, does it have to be unpacked, assembled, etc.?)

18. What has to be done to move it once it is there?

19. Does this requirement have special employment considerations? (For example, require a large, level area of land or a fresh water source; be located near an MSR; need refrigeration; require dedicated transportation; etc.)

20. How often will the commodity, supply, or service be required? How often must it be replenished?

21. Does the requirement have preparatory activities? [For example, engineers to berm a bag farm, airfield matting for forward arming and refueling points (FARPs), road and pad construction for an ASA]

22. What is the expected duration of the required preparation?

23. How do you request the preparation and who approves it? (For example, engineer work has to be approved through channels.)

24. What support is required for the preparatory activities?

CAPABILITIES

1. What are the units available that have the capability to fulfill the requirement?

2. What is the basis of allocation for the unit that has the necessary capability? (For example, is its basis of allocation one per corps or division, or is it based on supported populations or expected equipment densities?)

3. Is more than one unit required to provide the capability? [A few examples: the Petroleum, Oils, and Lubricants (POL) Supply Company is usually employed with the medium truck company (POL). Typically, a Water Purification and Distribution Company pairs up with a Field Service Company (SCLR & MA)]

4. What are the overall receipt, storage, and issue requirements for my area of support for this particular commodity, supply, or service?

5. Are receipts and issues exclusive capabilities? (For example, can a unit receive, store, *and* issue so much of a particular commodity, or can it only receive *or* store *or* issue *or* rewarehouse so much of a particular commodity?)

6. Will this capability be used to weight the battle logistically?

7. What is the total short ton (STON)/gallon/pallet/other distribution capability by mode? Line haul? Local haul? Other? *With today's delivery/distribution systems, focus on pallets!*

8. What distribution planning factors were used (DOS, gallons, STONs, *pallets*)?

9. How many locations require this capability?

10. Are any units with this capability already committed?

11. Are any units with this capability due in? When?

12. Do units depend on other units to function? (For example, to perform its mission, some mode transportation units must bring cargo to a cargo transfer company.)

13. Can a unit deploy elements (sections or platoons) to place the capability where it is required?

14. Does the unit have unique management/employment considerations?

COMPARISON/SHORTFALL

1. If there is no shortfall, go to the *analysis* portion of this methodology.

2. Which requirements exceed capabilities?

3. For requirements that exceed capabilities, is it overall or in a particular area, region, or time?

4. How much is the shortfall in terms of units of measurement (pallets, STONs, gallons, square feet)?

5. What does the shortfall equate to in terms of days of supply?

6. At what point in the battle is the requirement expected to exceed the capability?

7. What is the type of shortfall? Is it a supply availability shortfall, a resource [equipment, materials handling equipment (MHE), personnel, facilities, man-hours, etc.] shortfall, or a distribution shortfall?

ANALYSIS

The analysis process has to occur for all support operations even if there is no shortfall. The sustainment planner is required to determine how to support the operation.

1. What is the earliest the support operation can begin?

2. What is the latest the support operation can begin?

3. Is it better to be early or late?

4. What is the purpose of the support? (For example, is the purpose to build stocks at GS, to sustain a force for a given period of time at DS, or to resupply a user?)

5. Will support be provided from a fixed location or from a forward logistics element?

6. What is the significance of the shortfall?

7. What is the potential impact of the shortfall?

8. What is the expected duration of the shortfall?

9. What is the cause of the shortfall (battle loss, time-phased force deployment sequence, etc.)?

10. If the shortfall is a *supply availability* shortfall, consider the following:

a. Is the shortfall only at this level or is at higher levels as well?

b. Is it a result of higher commands' efforts and support priorities?

c. Is the supply available at other echelons and, if so, where?

d. How long will it take to get here?

e. Is there an acceptable alternative, a substitute, or an alternative source of supply?

11. If the shortfall is a *resource shortfall* (equipment, MHE, personnel, facilities, man-hours, etc.), consider the following:

a. Can similar resources be diverted or obtained from somewhere else

b. Is HNS a viable alternative? Contractor support?

c. How specialized is the shortfall resource? (For example, it is easier to train a mortuary affairs specialist than it is to train a doctor. It is easier to find an automotive mechanic than it is an M1 fire control specialist.)

d. Can a secondary or related military occupational specialty (MOS) be used?

e. Does a sister service, contractor or coalition partner have the capability?

12. If the shortfall is a *distribution shortfall,* consider the following:

    a.   Is the shortfall due to a lack of assets or to a time-distance problem?

    b.   Does the shortfall capability require special handling or any special distribution requirements?

    c.   Are there any alternative distribution modes?

    d.   What are the alternative mode requirements? (For example, a pipeline requires continuous pump and hose/pipeline maintenance, engineer support to lay the pipeline, etc.)

    e.   Are host nation distribution assets available?

    f.   Are sister service/coalition assets available?

    g.   Are they compatible? (For example, European and SWA host nation fuel tankers are metric and require a coupler adapter to interface US tankers or bags.)

    h.   Are there any airfields, field landing strips, or heli-pads near the requirement?

13. How will logistics capability be echeloned forward? Which units will be tasked to establish forward logistics bases?

SOLUTIONS

1.   Determine the most workable solutions based on analysis.

2.   Integrate with other support operations and commodities.

12.4 Commander's Guidance Worksheet.

OPORD #   **Unit HQs**   **DTG**   **Cdr's Signature**

1. Commander's Intent
   a. Broader purpose

   b. Key tasks

   c. Endstate

2. Decisive points/ actions:

3. COAs to consider (where/ when/ how to mass to accomplish mission and intent)
   a. Friendly

   b. Enemy

4. How we must posture for next phase (logistically/ geographically)

5. Recon guidance

6. Deception guidance (if applicable)

7. Priorities for:
    a. Human Resource

    b. Supply (Fuel, Arm)

    c. Maintenance

    d. Transportation

    e. Field Service

    f. Health Service Support

    g. Force protection/ security measures to be implemented

h.   EOD, Religious, and Fin Svc

8.   Risk (areas acceptable)

9.   CCIR
a.   PIR

b.   FFIR

10. Decisions I see myself making:

11. Time plan (confirm/ readjust proposed timeline)

12. Type order

13. Type Rehearsal

12.5 Personnel Estimate

Personnel Estimate

The S-1 prepares the personnel estimate, which is an analysis of how all human resources and personnel factors impact soldier and unit effectiveness before, during, and after the mission. It is includes a current overall personnel status of the organization, its subordinate units, and any attached or supporting elements. Personnel status includes assessments of the following factors, medical evacuation and hospitalization, unit strength maintenance, replacements, soldier's readiness, organizational climate, cohesion, and discipline, law and order. The personnel estimate predicts losses (where and when losses could occur) and when, where, and if such loses cause the culmination of an operation. It contains the feasibility of supporting major operational and tactical missions.

———————

(Classification)

Headquarters
Place
Date, time and zone
Msg ref no.

PERSONNEL (PERS) ESTIMATE NO_____

(U) **References:** Map, charts, or other documents.

(U) **Time Zone Used Throughout the Estimate:**

1. (U) **MISSION**: This paragraph lists the command's restated mission.

2. (U) **THE SITUATION AND CONSIDERATIONS:**

    a. (U) <u>Intelligence Situation</u>. This paragraph contains information from the intelligence officer. As the personnel officer, include a brief summary when the details are appropriate and there is a written estimate. Refer to the appropriate intelligence document or use an annex of the estimate. Include:

(1) (U) Characteristics of the area of operations.

(2) (U) Enemy strength and dispositions.

(3) (U) Enemy capabilities. Include enemy and non-enemy sponsored terrorist activities–

    (a) (U) Affecting the mission

    (b) (U) Affecting personnel activities.

b. (U) <u>Tactical Situation</u>. Information for this paragraph comes from the commander's planning guidance and from the S-3. Include –

(1) (U) Present disposition of major tactical elements.

(2) (U) Possible courses of actions. List all given courses of action.

(3) (U) Projected operations, if known. List projected operations and other planning factors required for coordinating and integrating staff estimates.

c. (U) <u>Sustainment Situation</u>. To list the Sustainment situation –

(1) (U) Present dispositions of sustainment units and installations that affect the personnel situation.

(2) (U) Show any projected developments within the sustainment WFFA field that might influence personnel operations.

d. (U) <u>Civil-Military Operations Situation</u>. Information for this subparagraph comes from the CMO officer at the Sus Bde (for CSSBs)/Div or Bde (for BSBs). Such information should help you:

(1) (U) Present dispositions of civil affairs units and installations that affect the personnel situation.

(2) (U) Show any projected developments within the CMO field that might influence personnel operations.

e. (U) <u>Troop Preparedness Situation</u>. Show the status in this subparagraph under the appropriate subheadings. Subparagraphs include-

(1) (U) Unit strength. Indicate authorized, assigned, and attached strengths. Include the effects of deployability, losses (combat or non-combat), critical MOS's and skill shortages, projections (gains and losses), and any other situations affecting strength.

(2) (U) Other personnel. Indicate personnel, other than unit soldiers, whose presence affects the unit mission. Include EPW's, augmentees (non-US forces), civilian internees and detainees, DA civilians, and others, depending on local circumstances.

(3) (U) Soldier personal readiness. Indicate those elements of quality of life and personnel administration and management which provide services, facilities, and policies affecting soldier personal readiness.

(a) (U) Soldier services. In this paragraph include –

(1) (U) Administrative services (pay, orders, evaluation reports, awards, reenlistment, eliminations, separations, promotions, assignments, transfers, personal affairs, leaves, and passes).

(2) (U) Health services (field medical support, disease, mental health, and other services).

(3) (U) Health care (medical, dental, entitlements, eligibility, and physical fitness).

(4) (U) Support services (transportation, commissary, PX, clothing, laundry, legal, spiritual, law and order).

        (5) (U) Personnel development (education and professional development).

        (6) (U) Community relations.

        (7) (U) Moral support activities (Army community services, libraries, community centers, clubs, movies, and post office).

        (8) (U) Family member assistance planning.

    (b) (U) Duty conditions, Include –

        (1) (U) Work facilities (location and quality).

        (2) (U) Work requirements (impact of frequency and length of field duty and rotation between remote and non-remote duty locations).

        (3) (U) Equipment (adequacy).

    (c) (U) Other.

  (4) (U) Human potential. Indicate factors affecting the stability and human potential of individual soldiers, teams, and crews to accomplish the mission. Consider, but do not limit yourself to, such factors as turbulence and turnover, experience, personal problems, and individual stress, status of crews, and MOS mismatch with the unit.

  (5) (U) Organizational climate. Indicate factors affecting personnel readiness. Include-

    (a) (U) Communications effectiveness with the chain of command.

    (b) (U) Performance and discipline standards.

    (c) (U) Incentives.

    (d) (U) Drug and alcohol abuse standards.

    (e) (U) Counseling.

    (f) (U) Human relations.

        (g)   (U) Supervision.
        (h)   (U) Planning
        (i)   (U) Ethics
        (j)   (U) Organization stress.
        (k)   (U) Other.

    (6)   (U) Commitment. Indicate the relative strength of the soldier's identification and involvement with the unit. Also note their:
        (a)   (U) Morale.
        (b)   (U) Motivations.
        (c)   (U) Confidence.
        (d)   (U) Trust.

    (7)   (U) Cohesion. Indicate factors which unite and commit soldiers to accomplish the mission such as:
        (a)   (U) Esprit.
        (b)   (U) Teamwork.

f.   (U) <u>Assumptions</u>. Until specific planning guidance from the commander becomes available, you may need assumptions for initiating planning or preparing the estimate. Modify assumptions as factual data becomes available.

3.   **(U) ANALYSIS OF COURSE OF ACTION**: For each COA, analyze personnel factors affecting each subheading in paragraph 2e indicating problem areas, trends, and deficiencies which might affect troop preparedness.

4.   **(U) COMPARISON OF COURSES OF ACTION**:

a.   (U) Evaluate deficiencies from a personnel standpoint. List advantages and disadvantages, if any, to accomplishing the mission.

b.   (U) Discuss the advantages and disadvantages of each COA under consideration. Include methods for overcoming deficiencies or modifications required in each COA.

5.   **(U) CONCLUSION:**

a.   (U) Indicate whether you have personnel to support the mission (paragraph 1).

b.   (U) Indicate which COAs you can best support from the personnel viewpoint.

c.   (U) List the major personnel deficiencies which the commander must consider. Include specific recommendations concerning methods of eliminating or reducing the effect of these deficiencies.

/s/ _____
(Personnel Officer S-1)

ANNEXES: (as required)

_____
(Classification)

12.6 Intelligence Estimate

_____
(Classification)

Headquarters
Place
Date, time and zone
Msg ref no.

INTELLIGENCE (INTEL) ESTIMATE NO____

(U) References: Map, charts, or other documents.

(U) Time Zone Used Throughout the Estimate:

1. **(U) MISSION**: This paragraph lists the command's restated mission.

2. **(U) THE SITUATION AND CONSIDERATIONS**:

    a. (U) <u>Characteristics of area of operation</u>.
        (1) (U) Weather. How will different military aspects of weather affect the intelligence area of concern and its resources?
        (2) (U) Terrain. How will terrain affect the intelligence area of concern and its resources?
        (3) (U) Other pertinent facts. Analyze political, economical, sociological, psychological, and environmental infrastructure, as they relate to the area.

    b. (U) <u>Enemy forces</u>. Enemy dispositions, composition, strength, capabilities, and COAs as they affect intelligence.

    c. (U) <u>Friendly forces</u>.
        (1) (U) Friendly courses of actions.

     (2) (U) Current status of intelligence resources within the responsibility of the S-3.

     (3) (U) Current status of other resources that affect the S-3.

     (4) (U) Comparison of requirements versus capabilities and recommended solutions.

     (5) (U) Key considerations (evaluation criteria) for COA supportability.

   d. (U) <u>Assumptions</u>.

3. **(U) ANALYSIS**: Analyze each COA using key considerations (evaluation criteria) to determine advantages and disadvantages.

4. **(U) COMPARISON**: Compare COAs using key considerations (evaluation criteria). Rank order COAs for each key consideration. A decision matrix should visually support comparison.

5. **(U) RECOMMENDATION AND CONCLUSIONS:**

   a. Recommended COA based on the comparison (most supportable from specific staff perspective).

   b. Issues, deficiencies, and risks with recommendations to reduce their impacts.

/s/ _____

(S-2 Officer)

ANNEXES: (as required)

ıinment Estimate

The S-4 prepares the Sustainment estimate, which provides an accurate and current assessment of the sustainment situation of the organization, its subordinate units, and any attached or supporting elements. The logistics estimate is an analysis of how service support factors can affect mission accomplishment. It contains the S-4's conclusions and recommendations about the feasibility of supporting major operational and tactical mission. This estimate includes how the functional areas of supply, transportation, services, and maintenance, labor, facilities, and construction affect various COAs.

(Classification)

Headquarters
Place
Date, time and zone
Msg ref no.

SUSTAINMENT ESTIMATE NO____

(U) References: Map, charts, or other documents.

(U) Time Zone Used Throughout the Estimate:

1. **(U) MISSION**: This paragraph lists the command's restated mission.

2. **(U) THE SITUATION AND CONSIDERATIONS:**

   a. (U) <u>Intelligence Situation</u>. This paragraph contains information from the intelligence officer. As the S-4 officer, include a brief summary when the details are appropriate and there is a written estimate. Refer to the appropriate intelligence document or use an annex of the estimate. Include:

(1) (U) Characteristics of the area of operations. Describe the general characteristics of the area of operations. Emphasize any specific aspects which might affect the sutainment effort.

(2) (U) Enemy strength and dispositions.

(3) (U) Enemy capabilities. Include:

    (a) (U) Any activities affecting the mission. Keep information general, but include both enemy and non-enemy sponsored terrorist activities.

    (b) (U) Any activities affecting sustainment activities. Give detailed information oriented toward possible effects of logistics operations. Include what you know about the enemy air assault and airborne capabilities, TACAIR, artillery, CBRN capabilities, guerrilla operations, and stay-behind or by-passed enemy forces.

b. (U) Tactical Situation. Information from this paragraph comes from the commander's planning guidance and from the S-3. Subparagraphs should be general and concise statements of tactical intentions. The S-4 should include:

(1) (U) Present disposition of major tactical elements. (Also put this information on the Sustainment overlay annex/LCOP, if appropriate).

(2) (U) Possible courses of action. Lit all given courses of action. (These courses of action are carried forward through the remainder of the estimate).

(3) (U) Projected operations. If known, list projected operations and other planning factors needed for coordinating and integrating staff estimates.

c. (U) Personnel Situation. Include information you obtain from the personnel officer. Include total strength, unit strength, and factors for casualties, replacements, hospital returnees, etc.

    (1)   (U) Present dispositions of personnel and administration units and installations which would affect the Sustainment/CSS situation.

    (2)   (U) Show any projected developments within the personnel field likely to influence sustainment operations.

  d. (U) Civil-Military situation. This paragraph details information from the civil-military officer The S-4 should include:

    (1)   (U) Present disposition of CMO units and installations affecting logistics operations.

    (2)   (U) Projected developments with the CMO field likely to influence sustainment operations.

  e. (U) Sustainment Situation. This subparagraph should reflect the current status. In the case of detailed information at higher levels of command, a summary may appear under the subheadings with reference to an annex to the estimate. You may use an overlay to show all sustainment units and installations, current and proposed. Include current status, capability, and any enhanced or reduced capability caused by attached, detached, or supporting units.

    (1)   (U) Maintenance. Provide a general statement about the present capability [such as repair time factors, posture of maintenance units, some references to Class VII and Class IX status if it affects maintenance capability, status of Class VII end items (such as repair parts, vans, wreckers) that may affect maintenance, etc.].

    (2)   (U) Supply. Provide overall status of controlled items and POL allocations, including pertinent comments on resupply availability, etc. Provide

information under subheadings of classes supply, list them in the most meaningful measure (days of supply, total line items, equipment shortages – Class VII) by unit.

(3) (U) Services. Provide present status, include both capabilities and problems.

(4) (U) Transportation. Provide present capabilities of mode-operating units to support transportation requirements. Detail adequacy of routes, facilities, and terminals to support distribution requirements. Discuss capability of movement control and in-transit visibility of movements and to assure sustained flow. Address time and distance factors which influence the capability to provide support at the right place and time. Consider factors such as facilities and terminals, airlift/drop, and in-transit visibility.

(5) (U) Labor. Provide present situation, status, restrictions on use of civilians, etc..

(6) (U) Facilities and construction. Provide availability of host nation facilities to serve as headquarters and support facilities. Provide status of construction to upgrade existing facilities and create facilities where needed.

(7) (U) Health service support. Provide present status of medical treatment and evacuation resources, projected location of patient-collecting points, and ambulance exchange points (AXP's), status of health service logistics (including blood, medical regulating, and any anticipated increase in casualty rates or EPW) work loads.

(8) (U) EPW operations. Provide facilities, construction, and sustainment functions.

(9) (U) Other.

f. (U) Assumptions. Until the commander provides specific planning guidance, you may need assumptions for initiating planning or for preparing the estimate. Modify assumptions as factual data becomes available.

NOTE: As you proceed with the estimate process, keep in mind the sustainment concept is intended to support the mission

2. **(U) ANALYSIS OF COURSES OF ACTION:** Analyze all sustainment factors for each subheading (paragraph 2e) for each course of action indicating problems and deficiencies. This paragraph, and any subparagraphs, should contain narrative analysis statements explaining mathematical and applied logic. (Mathematical calculations you perform to assess status of any class of supply, maintenance attrition rates, tonnage lift capacity, and so forth, are solely a means to obtain information for full analysis.) The result of your analysis for subheadings for each course of action should provide both sustainment and tactical impact.

    a. (U) <u>Sufficiency of Area</u>. Determine if the area under control will be adequate for sustainment operations. Will it be cleared of enemy units? Will other units be sharing the same area (units passing through one another)? Will boundaries remain unchanged? Etc.

    b. (U) <u>Material and Services</u>. Include all that apply:

        (1) (U) Maintenance.
        (2) (U) Supply.
        (3) (U) Services.
        (4) (U) Transportation.
        (5) (U) Labor.
        (6) (U) Facilities.
        (7) (U) Contract services
        (8) (U) Other

3. **(U) COMPARISON OF COURSES OF ACTION:**

    a. (U) <u>Evaluate Sustainment deficiencies</u>. List any advantages and disadvantages to accomplish the mission

    b. (U) <u>Discuss the advantages and disadvantages of each course of action you consider</u>. Include methods of overcoming deficiencies or modifications each course of action required.

4. **(U) CONCLUSIONS:**

    a. Indicate which course or courses of action is sustainable - sustainment can best support. If all are sustainable, focus on levels of efficiency and effectiveness.

    b. List the major Sustainment deficiencies and shortfalls the commander must consider. Include specific recommendations concerning the methods of eliminating or reducing the effect of these deficiencies. Note – not everyone needs to be supported equally. Use the derived Concept of Support to cross allocate or redistribute commodities/services. For example, if there is an identified shortfall of a specific type of artillery ammunition (such as D544 DPICM), then weight the main effort/decisive operations, minimizing to the safest extent possible the shaping/supporting efforts.

/s/ _____
(S-4 Officer)

ANNEXES: (as required)

12.8 Support Operations Mission Analysis Checklist

An effective checklist tool for SPOs, but note it does not cover everything. Make sure requirements are integrated. (Example: Identify the amount of Class V to be moved and stored. The Trans section then determines assets needed to move it. S&S section then identifies the fuel needed based on the anticipated mileage. Maint. Section identifies anticipated class IX and repair activities based on vehicle usage. S-2 identifies availability of and/or any security requirements.

1.	GENERAL REQUIREMENTS – ALL STAFF	
Tasked	**Item**	**Status**
	Understand Commanders Mission (Next two higher echelons)	
	Understand Commanders Intent (Next two higher echelons)	
	Review Area of Operations	
	Understand Concept of Operations from Higher	
	Review Task Organization	
	Identify Specified Tasks	
	Identify Implied Tasks	
	Identify Essential Tasks	
	Review Available Assets	
	Identify Any Attachments/Detachments	
	Determine Any Limitations	
	Identify Any Risks	
	Determine Critical Facts	
	Determine Critical Assumptions (OPLAN Only)	
	Review/Determine Time Line (1/3 - 2/3 rule)	
	Determine Current Status	
	Determine Projected Status by D-Day/Execution	

	Determine Critical Shortages (Effects/Impacts on Operations)	
	Predict Critical Shortages by Phases of Operations	
	Determine Resupply Rate and Method	
	Determine if Host Nation Support is Available	
	Determine Higher Supporting Units	
	Determine Resupply Unit Locations	
	Determine Any Supply Constraints	
	Determine Any Shortfalls/Warstoppers	
	Determine Any Contracting Support Required	
2.	**SERVICE SUPPORT - GENERAL (ALL)**	
Tasked	**Item**	**Status**
	Facts: Determine status of: CLASS I, II, III(P), IV, VI, VII, X, and maps	
	Determine any critical shortages	
	ASSUMPTIONS: Determine resupply rates	
	Determine availability of host nation support	
	CONCLUSION: Determine projected SUPPLY status on d-day	
	Review projected distribution system	
3a.	**SERVICE SUPPORT - FIELD SERVICES**	**Status**
	Facts: Determine status of field services (FS) field feeding, laundry & bath support, clothing repair, & water purification	
	Identify total number of soldiers to be supported	
	Identify critical equipment and supply shortages	
	Assumptions: Determine any host nation support available	
	Conclusions: Determine FS status on D-day and throughput operations	
	Other: Determine location of FS support units	
	Identify supplies to support FS operations	

	Determine transportation / time requirements to move FS units	
3b.	**SERVICE SUPPORT - FUELING**	
Tasked	**Item**	**Status**
	Facts: Determine current status of bulk carriers/ storage assets	
	Determine current supply status in terms of DOS and O/H gallons	
	Review bulk fuel distribution system	
	Identify any critical shortages of fuel or fuel support equipment	
	Assumptions: Determine amount of fuel required to support daily operations	
	Determine resupply rates	
	Determine host nation support available	
	Conclusions: Determine projected status of Class III at D-day and during phases of operation	
	Other: Identify any enroute movement requirements	
	Identify any RO/ FARP missions	
	Determine location of fuel resupply units	
	Identify fuel testing (lab) support	

Solving fuel shortfalls (1) set priorities; (2) increase tanker trips per day; (3) request assistance from higher		
3c.	**SERVICE SUPPORT - ARMING**	
Tasked	**Item**	**Status**
	Facts: Determine current Class V status	
	Review current distribution system	
	Identify known restrictions	
	Identify Class V critical shortages	
	Assumptions: Determine resupply rates	

	Determine any host nation support available	
	Conclusion: Determine projected supply status on D-Day	
	Other: Identify projected location of ammunition units/ supply points	
	Identify any lift problems	
	Identify emergency resupply procedures	
	Identify any required EOD support	
	Forecast requirements	
	Determine/ review CCL requirements	
	Solving ammunition shortfalls: (1) sub-allocate to subordinates; (2) establish restrictions to firing; (3) pre-draw/ cache critical items; (4) request an increase in CSR	

4.	MAINTENANCE - FIXING	
Tasked	**Item**	**Status**
	Facts: Determine current equipment maintenance status (FMC, NMC)	
	Determine Class IX status/ critical status	
	Identify maintenance and evacuation priorities	
	Establish maintenance repair timelines	
	Determine controlled substitution/ cannibalization procedures	
	Assumptions: determine any host nation support available	
	Determine projected equipment losses	
	Conclusions: Determine projected maintenance status on D-Day	
	Other: Identify critical weapons systems status	
	Review MST employment plan	
	Review distribution system for Classes VII and IX	
	Determine location of higher level maintenance units	

Improving material readiness rates: (1) Prioritize by unit and by equipment; (2) Re-look time guidelines; (3) Delegate authority to controlled exchange and cannibalization		
5.	**TRANSPORTATION - MOVING**	
Tasked	**Item**	**Status**
	Facts: Determine current readiness status of transportation assets	
	Determine status of critical LOCs/ MSRs	
	Determine any critical transportation shortages	
	Assumptions: Determine any host nation support available	
	Conclusions: Analyze projected transportation assets status on D-Day	
	Determine projected status on LOCs and MSRs on D-Day	
	Other: Determine transportation requirements	
	Determine movement and route use priorities	
	Analyze transportation network (ports, airfield, roads, waterways, railroads)	
	Determine locations of cargo transfer points	
	Determine transportation control requirements/ first destination, points, traffic control points, etc.)	
6.	**HEALTH SERVICE SUPPORT (HSS)**	
Tasked	**Item**	**Status**
	Determine HSS mission statement	
	Determine Enemy Situation (strength and disposition, combat efficiency, capabilities, logistic situation, state of health, weapons)	
	Determine Friendly Situation (strength and disposition, combat efficiency, present and projected operations, logistic situation, rear area protection plan, weapons)	
	Determine Characteristics of the Area of Operations (terrain, weather and climate, dislocated civilian population and EPWs, flora and fauna, disease, local resources, NBC and DE weapons)	

	Determine Strengths to be Supported (U.S. Army, U.S. Navy, U.S. Marines, U.S. Air Force, U.S. Coast Guard; DoD Civilians; Allied forces; Coalition forces; EPWs; U.S. National Contract Personnel; Indigenous civilians and Third Country personnel; detainees; internees; others)	
	Determine Health of the Command (acclimation of troops, presence of disease, status of immunizations, status of nutrition, clothing and equipment, fatigue, morale, status of training, other)	
	Determine Special Factors (items of special importance in the particular operation to be supported such as unique conditions to be encountered in CBRN/DE warfare or the impact of patients suffering from combat stress will have on the HSS system)	
	Determine patient estimates (indicate rates and numbers by type of unit)—number of patients anticipated, distribution within the AO, evacuation time, areas of patient density, possible MASCALs, lines of patient drift and evacuation)	
	Determine Support Requirements (patient evacuation and medical regulation, hospitalization, health service logistics—to include blood management, medical laboratory services, dental services, veterinary services, preventive medicine services, combat stress control services, area medical support, C4I (command, control, communications, computers, intelligence), others as appropriate)	
	Identify Resources Available (organic medical units and personnel, attached medical units and personnel, supporting medical units, civil public health capability and resources, EPW medical personnel, health service logistics, medical troop ceiling)	
	Determine courses of action (as a result of the above considerations and analysis, determine and list all logical COAs which will support the commander's plan and accomplish the HSS mission—consider all SOPs, policies, and procedures in effect)—courses of action are expressed in terms of what, when, where, how, and why.	
	Determine if the HSS mission can/ cannot be supported.	

	Determine which medical COA can best be supported from the HSS standpoint.	
	Identify the limitations and deficiencies in the preferred COA that must be brought to the commander's attention.	
	Identify factors adversely affecting the health of the command.	

12.9 Asset Availability Worksheet

Asset Availability Worksheet

1. Identify system capabilities not individual. Match up personnel with a complete system (i.e. Driver, Assistant Driver, Prime mover and mission trailer).
2. Identify capabilities in consistent and appropriate terms and state them (i.e. 30% local haul of four 60 km round trips, 60% long haul of two 180 km round trips, 10% maintenance or single lift capability of XXX). Identify manning, maintenance, trafficability, etc. as issues.

UNIT	SYSTEM	CAPABILITIES	ISSUES (STATUS, LOCATION, etc)

CHAPTER 13

COMMANDER'S GUIDANCE GUIDELINES

✫✫✫

This is a generic list of information commander's consider as they develop their guidance. The commander does not have to address every item. It should be tailored to meet specific needs and the commander will issue guidance on only those items appropriate to a particular mission.

Intelligence:
1. Enemy COAs to consider during the COA development and COA analysis phase of the planning process. This may be the enemy's most probable COA, most dangerous COA, or a combination of the two.
2. Enemy's critical decision points and vulnerabilities.
3. PIR (CCIR)
4. Targeting guidance
5. High-Value targets
6. Defining of the enemy commander's mission
7. Defining of the enemy commander's methods
8. Desired enemy perception of friendly forces
9. Intelligence focus for reconnaissance and security effort
10. Reconnaissance and surveillance guidance
11. Specific terrain and weather factors to consider
12. Use of organic assets: gun trucks, electronic warfare devices/systems, attached aviation.

Maneuver:
1. Initial intent
   - Purpose of operation
   - Method (phases/sequences)
   - Desired end state
2. Concept of operations (consider your customer as well as yourself):
   - Decisive operation (as well as Shaping and Sustaining)
   - Battlefield organization (close, deep, rear)
   - Task/purpose
   - Resources to be used for each
3. COA development guidance
   - Critical events
   - Number of COAs to be developed
   - COAs to consider or not consider and formations to consider
   - Shaping the battlefield
   - Defeat mechanism
   - Main and supporting effort
     * Task organization
     * Where/what risk to accept
     * Task/purpose of subordinate units
   - Reserve guidance (composition, mission, priorities, command and control measures)
   - Reconnaissance or counter reconnaissance guidance
   - Composition
   - Mission Command (MC) measures
   - FFIR
4. Intelligecne Collection (formerly reconnaissance and surveillance) guidance and priorities
5. OPSEC considerations

Maneuver Support and Survivability:
1. Priority of effort and support
2. Mobility:
   - MSR/ASR status, physical condiction & bridging guidance

- Employing protection assets guidance
3. Countermobility:
   - Obstacle effects/emplacement guidance
   - FASCAM use and duration
4. Survivability: Assets available to dig survivability positions
5. CBRN defense operations:
   - Chemical reconnaissance assets
   - MOPP posture
   - Decontamination guidance
   - Masking and unmasking guidance
   - Employment of smoke
   - Detection, reporting, marking
6. Management of engineer supplies and materiel
7. Environmental guidance

Air Defense:
1. Protection priorities
2. Positioning guidance
3. Weapons control status for specific events

Information Operations (IO):
1. Military deception guidance:
   - Amount and types of resources to commit to the deception plan
   - Intent for exploiting the enemy actions
   - EEFI (CCIR)
2. OPSEC considerations:
   - Identification of actions that can be observed by the enemy
   - Determination of indicators from which enemy intelligence systems can gain critical information
   - Selection of measures to reduce vulnerabilities
3. Electronic warfare (EW) considerations:
   - Measures for electronic protect (EP)
   - Support needed for electronic warfare support (ES)
   - Methods of electronic attack (EA)

4. Physical destruction considerations:
   - Planned indirect fire support targets to support C2W plan
   - Maneuver actions to suppress, neutralize, and destroy enemy
   - Air defense measures to nullify enemy aircraft
5. PSYOPS considerations:
   - Priority of effort for attached PSYOPS forces
   - Allocation of organic and/or supporting resources to support PSYOPS efforts (field artillery, close air support, unmanned aerial vehicles, security elements)
6. Public affairs (PA) considerations:
   - Effective publications that are dependent on credibility
   - Early deployment of public affairs personnel
   - Information security practiced at the source
7. Themes and Messages
   - Specific Themes that support the operation
   - Medium(s) to employ to convey messages

Sustainment:
1. Commander's guidance for sustainment:
   - Sustainment priorities in terms of manning, fueling, fixing, arming, moving, and sustaining
2. Location of sustainment assets
3. MEDEVAC treatment and evacuation guidance
4. Classes of supply:
   - Anticipated requirements and pre-stockage of Class III, IV, and V
5. Controlled supply rates
6. Guidance on construction and provision of facilities and installations

Mission Command:
1. Rules of engagement
2. CP position guidance

3. Position of commander
4. Integration of retransmission assets or other communications equipment
5. LNO guidance
6. Force protection measures
7. Time-line guidance
8. Type of order and rehearsal
9. Specific signal guidance

Design
1. Decision on employment of 'Design'
2. Size/composition of Design Team

CHAPTER 14

MISSION ANALYSIS BRIEFING FORMAT

★★★

MISSION ANALYSIS BRIEFING

SUBJECT	BRIEFER
1. Opening comments	CDR
2. Introduction (participants, purpose and desired conclusion)	XO
3. Roll Call, time plan for MA Brief (enforced by XO)	XO
4. Map overview of Brigade/Division AO, Friendly situation	S-3
5. Mission and commander's intent (two levels up)	S-3
6. Mission, commander's intent, concept of the operation, and deception plan or objectives (one level up)	S-3
7. Review of commander's initial guidance	S-3
8. Enemy situation with impact on logistics (deep, close, rear) Initial IPB products a. Area of Operation/Interest	S-2, Intel NCO

      b.   Avenues of approach

      c.   Weather/Terrain Analysis (affects of
          weather and key/decisive terrain)

      d.   Enemy intent and objectives

      e.   Enemy order of battle

      f.   Enemy capabilities

      g.   Enemy vulnerabilities

      h.   Enemy COAs: (graphically represented
          on two separate handouts)
          (1)   Most likely
          (2)   Most dangerous

      i.   Friendly intelligence capabilities
        (other than organic)

9.	Specified, implied and essential tasks	S-3
10.	Pertinent facts and assumptions	S-3
11.	Constraints on the operation	S-3
12.	Forces available (2 levels down/by type unit; include Avn sorties)	S-3
13.	Overview of Sustainment AO (LOC's, MSR/ASR's, airfields, rail, ports, Warehousing, other sustainement related infrastructure)	SPO
14.	Task Org for support (incl. Sustainment attachments/augmentation)	S-3/SPO
15.	Overview of supported unit support concept (para. 4 OPORD)	SPO
16.	Transportation requirements, capabilities and shortfalls with proposed recommendations	S4

17.	*HSS requirements, capabilities and shortfalls with proposed recommendations (BSB)*	C-Med Cdr
18.	*HSS augmentation and evac platforms (BSB)*	C-Med Cdr
19.	Results of requirements, capabilities and shortfalls analysis	SPO
20.	DS sustainment stocks required (min 3 DOS at CSSB/Sus Bde)	SPO
21.	CL III distribution plan	SPO
22.	CL V storage, transfer and distribution plan	SPO
23.	Results of material damage and combat power prior to LD estimates	SPO
24.	Support concept prior to higher HQ staff analysis	SPO
25.	Critical personnel and equipment shortfalls with impact on mission	S-1, S-4
26.	Hazards and Initial Risk Assessment	S-3
27.	Proposed theme and messages	S-3
28.	Recommended initial CCIR and EEFI's	S-3
29.	Proposed initial Information (Intelligence) Collection Plan	S-3, S-2
30.	Recommended time lines (planning, preparation, execution)	XO

31. Recommended proposed problem statement   XO

32. Recommended proposed mission statement   XO

33. Recommended COA evaluation criteria   XO

34. Approves support concept and mission statement CDR

35. Commander's intent   CDR

36. Commander's planning guidance and   CDR
    collaborative planning Sessions or work groups

CHAPTER 15

COURSE OF ACTION BRIEFING FORMAT

★★★

COURSE OF ACTION BRIEFING

<u>SUBJECT</u>	<u>BRIEFER</u>
1. Introduction (Purpose and desired conclusion)	XO
2. Update Status (RFIs and CCIR)	XO

3. Intelligence
    a. Updated IPB (weather and terrain)
    b. Possible enemy COAs (Event Template)
	S-2, Intel NCO

4. Mission Statement	S-3
5. Update of personnel and equipment (chart or projection)	S-1/S-4
4. Proposed COAs, in order (prepare handouts)	
a. Array of forces, logistics & medical support (sketch)	SPO/S-3
b. Scheme of support statement (before, during, and after operations)	SPO/S-3
c. Course of Action rational for each COA	SPO/S-3

(1) Considerations affected by possible
           enemy COA(s), logistics assets
           Available, missions assigned, or timeline imposed.	

      (2)   Why units are arrayed as shown on sketches

      (3)   Priorities of support, phasing, C2,
            and availability of assets

      (4)   Why selected control measures used

  d.   Discuss risk and end state of each COA   SPO/S-3

5.   Commander's guidance for war gaming   CDR

6.   Time and Location for War gaming   XO

CHAPTER 16

DECISION BRIEFING FORMAT

★★★

DECISION BRIEFING

<u>SUBJECT</u>	<u>BRIEFER</u>

1. Introduction (purpose and desired conclusion)   XO

2. Mission Statement/Intent of HHQs   S-3

3. Status of Friendly Forces   S-3
    a. TASKO changes
    b. Relative combat power ratios (friendly/enemy)
    c. Unit locations (own and adjacent)

4. Updated terrain analysis   S-2/Intel NCO

5. Facts updated (changes/additions only)   S-3/OPS NCO

6. Enemy COAs (most likely/most dangerous)   S-2/Intel NCO
    (flip slides)

7. Friendly COAs, in sequence (against   S-3
    "Most Likely" COA)
       ("Most Dangerous" COAs become branch CONPLANs)

8. Overall COA comparison with weighted   S-3
    comparisons

9.   COA comparisons (War fighting
     Functional Area specific criteria)
     a.   Movement & Maneuver   S-3
     b.   Mission Command (C2)   S-3
     c.   Fires (*if applicable*)   S-3
     d.   Protection (ADA, Survivability, CBRN)   S-3
     e.   Intelligence   S-2/Intel NCO
     g.   Sustainment   SPO/S-4/S-1
          (1)   Logistics   SPO/S-4
          (2)   Personnel/HSS   S1/(BMSO)
          (3)   CMO   S1

10.   Recommended COA   S-3/XO

11.   Decision   CDR

12.   Intent Statement (for re-approval/modification)   CDR

13.   Time and Location for Orders Briefing: _____   XO

CHAPTER 17

ORDERS BRIEFING FORMAT

✯✯✯

ORDERS BRIEFING

SUBJECT	**BRIEFER**
1. **INTRODUCTION**	XO

- Classification
- Purpose of briefing
- What do we need at the conclusion of the briefing

2. **PRELIMINARY DATA**	S-3

- Classification of OPLAN/OPORD
- Header Data
- OPLAN/OPORD Number
- References
- Time Zone

3. **TASKO**	S-3

- Area of Operations/Area of Interest Overview (permanently posted)
- *Brigade Overview (permanently posted) (BSB only)*
- *Corps/Division Overview (permanently posted) (Sus Bde/CSSB only)*
- Sustainment Bde detailed TASKO (permanently posted) (Sus Bde/CSSB)

4. SITUATION   S-3
  - Terrain & Weather Data
  - Enemy Forces (TASKO) (permanently posted)
  - Friendly Forces
  - Attachments/Detachments
  - Assumptions (OPLAN Only)

5. MISSION   S-3
  - CORPS/TSC/ESC Mission (permanently posted)
  - DIVISION Mission (if applicable – Sus Bde) (permanently posted)
  - BRIGADE Mission (permanently posted) (BSB only)
  - SUSTAINMENT BRIGADE (permanently posted for CSSB)

6. EXECUTION   S-3
  - HHQ's Intent (permanently posted)
  - SUSTAINMENT BDE CDR'S Intent (permanently posted) (CSSB)
  - DIVISION Concept of Operations (BSB)
  - BDE CDR's Intent and Concept of Operations
  - Movement of Sustainment units (all Phases)   SPO
  - FLE's, CRSP, TTPs, CSCs other special Log events
  - General Concept of Support (all Phases)   SPO
        Material and Services (by Phase)
        Priority of Support
        Priority of Movement (fwd & rear)
        Special events in any Phase
  - Concept of Support for each commodity   SPO
    (all Phases)
        Method of supply for each class
        Stockage for each class
        Operations of next higher supplying Div
        Control of command regulated items
        Critical / special activities
        Schedules

- Transportation   S-4/MCT (if avail)
     MSR's - primary, alternate, dirty (or SPO Trans if avail)
     Traffic circulation / control plan
     Priorities of support / movement
     Schedules / Taskings

- Maintenance (Air and Ground for   S-4
     each subparagraph)
     Approving authority for   (or SPO Maint if avail)
     controlled exchange/cannibalization
       Control of command regulated CL IX
       Priority of maintenance
       Location of facilities and collection points
       Repair time limits at each maint level
       Evac procedures

- Medical Concept of Support   S-1, Bde Surgeon
     Collection, evacuation, treatment   (C-Med Cdr if
     BCT) of US, Allied, EPW, Civilian
     sick, injured, wounded - facilities, evac routes
     CHS logistics (incl blood) - stockage
     objectives, next higher spt
     Combat stress control, preventive med,
     dental, optical, veterinary

- BSB/LSA/FOB defense plan   S-3
- CCIR (PIR, EEFI, FFIR)   S-3
- Tasks to organic units   S-3
- Tasks to attached units
- Tasks to other supporting units

7. **SERVICE SUPPORT** (Internal support unit logistics)
    - Internal Concept of Support   S-4
    - Personnel, Religious, Legal   S-1

8. COMMAND AND SIGNAL   S-6/S-3

CHAPTER 18

PLANS UPDATE TO CDR FORMAT (OR COMMANDER'S UPDATE BRIEF — CUB)

✮✮✮

PURPOSE: Update CDR on Plans/Contingencies for next 24 hours.

<u>SUBJECT</u>	<u>BRIEFER</u>
- General Support Changes Next 24 Hrs	S-3/SPO
- Decision Points that could require Command Group decision next 24 Hrs	XO/S-3
- Synchronization Matrix for next 24 Hrs	XO/S-3/SPO
- Contingency Plans in development 　　Status 　　Nature of Plan	S-3

CHAPTER 19

COMMON MDMP ERRORS AND MISTAKES

★★★

Having conducted well over 850 Military Decision Making Process training sessions from battalion to division level over the course of 14 years, as well as soliciting input from two highly experienced Sustainment Subject Matter Experts (Ben Terell and Roy Pond), I have listed below the most common errors Sustainment Unit Commanders and Staffs typically encounter while undergoing MDMP.

19.1. Receipt of Mission

1. **Take Stock in What You Have**. First action item required is to inventory and ensure you have received all documents associated with the OPORD or WARNORD that HHQ has produced. This requires reviewing what documents have been produced versus those identified as 'TBP' (To Be Published). In one case, a BSB staff rushed through the process, only to come to a complete halt when they realized they were missing the Brigade's Decision Support Matrix (kind of hard to conduct COA Analysis, especially when trying to sync moving the BSA when you do not know the Brigade's movement plan). Often times, graphics and overlays are overlooked. Missing these can have an impact especially during Intelligence/Logistics Preparation of the Battlefield when determining 'constraints' (locating bridges, overpasses, key terrain) and 'Specified/Implied' tasks (ID of No-Go and restricted areas, MSR speed limits, etc)

2. **Have everyone read the base OPORD/OPLAN**. Staffs are like anyone else – they focus strictly on their area of expertise or 'lane'. Having everyone read the Base OPORD/OPLAN establishes a common understanding what that the HHQ unit (and more importantly 'the customer') is doing. While the staff is reviewing it, reference the Map(s) or Ops graphics to ensure the staff can visualize the Operating Environment.

3. **Ask Questions**. Commanders at this point may be a tad bit overwhelmed in developing initial planning guidance, so don't be afraid to ask questions; Use Army Design Methodology (ADM) or MDMP, dispatch LNOs, commander involvement, etc. The only bad question is the one that doesn't get asked. This also impacts on the *time available*. Questions asked early on will always provide clarity and provide the staff more *time* to plan using valid information versus playing the guessing game.

19.2 Mission Analysis

1. **Analysis HHQ Order**. Typically, staffs will '*cut and paste*' the mission statement and commander's intent of the immediate two higher headquarters without really understanding what these HQ's are doing – in short understanding these organization's 'Operational Framework'. This consists of an understanding of what the HHQ's Decisive, Shaping, and Sustaining Operations are, and then asking the question '*Where do I fit within this operational framework?*' In the case of sustainment organizations, this is compounded by a lack of understanding what the customer is doing. Here, the supported unit's '*Concept of Support*' becomes the sustaining units '*Concept of Operation*', and thus sets the stage for an understanding of what is required of the sustaining unit.

2. **Understanding your capabilities**. If a sustainment unit is going to fail, it usually fails here. All too often during development of the Sustaining Running Estimate, the SPO provides an 'inventory' of equipment (x # of PLS, y # gals of fuel holding, etc) without really taking into account how many pallets or gallons can be pushed within 24 hours (DOS), or x number of miles/kilometers can be 'pushed' from the support area, or how many SECFOR gun trucks and personnel are available to support convoy operations. This also extends into support maintenance companies (how many are trained, how long have they worked together, how up to date is their equipment and test sets, etc). Taken all together, this provides an understanding of what is the sustainer's 'combat power' (or sustainment power if you wish). Just like maneuver forces develop their combat power ratios, sustainers need to develop their sustainment combat power towards supporting their customer.

3. **Understanding of the tasks assigned.** Often times, units develop an abounding list of specified tasks but seldom understand the breadth and depth of the tasks. Understanding a task begins with articulating the task as a tactical task with a purpose that addresses a problem the unit must correct or overcome to achieve the commander's end state. (A task that is not a tactical task and addresses a problem that leads to achievement of the commander's end state is not a valid task and should be dropped from the list of tasks.) As soon as the staff has articulated their tasks, they develop their assessment criteria in relation to the tasks (how are we going to measure success?). The staff continues mission analysis focusing only on the tasks articulated, thus saving time and effort.

4. **Define the Course of Action Evaluation Criteria early.** COA evaluation criteria are a by-product of the assessment plan. Staffs frequently wait until they are solidly within COA

development before beginning COA evaluation criteria. And when they do recommend COA evaluation criteria they are vague, irrelevant, and only partially developed. COA evaluation criteria are indicators of success derived during the development of the assessment plan while developing an understanding of the tasks assigned.

19.3 Course of Action Development

1. **Know Your Doctrine, Know Your Limits**. For sustainment units, COA development is all about extending the operational reach (ADRP 3-0) of the customer (and the sustainment) unit. Commander's need to articulate their desired method and manner of distribution when they provide their planning guidance during mission analysis. This will save staffs tremendous time and efforts.

19.4 Course of Action Analysis (Wargaming)

1. **Start with major 'muscle' moves**. A good sustainment TTP is to start with wargaming major sustainment actions (i.e. '*muscle moves*') such as deployment of Forward Logistics Element (FLE), or a large size Sustainment Replenishment Operations (SRO). Much of this many already have been accomplished during the HHQ's COA Analysis, and thus the Sustainment Sync Matrix can be refined at this point.

2. **Having all your tools available when Wargaming**. For sustainers to be successful, you need to know and coordinate on what your customer is doing. For this, you need to have the supported units Decision Support Template/Matrix (Appendix 3, Decisive Support Products of Annex C Operations). Knowing what their Decisive Operation (DO) and key Shaping Operations are, and synchronizing your support to them ensures the DO will not fail due to lack of sustainment (it's always a good excuse to blame the S-4 or SPO for lack of supplies).

19.5 Course of Action Comparison

1. **Identify the matrix template before you start**. Time is the one resource you do not have a lot of and like most staffs, you have probably already adjusted your timeline because Mission Analysis and Course of Action Development required more time than the XO forecasted. Trying to decide and agree upon a format as a staff for the COA Decision Matrix at this stage of the process is guaranteed to cause you to have to adjust your timeline yet again.

2. **SQUIDMAT**. If you do not have any good examples or are very inexperienced at this process, try 'Squidmat' which is a civilian version of a Decision Matrix (DECMAT) and is available on line. This was used extensively a few years ago when attendance at the Combined Arms Staff Service School (CAS³) was mandatory.

19.6 Course of Action Approval

1. **Be careful what you ask for**. Staffs will do exactly what they are told to do with the guidance provided by commanders, but on a handful of occasions, be advised – commanders make mistakes too! In some cases as staffs present COA Decision Briefs, Commanders may have epiphanies (something they may have overlooked, or undervalued). This is especially true when looking into the aspects of Sustainment Mission Command, such as asking 'how do I communicate with that FLE, or CSC, etc'. In these cases, COAs may have to be re-evaluated or even re-wargamed. After all, it's the Commander's prerogative to change, even at this step.

2. **Publishing WARNORD #3?** At this stage, many staffs have tremendous amounts of planning guidance available for subordinate HQ's to use in their parallel planning, but instead of issuing WARNORD #3, the staff will wait until they publish

the OPORD/OPLAN then in turn brief it. Push this information out to them as soon as possible – remember time is the one resource you don't have a lot of. Pushing WARNORD #3 out may seem like a pain, but consider it 'investment capital' in the form of higher quality subordinate commander confirmation/back briefs.

19.7 OPORD/OPLAN Production, Dissemination, and transition

Orders, in the past decade and a half, have evolved into something never intended, becoming something akin to the size of a typical Los Angeles phone book! The correct philosophy as described in doctrine today is the Mission Order – simple, concise, detailing the commander's intent, essential tasks, constraints (and authorities), coordination measures, and resourcing of the tasks.

1. **Use the synchronization matrix to write the order.** Staffs frequently write their portions of the order from scratch and with little, if any, reference to the work done during COA analysis. The purpose of the sync matrix is to detail tasks, priorities, and coordination measures for the operation; that is all that a mission order requires. Failure to include the details found on the sync matrix will lead to an incomplete order. Including details not found on the sync matrix overburdens and confuses subordinate commands during their mission analysis.

2. **Write a mission order, not a book.** One of the biggest mistakes in order writing today is the insistence of publishing attachments. The purpose of attachments is to provide detail that not everyone on the staff needs, but is essential to mission accomplishment. An attachment is not an opportunity to regurgitate information found anywhere else in the order, pontificate on sustainment philosophy and operations, or

delineate standard operating procedure. At brigade level, a mission order would typically have only three attachments (Annex B (Intelligence) Appendix 1 (Intelligence Estimate), Annex C (Operations) Appendix 2 (Operations Overlay), and Appendix 3 (Decision Support Matrix)), maybe less; and a battalion would seldom publish an attachment. So, what does right look like? Use the ten minute rule. No single portion of an order should take longer than ten minutes to read.

3. **Keep it simple.** Another huge problem is over-complicating an order just because higher headquarters developed a complex order. The purpose of phasing is to organize the operation. Phasing for one headquarters is not necessarily the correct answer for subordinate headquarters. Sustainment units should frequently organize their operations over different chronological lines of operations than the maneuver units they support, or sustainment headquarters for which they work. Even more, battalions should consider producing one order for each of their higher headquarters phases (especially if the higher headquarters is using "sub-phases" or "stages").

4. **Words have meaning.** Know your doctrine and know what you are talking about. All too often, staff officers/NCOs will use 'buzz' words that connote pseudo knowledge of doctrine, such as 'the Decisive Effort is...or the Shaping Efforts are..." as an example (there are no such doctrinal term). If the term used cannot be defined within contemporary ADP/ADRP/ATPs/FMs – '**don't use it**'! The same could be said for use of colorful adjectives to spice up OPORD verbiage. An example of this is 'Units will conduct *aggressive* patrolling outside the support area'. Does this mean we typically conduct *passive* patrolling? Of course not, but the use of the adjective '*aggressive*' juices up what would otherwise

be a mundane tasking. Also avoid the use of *'unqualified objectives'* and other meaningless expressions like <u>*as soon as possible* (ASAP)</u>. Indecisive, vague, and ambiguous language leads to uncertainty and lack of confidence.

For example, do not use:
- "*try to retain*" instead say "<u>retain until</u>"
- "*violently attacks*" or "*delays while maintaining enemy contact*". Use "<u>*attacks*</u>" or "<u>*delays*</u>" instead.

5. **Find your 'active' voice.** An OPORD/OPLAN is just that – <u>an order</u> and all orders are directive in nature. The order or plan reflects the commander's intention and will. Therefore, its language must be direct Write your portion using an '*active*' not a '*passive*' voice. An example of this is '286 CSSB *supports* versus 286 CSSB *will or could* support.

Blast from the Past

"An order that can be misunderstood will be misunderstood."

Field Marshal Helmuth Von Moltke,
Chief of the Prussian General Staff
Battle of Sedan, Sep 1870

1

CHAPTER 20

ORDERS BREAKDOWN FOR STAFF ANALYSIS

★★★

General. When the unit receives an OPORD from higher headquarters, the order is broken down and distributed per the below chart. It is not always possible or realistic to copy, disseminate, and read the entire OPORD from a higher headquarters. However, there are portions of the plan that must be read by various staff sections and key information must be disseminated to all staff and unit commanders. A complete copy of the Base OPORD will be given to BC, XO, CSM, 1 ea (S-1, S-4, HHC), 2 ea (S-2/3, SPO). A complete copy of all annexes will be made for the BC and XO. All other annexes are copied and distributed in the numbers listed below.

ANNEX	TITLE	COPIES (Total)	BC (Master Copy)	XO	SPO	S-1	S-2 &3	S-4	CSM
A.	Task Organization	7	X	X	X	X	X (P)	X	X
B.	Intelligence	3	X	X			X (P)		
C.	Operations Overlay	5	X	X	X		X (P)	X	
D.	Fires	3	X	X			X (P)		
E.	Protection	4	X	X			X (P)		X
F.	Sustainment	7	X	X	X	X (P)	X	X (P)	X

G.	Engineer	3	X	X			X (P)		
H.	Signal	3	X	X			X (P)		
I.	Not Used								
J.	Public Affairs	3	X	X		X (P)			
K	Civil Affairs Operations	6	X	X	X	X (P)	X	X	
L.	Information Coll	3	X	X			X (P)		
M.	Assessment	3	X	X			X (P)		
N.	Space Operations	3	X	X			X (P)		
O.	Not Used								
P.	Host Nation Support	3	X	X	X (P)			X	
Q.	Knowledge Management	4	X	X (P)	X			X	
R	Reports	7	X	X	X	X	X (P)	X	X
S.	Special Technical Operations	3	X	X			X (P)		
T.	Spare								
U.	Inspector General	4	X	X		X (P)			X
V.	Interagency Coordination	3	X	X		X (P)			
W	Operational Contract Support	5	X	X	X (P)	X		X	
X, Y	Spare								
Z.	Distribution		X	X		X (P)	X		

(P) Primary responsibility

NOTE: This chart illustrates the orders breakdown in an unconstrained environment. In a constrained environment, risk is assumed by reading only those products that time permits. All staff sections must read all of the base order.

CHAPTER 21

SET UP OF THE PLANS VAN/ROOM

★ ★ ★

The following maps are posted:
- 1:250,000 with Corps operations overlay.
- 1:50,000 Brigade Planning map with current operational and support graphics
- 1:100,000 S-3 Planning map with current operational and support graphics.
- 1:100,000 S-3 Planning map with enemy FS range fans, Mobility Corridors and Avenues of Approach down to Battalion level.

The following charts will be posted:
- Mission and Intent Statements for appropriate BCT, Division & Sustainment Bde
- Enemy intermediate and subsequent objectives
- OPLAN/OPORD Status Chart.
- CONTINGENCY PLAN Status Chart.
- HVT List (developed by Bde S-2 using Mission Analysis)
- HPT List
- Operational Framework worksheet.
- Synchronization Matrix. (developed during War Gaming)
- DST
- Task Organization.
- Time Analysis Chart.
- Posted FRAGORDs/INTSUMs/WOs/etc.
- Commander's Planning Guidance.
- Status board for assets requested from higher
- Relative Combat Power and Sustainment Power chart.

- Current Target Synchronization Matrix (BCT)
- Planning assumptions.
- Graphical Control Measures for division-level planning.
- WFFA Chart

Tools to be available in Van:
- Butcher Pad and Easel (with extra pads).
- Graphics Templates.
- 2 DVNTs (one attached to fax machine).
- Personal Computer and Laser Printer (PC Programs: MS Word, MS Excel, MS PowerPoint, Form Tool).
- Screen for viewing overheads.
- Alcohol and Non-Permanent markers (Broad, Medium, & Fine) in all colors.
- Tube-type markers of various colors (for butcher pad)
- Current operational graphics cartoons (paper and transparency versions)
- MCOO, DST.
- Screening criteria (offensive and defensive) for Decision Briefing.

CHAPTER 22

OPERATIONAL ENVIRONMENT FRAMEWORK

★ ★ ★

AREA OF INFLUENCE. A geographical area wherein a commander is directly capable of influencing operations by maneuver or fire support systems normally under the commander's command or control. (JP 3-16)

AREA OF INTEREST (AOI). Area of concern to the commander, including the area of influence, areas adjacent thereto, and extending into enemy territory to the objectives of current or planned operations. This area also includes areas occupied by enemy forces that could jeopardize the accomplishment of the mission.

AOI is based on the ability of the threat to project power or move forces into the AO. Also consider the geographical locations of other activities or characteristics of the environment that might influence COAs or command decisions. Consider also any anticipated future missions or "be prepared" and "on order" missions identified during mission analysis, and determine their effect on the limits of the AI. An additional consideration would be to divide the AI into several components, such as a ground AI, an air AI, or a political AI. Such a division accommodates the types of information relevant in each AI as well as their usually different geographical limits. (See FMs 3-0 (Para 6-72), JP 2-03, JP 3-16)

AREA OF OPERATIONS (AO) A geographical area, including the airspace above, usually defined by lateral, forward, and rear boundaries assigned to a commander, by a *joint force* higher commander, in which he has responsibility and the authority to conduct military operations. A thorough knowledge of the characteristics of this area leads to its effective use. Generally, because this is the area where the command will conduct its operations, the evaluation of the battlefield's effects is more thorough and detailed within the AO than within the Area of Interest (AOI). An area of operations should not be substantially larger than the unit's area of influence. The limits of the AO are normally the boundaries specified in the OPORD or contingency plan (CONPLAN) from higher headquarters that define the command's mission. (See FM 3-0 (C1) Para 6-68)

AREA OF RESPONSIBILITY (AOR). The geographic area associated with a combatant command within which a combatant commander has authority to plan and conduct operations. (See FMs 3-0, FM 5-0, and JP 0-2

CHAPTER 23

WARFIGHTING FUNCTIONAL AREA (WFFA)

★★★

WARFIGHTING FINCTIOAL AREAS

1. **INTELLIGENCE**
2. **MOVEMENT & MANEUVER**
3. **FIRES**
4. **PROTECTION**
5. **SUSTAINMENT**
6. **MISSION COMMAND**

TACTICAL SUSTAINMENT FUNCTIONS
See Support Concept Matrix

1. SUPPLY - CL I, CL II, CL III (B/P)CL IV, CL V, CL VI, CL VIII support

2. HUMAN RESOURCES – All Personnel management, CAO, OPMS/EPMS

3. MAINTENANCE - all maintenance management, CL VII, CL IX,

4. TRANSPORTATION - all ground, air, water transportation management, traffic control, routes, security

5. FIELD SERVICES – Shower, Clothing Repair, Laundry, Mortuary Affairs

6. HEALTH SYSTEMS SUPPORT - all Medical and CL VIII

7. EOD – Explosive Ordnance Disposal

8. FINANCIAL MANAGEMENT SERVICES – pay issues and financial dispersement operations

9. RELIGIOUS & LEGAL SUPPORT.

CHAPTER 24

COMMANDER'S CRITICAL INFORMATION REQUIREMENTS (CCIR) GUIDANCE

★★★

1. General. Commanders determine their CCIRs and consider the nominations of the staff. CCIRs are situation dependent and specified by the commander for each operation. Commanders continuously review the CCIRs during the planning process and adjust them as situations change. The initial CCIRs developed during mission analysis normally focus on decisions the commander needs to make to focus planning. Once the commander selects a COA, the CCIRs shift to information the commander needs in order to make decisions during preparation and execution. Commanders designate CCIRs to inform the staff and subordinates what they deem essential for making decisions. The fewer the CCIRs, the better the staff can focus its efforts and allocate sufficient resources for collecting them.

CCIRs are published within Para 3.j (2), Coordinating Instructions, of the Operations Plan (OPLAN) or Operations Order (OPORD). The S-3 is responsible for staff input and formulation of recommended CCIR for sustainment unit Cdr approval. From the time of receipt of a mission, there is always a lack of information available to planners. A system of developing information needs and requesting this information and monitoring responses from higher or lateral headquarters, must be in place immediately – supervised by the S-3 or SPO sections.

a. XO manages CCIR as directed by CDR and provides them to all staff sections.

b. Each staff section nominates CCIR's to the XO for inclusion in the final list.

c. Total number of PIR's should be **limited to ten or less and should be tied to any decisions identified within the organization's Decision Support Template/Matrix that the Commander will need to make.**

d. CCIR's should be limited to the information needed by the CDR to visualize the battlefield and thereby make critical decisions, especially those that either determine or validate a specific COA. Only that which is important to mission accomplishment should be in the CCIR's.

e. CCIR's are time sensitive. They are based on a specific time and space to drive identified decisions at designated decision points.

f. CCIR's generate RFI's to the support brigade/BCT or higher intelligence gathering systems and create the tasks for the Unit's R&S plan. These sources, together with internal status reports, answer the CCIR's.

g. CCIR's are composed of PIR's, and FFIR's as detailed in the CCRI Template. In addition to nominating CCIRs to the commander, the staff also identifies and nominates essential elements of friendly information (EEFIs). Although EEFIs are not CCIRs, they have the same priority as CCIRs and require approval by the commander. An EEFI establishes an element of information to protect rather than one to collect. EEFIs identify those elements of friendly force information that, if compromised, would jeopardize mission success. Like CCIRs, EEFIs change as an operation progresses.

2. CCIR

Helps the commander:
- Manage information to ensure they get a complete picture of the battlefield
- Create, confirm, or modify a COA
- Verify and update their assessment of current operations and their estimate of future operations and requirements
- Readily recognize when execution or adjustment of support operations may be necessary
- Assess the unit's ability to accomplish its mission in accordance with the higher commander's intent

3. PRIORITY INFORMATION REQUIREMENTS (PIR)

(How I see the enemy and current/future support operations). PIR is what the commander wants or needs to know about the enemy, changes to the AO, Task Organization, support requirements, or future support operations. For a Sustainment unit, these include (as a minimum) the following:

- Changes to missions
- Changes to task organization
- Changes in readiness (personnel, equipment, and systems)
- Enemy actions in AO

4. FRIENDLY FORCES INFORMATION REQUIREMENTS (FFIR)

(How the enemy sees me). FFIR allows the commander to determine the combat capabilities of their unit. These are not routine reports, but items that are critical enough that they are reported immediately over the command channel when their status changes. For a Sustainment unit, these include (as a minimum) the following:

- Status of forces in base and/or base cluster
- Status of units in AO

5. *ESSENTIAL ELEMENTS OF FRIENDLY INFORMATION (EEFI)

(What do I not want the enemy to know about me). EEFI allows the commander to determine how the enemy sees the friendly unit. For a BSB/CSSB, these include (as a minimum) the following:

- Location of assigned units
- Traffic patterns
- Location of BSAs, LSA, Sus Bdes, CRSPs, CSCs, TCPs, etc.
- Location of base or base cluster units

* Per Para 3-40 & 9-51 of FM 6-0, EEFI is no long a part of the Commander's CCIR

CCIR TEMPLATE

1. **How I See the Enemy (Priority Intelligence Requirements (PIR))**
   - Most probable enemy COA
   - Artillery/Rockets/Mortars (capabilities, location, range fans)
   - Air Insertion
   - Objectives
   - Use of Terrain
   - Formations in depth

   EXAMPLE
   - Location of SPF units/teams operating in the area
   - Reporting any units in CBRN posture.
   - Convoy ambushes
   - First enemy contact
   - Blocked or cut MSR

2. **How the Enemy Sees Me (Essential Elements of Friendly Information (EEFI))**
   - My most probable Spt Ops Concept COA
   - Location of sustainment facilities, stockage & fuel locations and activities.
   - MSR's
   - Supply stockages

   EXAMPLES
   - Location of March Unit Commanders during convoy movements
   - Location of BSB or LSA ATHPs
   - Location of the BCT/BSB TOC
   - Location of the BCT alternate TOC
   - Location of the BSB BMSC

3. **How I See Myself (Friendly Force Information Requirements (FFIR))**
   - Time distance factors in Area of Operations
   - Supported unit sustainment statuses
   - Supported unit tactical situation
   - MSR status
   - Supporting unit statuses

   EXAMPLES
   - Any traffic accidents reducing long convoy route mobility
   - Any non BCT elements operating in the BCT's area
   - Loss of 5K tankers
   - Loss of PLS systems
   - Loss of wheeled or tracked ambulances
   - PERSAT below 75% for the BSB/CSSB
   - Captured FBCB2-BFT device

CHAPTER 25

GENERAL PLANNING CONSIDERATIONS

★★★

1. Avoid predictability.
2. Use appropriate doctrinal terms.
3. Integrate reconnaissance into the battlefield framework.
4. CAV Sqdn's must be augmented if given a covering force mission.
5. Effective counter-reconnaissance is necessary forward of a main defensive area (MBA).
6. Make timely decisions to transition between phases. The target time (decision to contact) for transition from attack to defense is 24 hours, with 12 hours being the minimum to coordinate and emplace BCT obstacle plan. The correct identification of triggers for such a transition is essential.
7. Preparatory to transition to defense select the ground necessary for both the covering force and MBA and continue to attack, if necessary, to secure it.
8. Be clear about the nature of an area defense (focused on terrain) or a mobile defense (focused on the enemy).
9. The maneuver force(s) reserve, if committed, becomes the main effort.
10. Reserves should not be used piecemeal.
11. Reserve deployment options should be illustrated on a DST.
12. There is no requirement for an uncommitted TCF; it may be used for rear area counter-reconnaissance or other supplementary tasks.

13. Orders given in an OPORD/OPLAN base document should not be repeated in an annex.
14. The DST and Synchronization Matrix are decision aids for the Commander rather than components of the OPORD/OPLAN.
15. Maintain continuity of purpose throughout the OPORD/OPLAN.
16. Do not become overly focused on current and/or close operations to the detriment of future and/or deep operations.
17. Read subordinates' OPORDs/OPLANs.
18. Endeavor to destroy the enemy's will to win by the maintenance of tempo, effective reconnaissance, and attack by fire.
19. If a security zone is utilized, it should be 15-20 km deep and incorporate significant obstacles covered by fire.
20. A counter attacking enemy force should be attrited and fixed or delayed by obstacles and observed fire.
21. Artillery assets, particularly MLRS, need to be protected from local attack.

CHAPTER 26

NOTES FOR PREPARATION OF OPLANS/OPORDS

★★★

1. Staff sections with responsibility for annexes, appendices, tabs, and enclosures published separately from the plan/ order are responsible for preparation, coordination, and staffing. Distribution remains the responsibility of the S-1. **RECOMMEND USING STANDARD FONT TIMES NEW ROMAN, 12 PITCH.**

2. Margins and spacing. Left, right, top, and bottom margins are 1 inch. Within the document, left justification will be used and the page numbers will be centered at the bottom of the page.

3. Heading. The heading shown below is the standard for all brigade/division Plans/Orders. The heading will be typed at the top right of the first page of the basic plan/order, conforming to the margin requirements indicated above.

    Example: Copy Number ___ of ___ Copies
    Headquarters, 123 BSB, 1ˢᵗ BCT *(or*
    Headquarters, 52ⁿᵈ Sus Bde))
    Smallville, OH 12345-6789
    (DTG)
    (MRN)

4. Unless otherwise indicted, all pages will be indicated as (UNCLASSIFIED) at the top of each page and under the page number.

5. References. The basic plan/order and each annex will list only those references applicable to that element. References listed in the basic plan/order need not be repeated in subsequent annexes, appendices, tabs, or enclosures.

6. Paragraphing.

    a. When there is only one paragraph to any one element, that paragraph is un-numbered. When a paragraph is subdivided, it must have at least two sub-divisions. The tabs are 0.25 inches and the space is doubled between paragraphs. Subsequent lines of text for each paragraph may be flush left or equally indented at the option of the chief of staff or executive officer, as long as consistency is maintained throughout the order.

    b. When paragraphs are sub-divided, they will be numbered and lettered as follows:

        1., a., (1), (a), 1., a.

    c. Each progressive sub-division of a paragraph will be for-matted as follows: (double space)

        1. Upper and Lower Case - **BOLD.**

            a. <u>Upper and Lower Case and Underlined</u>.

                (1) Upper and Lower Case.

                    (a) Upper and Lower Case.

                        1. Upper and Lower Case.

                            a. Upper and Lower Case.

      b. Las subdivision is 0.25" indented from its parent.

7. Page numbering:

    a. Pages preceding the basic plan/order are numbered using lower case Roman Numeral (i.e., i, ii).

    b. Pages of the basic plan/order are numbered with Arabic Numbers (i.e., 1, 2, 3).

    c. Pages of annexes, appendices, tabs, and enclosures are numbered as follows:

        (1) Annex A, page 1 is number A-1.

        (2) Annex A, Appendix 1, page 2 is numbered A-1-2.

        (3) Annex A, Appendix 1, Tab A, page 2 is numbered A-1-A-2.

        (4) Annex A, Appendix 1, Tab A, Exhibit 1, page 2 is numbered A-1-A-1-2.

8. Capitalization and Punctuation.

    a. Names of geographic locations are capitalized (BALTIMORE).

    b. Paragraph titles are capitalized and underlined (SOLID CAPITALS).

    c. Full capitalization should be used on proper names (Task Force BRAVO, OBJECTIVE NAIL, AXIS RED, etc.).

    d. All title designations are in upper and lower case with the initial capitals (Task Force).

e. Whenever reference is made to a specific annex within the plan/order, use the following format:

(1) Capital letters will be used when identifying the title of annex referred to, i.e., IAW annex C (OPERATIONS).

(2) When referring to appendices, tabs, or enclosures, the title will be in upper and lower case, i.e., Appendix 12 (Fire Support) to Annex C (OPERATIONS).

(3) Do not use the word "See" when referring to an annex, appendix, enclosure, or tab.

9. Abbreviations.

a. Use abbreviations as authorized in AR 310-50. Be consistent. Do not use acronyms and abbreviations not found in FM 1-02 or JP 1-02.

b. Spell out the entire acronym or abbreviation and place the acronym or abbreviation between parentheses at first use in the document. After this first use, use the acronym or abbreviation throughout the document.

10. The final draft must be proof-read for punctuation, grammar, and spelling.

11. Ensure your staff principal concurs with your input to preclude controversies and delays during staffing of the final plan/order.

12. Ensure what is written is in consonance with the higher headquarters plan/order.

Blast from the Past

"An order that can be misunderstood will be misunderstood."

**Field Marshal Helmuth Von Moltke,
Chief of the Prussian General Staff
Battle of Sedan, Sep 1870**

CHAPTER 27

MOVEMENT RATES

★★★

UNOPPOSED RATE OF MOVEMENT	DAY	NIGHT
NON-RESTRICTIVE TERRAIN	24 kmp	24 kmph (w/lights)
RESTRICTIVE	16 kmph	8 kmph (black out)
SEVERELY RESTRICTIVE	1 kmph	1/2 kmph

AGAINST PREPARED DEFENSE (24+ hrs) OPPOSED RATE OF MOVEMENT*	Non-Restrictive	Restrictive	Severely Restrictive
Intense resistance (1:1)	.6	.5	.15
Very Hvy (2:1)	.9	.6	.3
Heavy (3:1)	1.2	.75	.5
Medium (4:1)	1.4	1	.5

Light (5:1)	1.5	1.1	.6
Negligible (6+:1)	1.7+	1.3+	.6+

*Bdes and below in kmph against **prepared defense**. Rates reduced by 1/2 at night. If there is surprise, multiply by (5) for complete surprise, (3) for substantial surprise, or (1.3) for minor surprise. Effects of surprise last 3 days (reduce effect by 1/3 on day 2 and by 2/3 on day 3)

AGAINST HASTY DEFENSE (2-12 hrs)

OPPOSED RATE OF MOVEMENT*	Non-Restrictive	Restrictive	Severely Restrictive
Intense resistance (1:1)	1	.8	.4
Very Hvy (2:1)	1.5	1	.6
Heavy (3:1)	2	1.3	.8
Medium (4:1)	2.4	1.75	.9
Light (5:1)	2.6	2	1
Negligible (6+:1)	3.0+	2.3+	1.1+

*Bdes and below in kmph against **prepared defense**. Rates reduced by 1/2 at night. If there is surprise, multiply by (5) for complete surprise, (3) for substantial surprise, or (1.3) for minor surprise. Effects of surprise last 3 days (reduce effect by 1/3 on day 2 and by 2/3 on day 3)

CHAPTER 28

TASK ORGANIZATIONS

★★★

DIVISION LEVEL	BRIGADE LEVEL
Task Forces (Bde Size)	Task Forces of Bn size
Named TFs (alphabetic order)	Named TFs (alphabetic order)
Named TFs (alphanumeric order)	Named TFs (alphanumeric order)
Brigade Combat Teams (alphanumeric order)	Battalions
Field Artillery Brigade (FAB)	Infantry
Aviation Brigade (CAB)	Air Assault
TFs of Bn size	Airborne
Named TFs (alphabetic order)	Combined Arms
Numbered TFs (alphanumeric order)	RSTA/Cavalry Squadrons
Maneuver Enhancement Brigade (MEB)	
Battlefield Surveillance Brigade (BSFB)	Separate ground maneuver battalions
Headquarters and Headquarters Battalion (HHB)	companies or both
DMAIN	
CP1	Named Teams (alphabetic order)
	Numbered Teams (alphanumeric order)
Band	Field Artillery Battalion
	Aviation Battalion
	Engineer Battalion

SUSTAINMENT BDE
STB
CSSB
TRANS BN
POL Supply BN
MVMT CNT BN (MCB)
MCT
ORDNANCE AMMO BN
EOD BN
TERMINAL OPERATING BN
Medical Co
Fwd Spt Co's

ADA Btry
Chemical Co
Engineer Co
Military Intelligence Co
Military Police
Network Signal/Support

Brigade Support Battalion
Distribution Co
Fwd Maint Co

CSSB
Quartermaster Supply Co (QSC)
Quartermaster Co (Mortuary
   Affairs or "MA")
POL Supply Co (GS)

Petroleum, Pipeline Terminal
   Operating Co
Truck Co (POL)
Truck Co (PLS)

Truck Co (LT/MED)

Truck Co (MDM)
Truck Co (HET)
Cargo Transfer Co (CTC)
Support Maintenance Co (SMC)
Component Repair Co (CRC)
Human Resource Co (Postal, R5)
Finance Co

Ammo Co (Modular)
Water Purification &
   Distribution Co
Quartermaster Field
   Service Co (FSC)
Quartermaster Heavy
   Aerial Supply Co
Aerial Delivery Co
Quartermaster Force
   Provider Co
Quartermaster Hvy
   Material Support Co

CHAPTER 29

COMMAND RELATIONSHIP DEFINITIONS

At the theater level, when Army forces operate outside the US, they are assigned under a "Joint Forces Command or "JFC". A JFC is a combatant commander, sub unified commander, or a joint task force commander (JTF) commander authorized to exercise COCOM or operational control (OPCON) over a joint force. Combatant commanders provide strategic direction and operational focus to forces by developing strategy, planning campaigns, organizing the theater, and establishing command relationships.

1. **ORGANIC**. An element assigned to and forming an essential part of a military organization.

2. **ASSIGNED**. Units or personnel placed in an organization where such placement is relatively permanent and/or where such organization controls, administers, and provides logistic support to units or personnel for the primary function, or greater portion of the functions, of the unit or personnel.

3. **ATTACHED**. Units or personnel temporarily placed in an organization. Subject to limitations imposed by the attachment order, the commander of the formation, unit, or organization receiving the attachment will exercise the same degree of mission command as he/she does over units and personnel organic to his/her command (parent organization retains responsibility for transfer/promotion of personnel).

4. **OPERATIONAL CONTROL (OPCON). (NATO)** Authority delegated to a commander to...
   - Direct forces assigned so he may accomplish specific missions or tasks usually limited by function, time, or location
   - Deploy units concerned.
   - Retain or assign tactical control of those units.

   OPCON does not include authority to assign separate employment of components of the units concerned, nor does it include service support control or matters of administration, discipline, internal organization, or unit training.

5. **COMBATANT COMMAND (COCOM). (DOD)** The non-transferable command authority exercised only by combatant commanders unless the NCA direct otherwise. Combatant commanders exercise it over assigned forces. COCOM provides full authority to organize and employ commands and forces to accomplish mission, they exercise COCOM through subordinate commands, to include sub-unified commands, service component commands, functional component commands, and JTFs.

6. **OPERATIONAL COMMAND (OPCOM). (NATO)** OPCOM is inherent in COCOM. The authority granted to a commander to assign missions or tasks to subordinate commanders, to deploy units, to reassign forces, and to retain or delegate operational and/or tactical control as necessary. OPCON may be exercised at any echelon at or below the level of the combatant command. It can be delegated or transferred. It does not include responsibility for administration or logistics.

7. **TACTICAL COMMAND (TACOM). (NATO)** The authority delegated to a commander to assign tasks to forces under his command for the accomplishment of the mission assigned by a higher authority.

8. <u>**TACTICAL CONTROL**</u> **(TACON). (NATO)** TACON is authority normally limited to the detailed and specific local direction of movement and maneuver of forces to accomplish a task. It allows commanders below combatant command level to apply force and direct the tactical use of sustainment assets but does not provide authority to change organizational structure or direct administrative or logistical support. TACON is often the command relationship established between forces of different nations in a multinational force. It may be appropriate when tactical level Army units are placed under another service headquarters. Army commanders make one Army force TACON to another when they want to withhold authority to change the subordinate force organizational structure and leave responsibility for administrative support or sustainment with the parent unit of the subordinate force.

IF RELATIONSHIP IS:		INHERENT RESPONSIBILITIES ARE:							
		Has Command Relation-ship with:	May Be Task Organized by:	Receives CSS from:	Assigned Position or AO By:	Provides Liaison To:	Establishes/ Maintains Communica-tions with:	Has Priorities Established by:	Gaining Unit Can Impose Further Com-mand or Sup-port Relationship of:
COMMAND	Attached	Gaining unit	Gaining unit	Gaining unit	Gaining unit	As re-quired by gaining unit	Unit to which attached	Gaining unit	Attached; OPCON; TACON; GS; GSR; R; DS
	OPCON	Gaining unit	Parent unit and gaining unit; gain-ing unit may pass OPCON to lower HQ. Note 1	Parent unit	Gaining unit	As re-quired by gaining unit	As required by gaining unit and parent unit	Gaining unit	OPCON; TACON; GS; GSR; R; DS
	TACON	Gaining unit	Parent unit	Parent unit	Gaining unit	As re-quired by gaining unit	As required by gaining unit and parent unit	Gaining unit	GS; GSR; R; DS
	Assigned	Parent unit	Parent unit	Parent unit	Gaining unit	As re-quired by parent unit	As required by parent unit	Parent unit	Not Applicable
SUPPORT	Direct Support (DS)	Parent unit	Parent unit	Parent unit	Supported unit	Supported unit	Parent unit; Supported unit	Supported unit	Note 2
	Reinforc-ing (R)	Parent unit	Parent unit	Parent unit	Reinforced unit	Rein-forced unit	Parent unit; reinforced unit	Reinforced unit: then parent unit	Not Applicable
	General Support Reinforc-ing (GSR)	Parent unit	Parent unit	Parent unit	Parent unit	Rein-forced unit and as re-quired by parent unit	Reinforced unit and as required by parent unit	Parent unit; then reinforced unit	Not Applicable
	General Support (GS)	Parent unit	Parent unit	Parent unit	Parent unit	As re-quired by parent unit	As required by parent unit	Parent unit	Not Applicable

NOTE 1. In NATO, the gaining unit may not task organize a multinational unit (see TACON).
NOTE 2. Commanders of units in DS may further assign support relationships between their subordinate units and elements of the supported unit after coordination with the supported commander.

Figure 29-1 Command and Support Relations

CHAPTER 30

SUSTAINMENT BATTLE STAFF DUTY DESCRIPTIONS

★★★

30.1 The Sustainment Brigade BATTLESTAFF

1. **Battlestaff** is a non-doctrinal term that describes the group of officers, NCOs, and soldiers that participate in the Sustainment Bde/CSSB planning process. This group expands as the mission and situation dictates, though there are constraints on its general size due to space limitations.

2. **S-1.** The S-1 is the brigade's principal staff officer frr internal human resources support and other issues impacting on the health, moral, and welfare of assigned and attached sustainment brigade soldiers. The S-1 coordiantes medical, religious, and legal support and is responsible for developing the human resource support portion of the operations plan or order. The S-1 is directly linked with the Human Resourcess Command (HRC) for strength management, replacement operationspersonnel accounting, and strength reporting. The S-1 provides technical guidance to all subordinate battalion S-1s.

   a. **MDMP Responsibilities**. Upon receiving the mission, the S-1 gives current friendly unit strength estimates, critical shortages, and available external personnel support.

Throughout the planning process, the S-1 is also the staff proponent for the Sustainment Brigade Chaplain, Surgeon, and in certain circumstances Safety. Beginning with Mission Analysis, the S-1 builds the personnel/human resources estimate, creating an all encompassing casualty estimation and casualty evacuation during war gaming. Simultaneously, based on availability from higher headquarters, the S-1 estimates replacement numbers, and in conjunction with S-4, and the XO, determines the priority of fill to the units. In COA development and COA decision brief, the S-1 makes recommendations to the command based on personnel supportability, i.e. casualty estimations, casualty evacuation, and the ability to maintain unit replacement flow.

b. **OPORD/OPLAN Responsibilities.** The S-1 develops the personnel and administration portions of Sustainment Brigade OPLANS and collects and compiles the following appendices: Annex F-Appendix 2 (Personnel Services Support) which includes Tab C (Legal Support), Tab D (Religious Support), and Annex F-Appendix 3 (Health Service Suport). The S-1 in conjunction with (ICW) the assigned Safety Officer, contributes to the development of Annex E-Appendix 2 (Safety) and Annex E-Appendix 9 (Force Health Protection) ICW the Brigade Suregeon.

References:	ADP/ADRP 3-0 Unified Land Operations
FM 1-0	Human Resources Support
FM 1-04	Legal Support to the Operational Army
ATP 1-01	S-1 Operations
ATP 1-02	Theater-Level Human Resource Support
ATP 1-05.1	Religious Support and the Operations Process

ADP/ADRP 5-0 The Operations Process
UNIT TACSOP

Participates: All Battlestaff planning sessions.

Brief: As required at: Mission Analysis, COA Decision Brief, Orders Brief

3. **S-2.** The Brigade Intelligecne Officer (S-2) identifies threat composition, strength, capabilities, and courses of action; conducts intelligence and sustainment preparation of the operational environment; and provides terrain and weather analysis. Support consists of monitoring the current situation, war gaming as the enemy commander, coordinating and synchronizing the IPB effort, conducting parallel planning with higher, adjacent, and subordinate headquarters, and providing intelligence input to all plans, orders, and fragos.

   a. **MDMP Responsibilities**. The S-2 monitors the intelligence requirements to support current and future operations; monitors intelligence analysis of higher, lower, adjacent, and subordinate units, coordinates with other intelligence agencies to effectively provide predictive and timely intelligence to support logistics missions. During Mission Analysis, provides threat Most Likely/ Most Dangerous Courses of Action (MLCOA/MDCOA). The S-2 (ICW the S-3) is responsible for the initial development of the Brigade's Intelligence Collection Plan, and serves as the opposing forces during Course of Action Analysis (Wargaming).

   b. **OPORD/OPLAN Responsibilities**. Responsible for the following OPLAN/OPORD/ FRAGORD input: Enemy Forces, Intelligence, Electronic Warfare, Deception, Coordinating Instructions, Annex B (Intelligence), and (ICW the S-3) Annex L (Intelligence Collection). The S-2 also provides input to the Decision Support Matrix and Synchronization Matrix.

References:

ADP/ADRP 3-0	Unified Land Operation
ADP/ADRP 5-0	The Operations Process
ADP/ADRP 2-0	Intelligence
ATP 2-01	Plan Requirements and Assess Collection
ATP 2-33.4	Intelligence Analysis
FM 2-01.3	C2, Intelligence Preparation of the Battlefield (IPB)
FMI 2-01.301	Specific Tactics, Techniques, & Procedures and Appl for IPB
FM 2-91.6	Solider Surveillance & Reconnaissance Fundamentals
FM 3-55	Information Collection

Participates: All Battle Staff planning sessions and all briefings from MA through Orders Briefing.

Briefs: Provides briefing input to all briefings from MA though Orders issue. In addition to briefing slides/input, products include:

Image maps

Slope image overlay

Elevation image overlay

Line of Communication overlay

Enemy Situation overlay

Enemy Event Template

NAI Overlay

Intelligence Priorities

Hydrology overlay

MCOO overlay

Key Terrain overlay

Avenue of Approach overlay

Intelligence Synchronization Matrix

Enemy COAs

Information Collection Plan

4. **S-3.** The Brigade Operations Officer (S-3) synchronizes and integrates sustainment operations with all warfighting

functions across the planning horizons in current operations, future operations, and plans integrating cells in accordance with the commander's intent and planning guidance. The sustainment Brigade S-3 performs the following:

a. Coordinates with supported units to synchronize future operations and the transition from the current operation to a future operation without loss of momentum and unit integrity. The S-3 also plans for and optimizes automation for mission planning, course of action development, rehearsals, operational planning, and after action reviews.

b. **MDMP Responsibilities**. The S-3 (ICW the SPO) leads the Battle Staff through the Military Decision Making Process and supervises development of briefings and written orders. During war gaming, the S-3 supervises the conduct of the war game and arbitrates disputes. The S-3 performs other duties as assigned by the XO.

c. **OPORD/OPLAN Responsibilities**. Responsible for the following input to the Sustainment Brigade OPLAN/OPORD: Friendly Forces, Attachments and Detachments, Assumptions (OPLAN only), Mission, Intent, Tasks to Subordinate Units, Coordinating Instructions, Command and Signal, Annex A (Task Organization), Annex C (Operations Overlay), Annex L (ICW the S-2) (Information Collection), Annex M (Assessment), Annex Q (Knowledge Management ICW Knowledge Management Officer), Annex R (Reports), Annex V (Interagency Coordination), and Annex Z (Distribution).

References: FM 3-06 Series
FM 3-07   Stability Opns and Support Opns
FM 6-0   Commanders and Staff
　　　　　 Organizations and Operations Guide

ADP/ADRP 1-02 Operations Terms and Graphics
ADP/ADRP 3-0 Unified Land Operations
ADP/ADRP 5-0 The Operations Process
ADP/ADRP 6-0 Mission Command
ATP 4-0.1 Army Distribution
ATP 4-90 The Brigade Support Battalion
ATP 4-93 The Sustainment Brigade
ATP 4-94 The Theater Sustainment Command
TACSOP, SUSTAINMENT BRIGADE TACSOP

Participates: Mission Analysis, COA Development, War Gaming, OPORD/OPLAN review and production.

Brief: Mission Analysis, COA Briefing, Decision Brief, Warning Orders, Contingency Plans

5. **PLANS OFFICER.** As required, the Brigade Plans Officer prepares, coordinates, and publishes operation orders and plans. The Plans Officer assists the S-3 in the execution of his/her duties and plans for operations for mid-range to long range time horizons and developing plans, orders, branches, and sequels based on ordrs for HHQ, projected outcome of current operations, and sustainment brigade commander's guidance. Normally, the Plans Officer will assist in the following tasks: Fighting friendly forces during the war game, assisting the S-3 producing portions of the order. He/she is directly responsible to write and proofread OPLANs/OPORDs before release, manages task organization, writes FRAGORDs, briefs subordinate commands, and takes briefings from higher commands. Primary responsible individual for LSA/Base Cluster defense plans. Performs other duties as assigned by the S-3.

References: Same as for S-3

Participate: In all of the Sustainment unit and higher headquarters related planning activities and responsibilities and War Gaming.

Brief: None. (Be prepared to brief in absence of S-3)

6. **S-4.** The Logistics Officer (S-4) is responsible for all aspects of internal sustainment and readiness. Primary task include: tactical maintenance, supply, transportation and field services planning for contingency missions and training exercises. Responsible for integrating and synchronizing sustainment support considerations internal to the sustainment unit with other warfignting functional areas in the development of estimates, plans, annexes, and orders for internal sustainment operations, tracks the current operation, provides staff oversight of food service operations, property book operations, and maintenance operations. Monitors current operations to endure sustainment systems continually support the Sus Bde forces. Maintains liaison with higher, supporting, and supported organizations to rapidly and effectively transfer logistical planning and operational information between affected units.

   a. **MDMP Responsibilities.** The S-4 (ICW the SPO) recommends priorities for allocating resources and determining the Units Concept of Support. Determines the adequacy of and recommends priorities for employing logistics support units. The S-4 performs other duties as assigned by the XO.

   b. **OPORD/OPLAN Responsibilities.** Responsible for the following input to the Sustainment Brigade OPLAN/OPORD: Sustainment Para, Coordinating Instructions (where applicable), Annex F (Sustainment) ICW the SPO.

References:	FM 3-06 Series
FM 3-07	Stability Opns and Support Opns
FM 4-95	Logistics Operations
FM 6-0	Commanders and Staff Organizations and Operations Guide
ADP/ADRP 1-02	Operations Terms and Graphics
ADP/ADRP 3-0	Unified Land Operations
ADP/ADRP 4-0	Sustainment
ADP/ADRP 5-0	The Operations Process
ADP/ADRP 6-0	Mission Command
ATP 4-0.1	Army Distribution
ATP 4-90	The Brigade Support Battalion
ATP 4-93	The Sustainment Brigade
ATP 4-94	The Theater Sustainment Command

Modular G1-G4 Battlebook

OPLOGPLNR Software, Logistics Estimator, Log Est Worksheet (LEW)

SUSTAINMENT BRIGADE TACSOP

Participate: Mission Analysis, COA Development, War Gaming, OPLAN/OPORD production, Sustainment Synch Matrix Development, Movement Rehearsals, Sustainment Rehearsals, and Decision Support Matrix (DSM) Development.

Brief: Mission Analysis (internal sustainment – man, arm, fix, sustain, and move the force), Decision Brief, and Orders Brief.

7. **MOVEMENT CONTROL OFFICER (ATTACHED).** Develops guidance, plans and policies for the Division's transportation requirements for highway, rail, air, sea transportation and military ocean terminal services. Plans, coordinates, and monitors the Division's transportation assets to meet movement requirements. Prepares the transportation/ mobility appendices for Division support plans/orders. Plans and coordinates with higher and adjacent headquarters/

agencies for transportation services in support of strategic deployments. Provides continuous coordination with and technical assistance to the General Staff, brigades, and subordinate units on all transportation logistic matters. Provides staff supervision for all Division movements.

References:	FM 3-06 Series
FM 4-95	Logistics Operations
FM 6-0	Commanders and Staff Organizations and Operations Guide
ADP/ADRP 1-02	Operations Terms and Graphics
ADP/ADRP 3-0	Unified Land Operations
ADP/ADRP 4-0	Sustainment
ADP/ADRP 5-0	The Operations Process
ADP/ADRP 6-0	Mission Command
ATP 4-0.1	Army Distribution
ATP 4-16	Movement Control
ATP 4-90	The Brigade Support Battalion
ATP 4-93	The Sustainment Brigade
ATP 4-94	The Theater Sustainment Command
FM 4-01.011	Unit Movement Opns, Oct 02
FM 4-0.30	Movement Control
FM 55-1	Transportation Operations
FM 55-15	Transportation Reference Data, Oct 97
Modular G1-G4 Battlebook	
MTMCTEA Ref 94-700-2	

Participate: Mission Analysis, COA Development, Movement Rehearsals, War-Gaming, Sustainment Rehearsal

Brief: By exception only

8. **Sustainment Brigade S-6 (Signal Officer).** The Brigade Signal Staff Officer (S-6) major tasks involve network operations and information management. The S-6 provides the

technical supervision over signal support activities through-out the sustainment brigade. The S-6 further provides tech-nical supervision of all communications asset attachments, coordiantes with supporting signal unit to maintain access to higher echelons common user signal networks, develops an dcoordinates signal support plans, and through the devel-opment of the signal estimate, identifies potential informa-tion network contraints and takes action to offset or adapt to these contraints by ensuring redundant signal means are available to maintain the network.

References:	ADP/ADRP 1-02	Operations Terms and Graphics
	ADP/ADRP 3-0	Unified Land Operations
	ADP/ADRP 5-0	The Operations Process
	FM 6-0	Commanders and Staff Organizations and Operations Guide
	FM 6-02	Series manuals
	FM 6-02.43	Signal Soldier's Roles and Responsibilities
	FMI 6-02.45	Signal Support to Theater

Operations

a. **MDMP Responsibilities.** Develop Signal staff estimate. Identify all non-doctrinal communications require-ments. Identify all communications restrictions to the Battle Staff. Ensure that any course of action developed is communications supportable. Provide mission com-mand evaluation to course of action selection.

b. **OPORD/OPLAN Responsibilities.** Prepare all signal and distribution annexes to Sus Bde OPLANs/OPORDs. Provide information exchange with the Signal Battalion S3 for concurrent planning. Responsible for ISSO. ISSO responsibilities are as follows: Responsible for tactical distribution and CP reproduction for the Sus Bde. Manages the Sus Bde Communications Security (COMSEC) distribution, accountability, and destruction within the Sus Bde. Prepares Annex H (Signal) to Sus Bde OPLANs/OPORDs

Participates: Mission Analysis, COA Development, COA Analysis, War Gaming, and OPLAN/OPORD Development/Production.

Brief: OPLAN/OPORD para 5 Command and Signal; other by exception

9. **CBRN Officer.** The Sustainment Brigade CBRN Officer is overall responsible for any and all related NBC issues for the Sus Bde during tactical operations. Upon receiving the mission, the Sus Bde CBRN Officer provides information on the Sus Bde's MOPP and radiation exposure status, currently assigned chemical units, availability of external chemical support, and a summary of recent and present enemy CBRN events that may indicate future actions. Along with the S-2, he/she develops possible enemy courses of action, determines enemy capabilities, and recommends PIR/IR and NAIs as related to CBRN operations. During Mission Analysis, the Sus Bde CBRN Officer provides constraints from higher headquarters on the use of nuclear weapons and acceptable risks, riot control agents, and herbicides. He also identifies any terrain restrictions relevant to unit dispersion, decontamination, and smoke operations. In the development and analysis of each COA, he makes recommendations on each COA in regards to the principles of NBC defense, contamination avoidance, protection, and decontamination. He continuously analyzes the vulnerability of friendly dispositions to CBRN strikes and makes recommendations and coordination with the S-4, supported unit CBRN (Chem) Off, G5, AC2, and

ADA on the supportability and feasibility of decontamination and smoke operations. As a member of the Brigade's Special Staff, and the Battle Staff, the Brigade CBRN Officer is the tactical POC for all CBRN issues in the Brigade, and is in constant communication with the CBRN personnel manning the Main CP, CP1 and Major Subordinate Commands. Collects and compiles the CBRN paragraph (Annex E 'Protection', Para 3a(6)) to Brigade's OPLANs/ OPORDs.

References: ADP/ADRP 1-02 Operations Terms and Graphics
FM 3-11.3   Multiservice TTPs for CBRNE Containment, Feb 06
FM 3-11.4   Multiservice TTPs for CBRNE Protection
FM 3-11.5   Multiservice TTPs for CBRNE Decontamination
FM 3-50   Smoke Operations, Dec 90
FM 3-101   Chemical Staffs and Units, Nov 93
FM 3-11 Multiservice TTPs for NBC Defense Ops, Mar 03

Participate: All Battle Staff Planning Sessions and War Gaming

Brief: None

10. **Support Operations Officer/Plans Officer (SPO).** The Sustainment Brigade SPO in conjunction with his/her staff plans and cooridnates support operations. Support Operations is the logistics function of planning, coordinating, and distributing all classes of supply, maintenance, and field services to supported organizations. The SPO balances external sutainment support requirements with sustainment capabilities. The SPO along with his/her staff conducts distribution operations, maintenance

management, operational contract support, and commodity management of general supplies, ammunition, fuel, and water.

a. **MDMP Responsibilities.** The S-4 (ICW the SPO) recommends priorities for allocating resources and determining the Units Concept of Support. Determines the adequacy of and recommends priorities for employing logistics support units. The S-4 performs other duties as assigned by the XO.

b. **OPORD/OPLAN Responsibilities.** Responsible for the following input to the Sustainment Brigade OPLAN/OPORD: Sustainment Para, Coordinating Instructions (where applicable), Annex F (Sustainment) ICW the SPO.

References:	FM 3-06 Series
FM 3-07	Stability Opns and Support Opns
FM 4-95	Logistics Operations
FM 6-0	Commanders and Staff Organizations and Operations Guide
ADP/ADRP 1-02	Operations Terms and Graphics
ADP/ADRP 3-0	Unified Land Operations
ADP/ADRP 4-0	Sustainment
ADP/ADRP 5-0	The Operations Process
ADP/ADRP 6-0	Mission Command
ATP 4-0.1	Army Distribution
ATP 4-90	The Brigade Support Battalion
ATP 4-93	The Sustainment Brigade
ATP 4-94	Theater Sustainment Command

Modular G1-G4 Battlebook
OPLOGPLNR Software, Logistics Estimator, Log Est
  Worksheet (LEW)
SUSTAINMENT BRIGADE TACSOP

Participate: Mission Analysis, COA Development, War Gaming, OPLAN/OPORD production, Sustainment Synch Matrix Development, Movement Rehearsals, Sustainment Rehearsals, and Decision Support Matrix (DSM) Development.

Brief: Mission Analysis (external sustainment – man, arm, fix, sustain, and move the force), Course of Action Development, Analysis/War Gaming, Decision Brief, and Orders Brief.

30.2 CSSB/BSB BATTLESTAFF

1. <u>Battalion Commander (BC)</u>

a. Prvovides mission command of all untis assigned and attached to the sustainment organization. The commander creates a positive command climate to inculate and foster trust and mutal understanding. The BSB Commander is 'dual-hatted' as Senior Tactical Commander of Brigade Support Area (BSA) (BSB only).

b. Approves Warning Orders (WARNORDs).

c. Approves restated mission. –

d. Provides initial planning guidance and initial Commander's Intent (written if time available).

e. Approves courses of action (COAs).

f. Decides on a COA.

g. Approves Commander's Critical Information Requirements (CCIR) list.

h.   Provides final Commander's Intent.

i.   Approves final operations plans and orders (OPLANs/ OPORDs).

j.   Approves fragmentary orders (FRAGORDs).

k.   Approves command priorities for internal support.

2.   **Battalion Executive Officer (XO)**. In addition to commanding in the Battalion Commander's absence:

a.   Serves as the Comamnder's chief of staff. The XO directs, coordinates, supervises, trains, an synchronizes the work of the staff ad ensures effective and prompt staff actions.

b.   Serves as Command Post (CP) OIC.

c.   The XO must understand the Comamnder's intent and ensures the battalion staff implements it. He/she provides the comamnder with the tools to visualize, describe, direct, and assess operations. Implements BCs directives and supervises MDMP. The XO ensures staff unity of effort and coordination.

d.   Rehearses the staff for all staff briefings, rehearsals, and battle update briefs (BUBs).

3. S2 & S3 (Operations and Intelligence Officers).

a.   Serves as plans and orders officer-in- charge (OIC). Responsible principally for planning of sustainment unit deployment flow of personnel and equipment from home station through staging base(s) into the area of operations (AO).

    *   "WFFA" - Responsible for coordinating and synchronizing the following war fighting functional area for the BSB and BSA:
- Protection (Air Defense Artillery (ADA), Survivability)
- Movement and Maneuver (Countermobility-Mobility Engineer Support)
- Fire Support (FS)
- Intelligence (Intel)
- Mission Command (MC).

  * Also supervises & coordinates:
- Terrain/Land management
- Tenant unit perimeter defense integration
- Military police/Security Forces (SECFOR) integration support
- Tactical combat force (TCF) integration -
- BSA quick reaction force (QRF) (BSB)
- Perimeter and area of influence defense planning
- Communications
- Operations, physical, logistics, and signal security (OPSEC. PHYSEC, LOGSEC, & SIGSEC).
- Tactical movements (convoys, displacements and occupation plan).
- Sustainment Engineering

b. Serves Officer-in-Charge (OIC) of Sustainment Unit Movement Plans Cell.

c. Performs time-available analysis in concert with (ICW) XO for each step in the planning process (adhering to "1/3-2/3 rule" - 1/3 of time available given to Bn staff, and 2/3 to subordinate elements).

d. Issues coordinated WARNORDs when approved by BC.

e. Maintains Battalion tactical map overlays/situation map of Brigade and Division and friendly and enemy situation.

f. Prepares and maintains battalion consolidated reports matrix showing reports requirements, time due-in and -out, and when they arrived and were sent.

g. With other staff input, formulates the recommended Commander's Critical Information Requirements (CCIR).

h. Maintains status of answers to CCIR/ISSUES. Significant Activities and detailed Daily Staff Journal Duty Officer's Log (DA Form 1594) for the battalion.

i. Drafts, coordinates, and consolidates staff input for OPORDs, OPLANs and FRAGORDs:

(1) Drafts Map Sheets, References, Time Zone. Used, and Task Organization sections.

(2) ICW Spt Ops Section, drafts Para 1, <u>Situation</u>, and any associated annexes.

(3) ICW Spt Ops Section, drafts restated mission and Para 2, Mission.

(4) ICW Spt Ops Section, drafts Para 3, Execution, and any associated annexes. Ensures Commanders Intent is incorporated.

(5) Includes the S4 and S1 input for Para 4, Service Support, and any associated annexes.

(6) Drafts Para 5. Command and Signal

4. **<u>Support Plans Operations Officer. (SPO)</u>** The SPO is principally responsible for developing the concept of support for assigned support area. The SPO synchronizes operations to maximize efficiencies and ensure priorities are executed in accordance with published orders. The SPO section is responsible for establishing and maintaining the logistics common operating picture for the command.

    a. **BSB**. Principally responsible for taking <u>BCT estimated requirements</u> (from the Bde S4) and recommending to the Battalion Commander how the BCT is best supported by available capabilities. Responsible for taking the BCT order/DSM and synchronizing with subordinate Bn's and FSC's replenishment operations (RO) mission taskings and recommending to the Battalion Commander how the BSB can best execute with available assets and capabilities.

CSSB. Responsible for taking Sustainment Bde replenishment operations (RO) mission taskings and recommending to the Battalion Commander how the CSSB can best execute with available assets and capabilities.

    (1) Applies sustainment capabilities in synchronization with forecasted Bde requirements to ensure the right amount is provided at the right place at the right time.

    (2) Provides input to S-3 for determination of specified tasks to unit subordinate elements in OPLAN/OPORD or FRAGORD in Para 3.j. <u>Tasks to Subordinate Elements</u> and 3.i. <u>Coordinating Instructions</u>.

(3)   Provides input to S-3 on concept of operation and mission statement for WARNORDs. OPLANs/ OPORDs and FRAGORDs.

(4)   Prepares and maintains the sustainment map overlay/LCOP and current status of BSB/CSSB DS assets for reporting and CCIR.

(5)   Recommends liaison personnel and locations to Bn Cdr. Normally a 24-hour requirement at HHQ Main Command Post and/or Sustainment Unit HQ.

(6)   Principal coordinator, parallel planner, and battalion liaison for BCT (Sus Bde) planning sessions, higher echelon support, host nation support (HNS) and/or commercially contracted support to the HHQ or on an area support basis.

b.   **BSA – BSB**. Recommends to BCT S3 where to position locations of the BSA, Logistics Release Points (LRPs) and Forward Logistics Elements (FLE). Coordinates CAB/IN/RSTA/Fires Battalion Support Areas ICW with Bn S-4s. Assures these positions are on posted to BCT graphics. Provides representative to BSA Movements Plans Cell.

CSSB. Recommends to the Bn Cdr/Sus Bde SPO/S-3 where to position locations of any projected CRSPs, TTPs, CSCs, "Mini-Marts", and Forward Logistics Elements (FLE). Assures these positions are on posted to HHQ and supported unit graphics. Provides representative to Sus Bde Movements Coordination Cell.

5. S1 (Personnel and Administration Officer).

    a.   Principally responsible for unit human resources and other personnel-related functions and is responsible for coordinating internal HR and administrative support to include coordinating HR support services, personnel accountability, medical & legal services, preventive medicine, Enemy Prisoners of War (EPW) collection, stress management, financial, and civil-affairs ("S5") matters. Prepares personnel estimate.

    b.   Principally responsible for personnel status to assist S-3 in determining relative combat power. Develops unit casualty collection points (CCPs) and EPW/Displaced Civilian (DCs) plans. Serves as the unit Public Affairs Officer (PAO).

    c.   In conjunction with the S4, drafts personnel and administration portions of Para 4, <u>Sustainment</u>, and any associated annexes.

6. <u>S4 (Logistics Officer)</u>.

    a.   Principally responsible for the internal supply, transportation, and service support to the unit's assigned or attached units. Monitors unit field sanitation, Plans for BSA/LSA/FOB damage control, Prepares logistics estimate, Supervises and coordinates the "Sustainment" WFF internal to the unit ICW S1 and BMT.

    b.   Within the BSA/LSA/FOB:

        (1)   Serves as key member of the unit's Movements Plans Cell/Movement Coordination Cell (MCC).

Authority to control of all convoy/vehicle movements and monitors checkpoints, release points, start points, and BSA/LSA/FOB exit and entrance gates.

(2)   Prepares unit feeding plan to include provisions for EPWs, DCs. and Mortuary Affairs Collection point (MACP) site.

(3)   Prepares Traffic Control Plan for the BSA/FOB.

7. S6 (Signal Officer).

a.   Principally responsible for the electromagnetic spectrum operations and networks within the sustainment unit's assigned support area. The sutainment unit may operate remotely from its HHQs and therefore must maintain communications with its Main Command Post. The S-6 focuses on maintaining the integrity of the freency modulation radio and digital communications network, ensuring links, and planning back up systems. Responsible for the full range of tasks associated with network management, systems administration, and systems/software security for all tactical automation.

b.   The S-6 uses the command post node to establish a secure wireless local area network for the logistics network.

c.   The S-6 also coordinates with the Sustainment Automation Support Management Officer (SASMO) making sure functions are reflected in the unit's electronic warfare plan to ensure the security and use of the Very Small Aperture Terminal (VSAT) and wireless Combat Service Suupport Automated Information System Interface (CAISI) network.

CHAPTER 31

INFORMATION UPDATE

★ ★ ★

SUBJECT	BRIEFER
1. **INTRODUCTION**	XO

- Purpose of the Briefing
- What is required at the conclusion of the Briefing

2. **MISSION**	S-3
3. **TASKO**	S-3
4. **ENEMY SITUATION**	S-2/Intel NCO

A - COMPOSITION
B - DISPOSITION
C - COMBAT POWER
D - STRENGTHS
E - WEAKNESSES/VULNERABILITIES
F - CAPABILITIES

5. **WEATHER**	S-2/Intel NCO
6. **TERRAIN**	S-2/Intel NCO
7. **SIGNIFICANT EVENTS SINCE LAST UPDATE**	S-2/Intel NCO
8. **FRIENDLY SITUATION**	S-3

A - MAIN EFFORT

B - PRIORITY OF FIRES

C - BRIEF DESCRIPTION OF RESULTS OF
    OPERATIONS

D - BATTALIONS IN CONTACT

E - BATTALIONS NOT IN CONTACT

F - RESERVES

G - CURRENT FLOT/LOCATION OF
    LEAD ELEMENTS

H - SIGNIFICANT EVENTS SINCE LAST
    UPDATE

I - PROBLEMS (FRIENDLY)

J - OPPORTUNITIES (FRIENDLY)

K - KNOWN STATUS OF FLANKING UNITS

9. <u>SUSTAINMENT CONSIDERATIONS</u>   SPO/S-1/S-4

A - CRITICAL EVENTS SINCE LAST
    UPDATE

B - PROBLEMS

C - OPPORTUNITIES

10. <u>DETERMINATION OF NEED FOR</u>   XO
<u>MORE DETAILED</u> ANALYSIS

Note: This briefing will be conducted at predetermined times as directed by the XO or CDR. The specific intent of this briefing is to update the CDR as soon as possible after his arrival back at unit TOC during tactical or field operations. Additionally, upon receipt of a new mission/order from higher HQs, the CDR may request an initial facts brief/update.

CHAPTER 32

LOGISTICS AUTOMATION REFERENCE

★ ★ ★

ACRONYMS	NAME	FUNCTIONS
BCS3 (S2MC)	Battle Command Sustainment Support System /Sustainment System Mission Command	Interfaces with GCCS-A; Interfaces with Sustainment STAMIS(s); Sustainment information for tactical/Sustainment Commanders; Collect and analyze technical sustainment data; Near real-time sustainment information.
DAMMS-R	Department of the Army Movement Management System-Redesign.Primarily used at Installation level. Is being replaced by TCAIMs-II	Movements Management; Transportation Management; Transportation Resources; Management at Division Through Theater
SAAS	Standard Army Ammunition System	Class V Management; Total Asset Visibility; Inventory Accountability; Material Management Activities
MTS	Movement Tracking System	Near Rear Time (NRT) tracking of sustainment assets on the battlefield with encrypted text messaging; designed to provide command and control over distributed assets supporting and conducting theater operations

SARSS (All Versions)	Standard Army Retail Supply System	Supply Mgt; Stock Control; Receipt/Storage; Requisition/Issue; War reserve; Material Rebuild; Major Item Acquisition; Catalog Processing; Demand/Document History. Used for Class II, III(P), IV, VII, IX
ILAP	Integrated Logistics Analysis Program	Produce Information Management Reports Combining Data from several Standard Systems
SDS	Standard Depot System	Industrial Log System; Industrial Ops/Ammo/AMC; Installation Mgt Standard System; Seamless Info. Processing; Processing Transactions while creating Mgt. Info.
SAMS E /1E /2E (replaces SAMS-1/SAMS-2)	Standard Army Maintenance System–Installation/Table of Distribution and Allowances. Refer to SAMS-E below	Shop Production; Maint. Control Records; Shop Supplies; Order Repair Parts; Equipment. Performance Report; Selected Maint; Equip. readiness; Engineering Data; Life – Cycle Mgt
PBUSE	Standard Property Book System–Redesign	Property/Accountability Reporting; Unit Hand Receipts; SSA Equip. Request /Receipt Interface; Authorization Asset Control; Serial Number Tracking; CBS-X, Reqval
MC4	Theater Army Medical Management Information System	Med. Supply; Med Maint; Med. Assemblage Management; Track Patients
TCAIMS-II	Transportation Coordinator Automated Information Management System	Selected Trans. Functions; Unit Equipment/Pers. Deployment

CTASC	Corps/Theater Automated Data Processing Service Center	Information systems that satisfy tactical information requirements under wartime conditions. CTASC uses SARSS-O to process and monitor the flow of logistics data and to support Class II, III(P), IV, VII, and IX supply actions.
SAMS-E/1E/2E	Standard Army Maintenance System – Enhanced	Motor Pool Ops; Flight Line Ops; BN S-4 Ops; Process PLL; Army Maint. Mgt; SARSS/SAMS Interface; Request Supplies; Forecast Basic Loads; Hand Receipt Asset Visibility; Unit Load Planning; Bulk POL Mgt; Facility Mgt; Produce Flight Packs; Track Aircraft Readiness; Maintain Historical Data; Order Repair Parts

CHAPTER 33

QUICK REFERENCE DATA

★★★

The data listed in the following enclosures provide quick reference data and planning factors. This data must be modified based on METT-TC and equipment availability (026 Report).

33.1 Logistical Planning Data

1. Transportation

Nomen	Model	LIN	Useable cargo area Length	Width	Pallets (40" X 48")	463L Pallet
LMTV	M1078	T60081	147	88	6	1
HEMTT	M977	T59278	216	90	8	2
MTV	M1083	T61908	168	88	6	1
Trailer, 22 1/2 Ton	M871	S70027	350	88	14	3
Trailer, 34 Ton	M872	S70159	485	93	20	4
PLS	M1075	T40999	227	90	8	2

2. Medical

Unit type	Assets
BSB – ABCT	11 ea M997 ambulance (wheel)
	38 ea M113 ambulance (track)

BSB – Stryker	16 ea M1133 Stryker Medical Evac Vehicle (MEV) 20 ea M997 ambulance (wheel)
BSB - IBCT	45 ea M997 ambulance (wheel)
CAB/Cav Sqdn	8 ea M113 ambulance (track)
IN BN/Cav Sqdn	8 ea M997 ambulance (IN)/4 ea M997 ambulance (Cav)
IN BN (Stryker)	4 ea M1133 Stryker Medical Evac Vehicles (MEV)
Fires BN (all BCTs)	3 ea M997 ambulance

3. **Tactical organic unit fuel distribution capacity**

Forward Support Company (FSC)

Type Unit	#/Type Veh/Cont	Mobile Gal Avail	Total Fuel Storage Cap
IN BN	4 x Fuel Tank Rack (2.5K)	9,000	15,520 Gal
CAB	6 x M978/6 x Fuel Tank Rack	27,000	61,737 Gal
IN BN (SBCT)	2 x M978/2 x Fuel Tank Rack	9,000	19,143 Gal
FA BN (ABCT)	3 x M978/4 x Fuel Tank Rack	15,750	41,269 Gal
FA BN (IBCT)	4 x Fuel Tank Rack	9,000	21,143 Gal
FA BN (SBCT)	2 x M978/2 x Fuel Tank Rack	9,000	21,236 Gal
Cav Sqdn (ABCT)	3 x M978/1 x Fuel Tank Rack	9,000	24,886 Gal

| Cav Sqdn (IBCT) | 4 x Fuel Tank Rack | 9,000 | 15,785 Gal |
| Cav Sqdn (SBCT) | 2 x M978/2 x Fuel Tank Rack | 9,000 | 17,755 Gal |

Distribution Company, Brigade Support Battalions

Type Unit	#/Type Veh.	Mobile Gallons Avail
ABCT	18 x M978	40,500
	18 x Fuel Tank Rack (2.5K)	72,000
IBCT	5 x M978	11,250
	5 x Fuel Tank Rack (2.5K)	11,250
	2 x Fuel Blivots (500 Gal)	1,000
SBCT	11 x M978	22,500
	12 x Fuel Tank Rack (2.5K)	27,000
	4 x Fuel Blivots (500 Gal)	2,000

TOTAL BRIGADE FUEL HOLDING CAPABILITY (IN GAL)

	BSB	FSCs	UNIT	TOTAL
ABCT	81,000 (21%)	119,250 (31%)	184,200 (43%)	384,450 (100%)
IBCT	23,500 (16%)	58,500 (39%)	67,488 (45%)	149,488 (100%)
SBCT	51,500 (27%)	54,000 (28%)	86,359 (45%)	191,859 (100%)

4. SUSTAINMENT BRIGADE/CSSB FUEL HOLDING UNIT CAP.

a. POL SUPPORT PLT (50K)

(1) Store *600,000* gallons at one location or *300,000* gallons each at two locations.

(2) Can receive and issue up to 200,000 gallons of bulk petroleum per day.

(3) The Area Support Section can store up to *120,000* gallons of bulk petroleum at one location and *60,000* gallons at each of two locations. It can receive and /or issue in any combination up to *120,000* gallons daily.

(4) The distribution section can distribute *48,750* gallons of fuel daily based on 75% availability of fuel dispensing vehicles at two trips per day.

(5) Can establish and operate two hot refueling points using two FARE systems for transitory aircraft operating in their area.

b. POL SUPPORT PLT (210K)

(1) Store up to *1,680,000* gallons at one location or *840,000* gallons each of two locations.

(2) Can receive and issue up to *300,000* gallons of bulk petroleum per day.

(3) The Area Support Section can store up to *120,000* gallons of bulk petroleum at one location and *60,000* gallons at each of two locations.

(4) It can receive and/or issues in any combination up to *120,000* gallons daily.

(5) The distribution section can distribute *48,750* gallons of fuel daily based on 75% availability of fuel dispensing vehicles at two trips per day.

(6) It can also establish and operate two hot refueling points using two FARE systems for transitory aircraft operating in their area.

6 WATER GENERATION

a. Requirements, Appendix B, FM 10-52

AREA	SUSTAIN	MIN
Temperate area	6.1 gal/man/day	3.4 g/m/d
Tropical area	7.7 "	5.0 g/m/d
Arctic area	6.6 "	3.9 g/m/d
Arid area	7.9 "	5.2 g/m/d

b. Sustainment unit capabilities:

(1) BSB equipped with 1 TWPS: 30,000 gal/day (20 hr operation/fresh water source)
" " 2 LWS (Lightweight Water Pur): 5,000 gal/day (20 hr opn/fresh)
Total BSB Water Production: *35,000* gal/day

(2) Water Purification & Distribution Company,

(a) Production: 6 ea 3K ROWPU: *360,000* gal/day (20 hr/day/fresh source)
3 ROWPU/PLT x 2 PLTs

(b) Storage: Water storage for *168,000* gal. Distribution Plt can provide storage of *168,000* gals at one location or *80,000* gals at two locations.

(c) Distribution: Can distribute up to *66,000* gal of water/day base on 75% equipment availability and two trips/day

c. Doctrinal notes (Ref Figure 33-1)

(1) Water is provided through supply point distribution and transported by units via the 900 gallon hippo

trailer. In an arid environment, where insufficient water sources are available, any additional water is provided by corps.

(2)   Sustainment Bde medium truck companies may augment Water Purification & Distribution Companies in distributing water using 5,000 gallon semi trailers, or using 4,750 or 3,000 gallon Semi Mobile Fabric Tanks (SMFT) on semi trailers.

(3)   Sustainment Bdes/CSSBs use SMFTs to haul water to Support Brigades without operational water purification sources to Spt Bdes/BCTs who have shut down their ROWPUs as a result of tactical operations. FAWPSS are used for remote locations. FAWPSS and full 500 gallon drums can be loaded on vehicles, towed short distances, or sling loaded by aircraft.

Modular Water Support

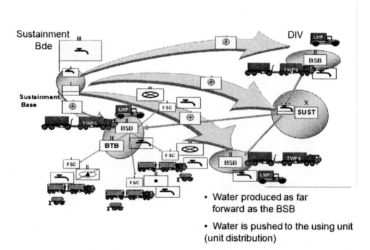

* Water produced as far forward as the BSB

* Water is pushed to the using unit (unit distribution)

Figure 33-1 Modular Water Distribution within Corps AOR

7. Planning Factor Rates in Pounds Per Person Per Day (PPD) (References: CDRSC ST 101-6, Theater Sustainment Handbook, Chapter 4)

Class II   1.6 PPD Southwest Asia (SWA)
            2.2 PPD Northeast Asia (NEA)
            1.9 PPD Other

to include Chemical Defense Equipment add:
            NATO +2.205 PPD
            SWA   +3.270 PPD
            NEA   +4.038 PPD

Class III (P)   .51 PPD

Class IV   9.92 PPD (NEA)
                           8.09 PPD (SWA)
                           9.01 PPD (Other)

Class VI (after D+60)   2.06 PPD temperate
                           3.74 PPD tropical/arid
                           1.78 PPD artic

Class VIII   1.03 PMD Southwest Asia

Class IX   N/A – calculated in tonnage

33.2 Personnel Loss Estimates.

a. Short Term Loss Estimates (Up to 5 days)

(1) Table 4-17. Distribution of Battle Losses by Branch.

Infantry	62.0%
Artillery	3.6%
Armor	23.1%
Engineers	3.3%
All Others	8.0%

b. Units in contacts (% Loss)

	Battle Loss	Non-Battle Loss	Total
Covering & Security Force			
Action ATTACK	0.9	0.3	1.2
Meeting Engagement	2.4	0.3	2.7
Of a position 1st day	3.8	0.3	4.1
Succeeding days	1.9	0.3	2.2
Of a fortified zone 1st day	6.3	0.3	6.6
Succeeding days	3.2	0.3	3.5
Defense:			
Meeting Engagement	1.5	0.3	1.8
Of a position 1st day	1.9	0.3	2.2
Succeeding days	1.0	0.3	1.3
Of a sector 1st day	3.2	0.3	1.9
Succeeding days	1.6	0.3	1.9
Inactive situation (In contact,			
neither attacking)	0.7	0.3	1.6
Pursuit	1.3	0.3	1.6
Retirement and delaying action	0.7	0.3	1.0

33.3 CHEMICAL PLANNING FACTORS

* FOG OIL CONSUMPTION RATE FOR SMOKE GENERATION:
  ONE (1) GAL DRUM/GENERATOR/MISSION HOUR

* WATER CONSUMPTION FOR OPERATIONAL DECON:
  100-150 GALS/WHEEL VEHICLE
  150-200 GALS/ARMORED OR LARGER VEHICLE

  (UNIT LEVEL VEHICLE WASHDOWN 1-3 MINUTES/ VEHICLE)

* WATER CONSUMPTION FOR THOROUGH DECON:
  400-500 GALS/VEHICLE
  (1 CHEMICAL DECON PLT CAN DECON 12 VEHICLE/HOUR)

* DEGREDATION EFFECT OF MOPP 4:
  MULTIPLY TASK TIME BY 1.5 TO 2.5

HISTORICAL PLANNING RATES FOR THE ARRAY OF FRIENDLY FORCES:

FRIENDLY MISSION	FRIENDLY:ENEMY	NOTES
DELAY	1:6	
DEFEND	1:3	Prepared and Fortified
DEFEND	1:2.5	Hasty
ATTACK	3:1	Prepared and Fortified
ATTACK	2.5:1	Hasty Position
COUNTERATTACK	1:1	Flank

33.4 AVIATION REFERENCE DATA

AERIAL RESUPPLY - GENERAL

Aerial resupply operations are extremely important in both heavy and light divisions. Units can use aerial resupply to reduce the impact of time/distance factors on logistical operations. Detailed planning and execution are necessary to effectively utilize air assets for logistical operations. Proper training for ground support personnel at the Landing Zone/Pickup Zone and the Drop Zone is critical to mission success.

AERIAL RESUPPLY

Aerial resupply is a method of delivering supplies and equipment from an aircraft to ground elements. Airdrop support units are organic to the separate airborne brigade and to the airborne division which rely heavily on air lines of communication for logistics support. Armored, infantry, and mechanized divisions have no organic support. They rely on corps units or teams for airdrop support.

Aerial resupply is accomplished using airland and airdrop techniques. The air dropping of supplies is a joint effort involving the Army and the Air Force. Air Force aircraft are used most often. Air Force assets are used for airdrop, and airland resupply operations. Army helicopters may drop supplies, but are most often used to sling load supplies.

1. Selecting the Drop/Landing (DZ/LZ) Zone. The selection of a usable drop/landing zone is extremely important. Logistical and tactical considerations are analyzed to ensure the DZ/LZ is correctly placed to support the mission. The area must be accessible to the aircraft that will use the site. The unit requesting an aerial resupply mission (preplanned, immediate, or emergency) coordinates with the support operations officer and is

responsible for selecting, securing, preparing, and marking the drop/landing area, and providing qualified ground guides and unloading teams to expedite aircraft turnaround time.

As a general rule, a DZ/LZ must provide for 30 meters separation between utility aircraft and 40 meters between cargo aircraft. Obstructions such as tree stumps, bushes, or man-made objects that could damage the aircraft or the load must be removed before operations can begin. The number of expected aircraft, weather, and light conditions at the time of delivery are also considered in the planning process. If night resupply is scheduled, a larger area is normally needed. The surface should be solid enough to prevent an aircraft or load from bogging down. Excessive slope may preclude helicopter landing. The avenue of approach and departure should be over the lowest obstacle in the direction of the prevailing winds.

Weather conditions often determine the size of the landing zone. Generally, hot and humid conditions at a landing site will decrease the lift capabilities of helicopters. Therefore, a large area with a longer approach and/or departure route is required for fully loaded helicopters.

2. Coordination Procedures For Aerial Supply. The unit request goes to the battalion S-4, through the supporting support battalion's support operations section to the MCO in a division environment. The MCO coordinates movement of supplies with the MSB and the FSB support operations sections. If the MCO determines that air resupply is appropriate, the request is passed through the DTO to the G-3. The G-3 operations section allocates helicopters. The G-4 ensures the CSS role for helicopters is considered concurrently with the tactical mission. The priorities for helicopter resupply should be addressed in the division OPORD and used by the MCO. Emergency requests are concurrently passed through both the logistics and operations channels to the brigade S-3 and division G-3. The G-3 operations section approves emergency requests and tasks the aviation brigade to perform the mission.

At the same time, the G-4 coordinates with the SUSTAINMENT BRIGADE support operations branch who coordinates with the RSS, MSB or FSB support operations section to prepare the shipment. A liaison officer from the Aviation Brigade S-3 Air, normally a pathfinder, coordinates with the MCO and support operations section. Throughput of aerial resupply to the using unit is the preferred method of delivery. Regardless of whether the mission is preplanned or emergency, if division helicopters cannot perform it for any reason, the request goes from the division TOC to the corps TOC. The diagram below shows the flow of a preplanned airdrop request.

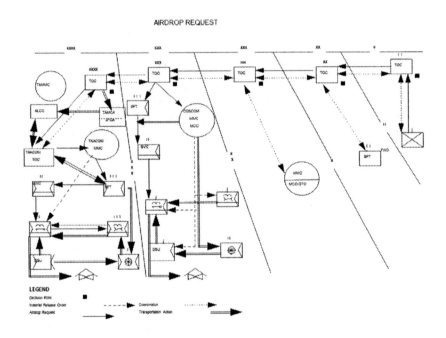

Figure 33-2 Airdrop Request Flow

Aerial resupply is divided into two categories, rotary wing and fixed wing. Rotary wing resupply is normally performed with Army aviation assets. Fixed wing resupply is primarily performed with Air Force assets and requires additional planning and coordination.

ROTARY WING RESUPPLY

Rotary wing aircraft use two methods of delivery - internal load and external load (slingload). The majority of rotary wing resupply will be conducted using UH-60 Blackhawk, CH-47 Chinook, or UH-1 Huey Helicopter. Average expected endurance is between 2 and 2.5 hours.

Aircraft capabilities and Characteristics

Type Aircraft	Weapon System	Max number of rounds	Max effective range	Max external payload	Max internal payload	Ave/Max speed (knots) (KPH) (MPH)	Fuel capacity (pounds) (gallons)	Average fuel consumption (pounds) (gallons)
AH-64	30mm chain gun	1200	3000			120/185 222/342 138/214	2405 370	810 179
	2.75 rkt	76 (4, 19 shot pods)	9000 indirect					
	Hellfire	16	7000+					
OH-58D	50-cal MG	500	2000			80/120 148/222 92/138	780 112	225 43
	2.75 rkt	14 (2, 7 shot pods)	9000 indirect					
	Hellfire	4	7000+					
	Stinger	4	5000					
UH-60				9000	3360	120/193 222/356 138/222	2360 362	960 181
CH-47D				26,000	20,206	125/165 232/306 144/190	6695 1030	2600 522

Type	Max Load (External)	# of Hooks	Usable Length	Usable Width	Usable Height
UH-1	4000 lbs.	1	39 in.	50 in.	50 in.
UH-60	8000 lbs.	1	110 in.	72 in.	54 in.
CH-47	10k - 26k	3*	366 in.	90 in.	78 in.

* Depending on model, may have one center hook and one hook forward and aft

Sling Load Operations:

Ground crew teamwork and proficiency are the most important part of sling load operations. All units should have an ongoing training program to keep ground crews current on unit equipment and train new ground crew personnel. The size of the crew may vary depending on the situation. Generally, three people make up the crew: the signal man, the hook up man, and an assistant. Each crew member will need a separate issue of equipment to perform their mission. Sample Ground Crew Equipment Listing:

Goggles	4240-00-052-3376
Snap Ring Pliers	5120-00-023-0049
Flashlight w/wand	6230-00-163-1856
Static Discharge Probe	1670-01-194-0926

External Load Carrying Devices

- Sling Sets: There are two types currently in use; the 10,000 and 25,000 pound capacity set.

VISIBLE DIFFERENCES BETWEEN THE 10,000 AND 25,000 POUND CAPACITY SLING SETS		
ITEM	10,000 lb. CAPACITY	25,000 lb. CAPACITY
Sling Rope Color	Olive Drab	Black
Sling Rope Diameter	7/8 in	1 1/4 in
Clevis Color	Dull Gray Aluminum	Gold Steel
Number of Chain Links	111	88
Weight	52 lbs.	114 lbs.

- Pallet Slings. Pallet slings have a carrying capacity of 4000 pounds. Two types of slings are in use: The MK 100 and MK 86.

DIFFERENCES BETWEEN THE MK 86 AND MK 100 PALLET SLINGS			
Type	Color of Coded Tubing	Load Height 40 x 48 in pallet	Weight
MK 86 MK 100	Black Yellow	29 to 40 in. 48 to 70 in.	13 lbs. 15 lbs.

- Cargo Nets. There are two types currently in use; the 5,000 and 10,000 pound capacity net.

VISIBLE DIFFERENCES BETWEEN THE 5,000 AND 10,000 POUND CAPACITY CARGO NETS		
ITEM	5,000 lb. CAPACITY	10,000 lb. CAPACITY
Net Color Material Load Zone Size Weight	Olive Drab Nylon Cord 5 ft. sq. 58 lbs.	Black Nylon mesh Cord 6 ft. sq. 96 lbs.

- A-22 Cargo Bag. The bag is an adjustable cotton duck cloth and webbing container consisting of a sling assembly, cover, and four suspension webs. The bag can transport 2000 lbs. of cargo. It can be rigged with or without the cover.

Return of Air Items. Units must develop a detailed plan to return all air items (sling sets, nets and bags) to their supporting unit. The supporting unit will not be able to sustain aerial resupply operations without an effective plan to return these items.

AERIAL RESUPPLY - FIXED WING

Fixed wing aircraft use a variety of methods to deliver supplies- Combat Off Load (COL), Containerized Delivery System (CDS), Door Bundles and Low Velocity Air Drop (LVAD).

Combat off load requires an operational and secure airfield/ field landing strip, material handling equipment is not required to unload palletized supplies. However it should be available to move supplies of the runway or parking area. Fuel storage containers need to be available when using the Aerial Bulk Fuel Delivery System (ABFDS) or "Bladder Birds".

The CDS is the primary method of fixed wing resupply to combat units. Rigger units "rig" the supplies using A-22 containers. Max planning weight is 2000 lbs.

Door Bundles are used to resupply small elements, such as Special Operations Forces (SOF) and Long Range Reconnaissance Detachments (LRSD). Rigger units "rig" the supplies using A-21 containers.

The LVAD (Heavy Drop) uses aerial delivery platforms to deliver Maneuver, Maneuver Support, and Sustainment assets to the battle area. Rigger support and sufficient preparation time is critical to ensure a successful operation.

Parachute rigger units are necessary to configure/pack CDS, Door Bundles and LVAD loads. A rigger detachment can "rig" 50 short tons/day and a rigger company can "rig" 200 short tons/day of all classes of supply. The amounts can increase significantly if rigging involves only like items, i.e. Class I MREs only.

Cargo Aircraft Capabilities and Dimensions

| Type | Cargo Compartment | | | # 463L Pallets | Fuel | CDS Bundles | PAX |
	Length	Height	Width				
C-130	492 in.	108 in	120 in	6	6k	16	90
C-141B	1120 in.	110 in.	123 in.	13	9k	40	200
C-17	986 in.	*162 in.	216 in.	18	N/A	40	**102
C-5A	1452 in.	162	228 in.	36	N/A	N/A	***73
KC-10	1508 in	96 in ****	218 in ****	25	N/A	N/A	69

* 162 in. aft of wing and 147.5 in. under wing

** Potential for 84 additional seats

*** Contingency for 255 seats in cargo compartment

**** Some restrictions due to fuselage profile

CHAPTER 34

SUSTAINMENT ASSETS

★★★

TRANSPORTATION – VEHICLE TYPES

FMTV

TRK CARGO, LMTV: M1078

TRK CARGO, LMTV: M1078
w/CANVAS CARGO TOP

TRK CARGO, LMTV: M1078
w/S-280 SHELTER

LMTV VAN: M1079

TRAILER, CGO, LMTV, DROPSIDE:
M1082

TRK CARGO, MTV: M1083

TRK CARGO, MTV: M1083
w/CANVAS CARGO TOP

TRK CARGO, MTV: M1083
w/S-280 SHELTER

TRK CARGO, MTV: M1083
w/HEIGHT REDUCEABLE SHELTER

TRK CARGO, MTV w/MHE: M1084

TRK CARGO, MTV, LWB: M1085

FMTV

TRK CARGO, MTV, LWB: M1085
w/CANVAS CARGO TOP

TRK CARGO, MTV, LWB: M1085
w/S-280 SHELTER

TRK CARGO, MTV, LWB w/MHE: M1086

TRK, VAN EXPANSIBLE, MTV: M1087

TRK TRACTOR, MTV: M1088

TRK WRECKER, MTV: M1089

TRK 5 TON DUMP, MTV: M1090

TRK TANK POL, MTV, 1500 GAL:
M1091

TRAILER, CGO, MTV DROPSIDE:
M1095

HEMTT'S

TRUCK, CGO, HEMTT: M977

TRUCK, CGO, HEMTT, w/MHE (LT CRANE):
M977 TRUCK, CGO, HEMTT
w/MHE (MED CRANE): M985

TRUCK, ELECT POWER PLANT , HEMTT:
M977EPP

TRUCK, TANK FUEL SERVICEING, HEMTT,
2500 GAL: M978

TRUCK, POTABLE WATER SERVICEING, HEMTT:
M978

TRUCK, TRACTOR, HEMTT: M983

HEMTT'S

TRUCK, WRECKER, HEMTT: M984A1

TRUCK, GUIDED MISSILE TRANSPORTER,
HEMTT: M985GMT

TRUCK, HEMTT-LHS: M977 (XM-1120)

TRUCK, CGO, HEMTT- LHS
w/ 20 FT CONTAINER

TRUCK, CGO, HEMTT- LHS
w/MECC

TRUCK, CGO, HEMTT- LHS
w/FRS (NOTIONAL)

M939 SERIES 5 TON VEHICLES

TRUCK, CARGO, 5 TON: M923

M931 TRACTOR w/5000 GAL TANKER

TRUCK, CARGO, 5 TON: M923
w/CANVAS

M931 TRACTOR w/M871 (30FT FLAT BED TRAILER)

TRUCK, VAN EXPANSIBLE, 5 TON
6x6: M934

M931 TRACTOR w/M871 (30FT STAKE BED TRAILER)

TRUCK, TRACTOR, 5TON: M931

M931 TRACTOR w/M871 (30FT TRAILER) & 20 FT CONTAINER

M915 SERIES TRUCK, TRACTOR, LINEHAUL

TRUCK, TRACTOR, LINEHAUL: M915

M915 TRACTOR w/M872 (40FT FLAT BED TRAILER)

M915 TRACTOR w/7500 GAL TANKER

M915 TRACTOR w/M872 (40 FT STAKE BED TRAILER)

M915 TRACTOR w/M872 TRAILER & 40 FT CONTAINER

HET

TRUCK, TRACTOR, HEAVY EQUIPMENT TRANSPORT (HET): M1070

TRUCK, TRACTOR, HET w/M1000 TRAILER

TRUCK, TRACTOR,HET w/M1000 TRAILER & M1A1 ABRAMS MAIN BATTLE TANK

MISCELLANEOUS ITEMS

FORKLIFT 4K

FORKLIFT 6K

FORKLIFT, 10K

MOBILE EXPANDIBLE CONTAINER
CONFIG. (MECC)

FORKLIFT, EXTENDED REACH
50K

CONTAINER 20FT

CONTAINER 40FT

ARMORED SECURITY VEHICLE
(ASV)

INTERIM ARMORED VEHICLE
(IAV) (WHEELED) (NOTIONAL)

CUCV: M1008A1

CUCV: M1009

CHAPTER 35

MILITARY SYMBOLS GUIDE

MILITARY SYMBOLS: UNIT TYPE

Symbol	Name	Symbol	Name	Symbol	Name
AG	Adjutant Gen.	(CHEM. cont) Recon.	(CHEM. cont) Recon.	MI	Military Intelligence
Air Force (surveillance) / Army	Aerial Obser.	SMOKE	Smoke	MP	Military Police
US / NATO	Airborne	CA	Civil Affairs		Motorized
Y	AIR ASSAULT	DPU	Data Process.	▲	Mountain
V	(no air)	D	Dental	⋈	Ordinance
	Air Cavalry		Engineer	▽	Petroleum
⋈	Air Defense	EW	Elec. Warfare		PSYOPS
	AMPHIBIOUS	●	Fld. Artillery	0	Quartermaster
	Engineer		Finance	RGR	Ranger
▽	Antiarmor	⊠	INFANTRY	RHU	Replacement
○	Armor	⊠ LI	Light		Rocket ARTY
⊘	Armored CAV	⊠	Mechanized	SVC	Service
✠	ARMY AVIATION (rotary)	⊠	BIFV mount.		Signal
✠	(fixed)	⊠	" dismount.		Sound Ranging
✠	Attack Heli.	⊠	Motorized	SF	Special Forces
	Bridging	L	Labor		SUPPLY
	Cavalry/recon.		Maintenance		" & Maint.
✗	CHEMICAL (NBC)		Medical	✳	" & Trans.
DECON	Decon	MET	Meteorological	SPT	Support

MILITARY SYMBOLS: SIZE & MARKING/INSTALLATION ROLE IND

UNIT SIZE

The size of units and installations is shown by placing the appropriate size indicator directly above the basic symbol.

US Description	STANAG 2019 Description	Symbol
Squad/crew	Smallest unit/UK section	
Section or unit larger than a squad but smaller than a platoon	Unit larger than a US squad/UK section but smaller than a platoon equivalent	
Platoon or detachment	Platoon/troop equivalent	
Company, battery, or troop	Company/battery/squadron equivalent	
Battalion or squadron	Battalion equivalent	
Group or regiment	Regiment/group equivalent	
Brigade	Brigade equivalent	
Division	Division	
Corps	Corps	
Army	Army	
	Army group/front	
	Battalion task force	
	Company team	

COLLECTING POINTS

(CAN)	Canibalization
(CIV)	Civilian
(DECON)	DECON Station
	Maintanance
(EPW)	Prisoners of War
(SALV)	Salvage
(S)	Stragglers

MISCELLANEOUS

	Graves Reg. SVC
	Hospital
(MMC)	Material MGT CTR
	Parking
(A)	Topographic
	Traffic Control
	Water

MARKING SYMBOLS

size of unit

unit designation

higher echelons of command

branch or duty performed

other information (DTG)

Unit Symbols:
Friendly   Enemy

EXAMPLES

	10th Infantry Division, III Corps, Eighth Army
	2d Platoon, A Company, 2d Battalion, 15th Infantry, 10th Infantry Division
	125th Infantry Brigade (Mech), III (US) Corps

MILITARY SYMBOLS: UNIT TYPE/INSTALLATION ROLE INDICATOR

Symbol	Description
	SAM
	SSM
	Survey
	Topographic
	Transportation
	RPV (unmanned air recon.)
	Veterinary

COMMUNICATIONS & ELECTRONICS INSTALLATIONS

Symbol	Description
	ADA Radar
	ARTY Loc. Radar
ADP	Data Proc. CTR.
	Direction Finding
EW	Elec. Warfare
	GND Surv. Radar
	Intercept
	Jamming
	Radio Relay
	Radio

Symbol	Description
	(C & E cont.) Dummy Radio
	Commo. CTR
	TGT Designator
	Telephone CTR
	Teleprinter
?	Unknown

LOGISTICS INSTALLATIONS

Symbol	Description
	Class I Subsistence
	Class II Clothing/Equip
	Class III(POL) Air Force
	Army Air
	Ground
	Solid Fuel
	Class IV Construction
	Class V Ammunition All
	Air Defense
	Air Force
ATP	AMMO Transfer Point

Symbol	Description
	CL V (cont.) Army Air
	Artillery
CHEM	Chemical
	Mines
NUC	Nuclear
	Rocket ARTY
	Small Arms
	Tank (main)
	Class VI Pers. Demand
	Class VII Major End
	Class VIII Medical
	Class IX Repair Parts
CA	Class X Non-Military
	All Classes
	Multiple Classes

GLOSSARY

✮✮✮

AA – Avenue of approach – where the enemy could come. Typically, two or more adjacent AAs become a Mobility Corridor.

AO – Area of operation

AOR – Area of Operational Responsibility. Usually Corps or higher

ADA – Air Defense Artillery. Now a part of the Fires Branch and Fires Warfighting Functional Area.

ASL – Authorized Stockage List. A stockpile of Class IX repair parts usually associated with a Service Support Activity (SSA)

BFSB – Battlefield Surveillance Brigade. This structure is programed to be removed in TAA 18-22

BSA – Brigade Support Area – A designated area in which sustainment elements of the Brigade Combat Team provide support to a brigade. The Brigade Support Battalion (BSB) manages the terrain and unit locations.

BSB – Brigade Support Battalion. BSBs assigned to Brigade Combat Teams (BCTs) have three companies (Distro, Fwd Maint, and Medical). BSBs assigned to Support Brigades (CAB, MEB, Field Artillery) only have two companies (Distro, Maint).

CCIR – Commander's Critical Information Requirements – Information required by the commander that directly affects his/her decision and dictates the successful execution of operational or tactical operations. CCIR normally result in the generation of two types of information requirements: priority intelligence requirements (PIR), and friendly force information requirements (FFIR).

CCL – Combat Configured Load – A planned package of ammunition or other supplies that are transported as a single load to support a type unit or weapon system. This can be air, rail, or other means of transport. This may also be referred to as "OCL" (Operational Configured Load) or "MCL" (Mission Configured Load)

CDS – Container Delivery System

COA – Course of Action

CRSP – Centralized Receiving & Shipping Point. A CRSP provides a centralized supply distribution operation within an AO where cargo is delivered and backhaul is picked up. This is accomplished using regular sustainment deliveries between FOBs. CRSPs employ the familiar "hub and spoke" concept.

CSC – Convoy Support (or Service) Center

CSSB – Combat Sustainment Support Battalion

CSR – Controlled Supply Rate – The rate of ammunition consumption that can be supported, considering availability, facilities, and transportation. It is expressed in rounds per unit, individual, or vehicle per day. A unit may not draw ammunition in excess of its CSR without authority from its next higher headquarters.

CSS – Combat Service Support – The essential capabilities, functions, activities, and tasks necessary to sustain all elements of operating forces in theater at all levels of war. This term is now considered obsolete with the publication of the Feb 08 FM 3-0 *Operations* and FM 4-0 *Sustainment.*

DS – Direct Support – A mission requiring a force to support another specific force and authorizing it to answer directly the supported force's request for assistance.

EEFI – Essential Elements of Friendly Information – Key questions likely to be asked by adversary officials and intelligence systems about specific friendly intention, capabilities, and activities so they can obtain answers critical to their operational effectiveness. The critical aspects of a friendly operation that, if known by the enemy, would subsequently compromise, lead to failure, or limit success of the operation, and therefore must be protected from enemy detection.

EN – Engineers

EOD – Explosive Ordnance Disposal – The detection, identification, on-site evaluation, rendering safe, recovery, and final disposal of unexploded explosive ordnance.

ESC – Expeditionary Support Command.

ESP – Engineer Supply Point, sometimes also known as a Class IV point.

FDRP – Final (or First) Destination Release Point

FFIR – Friendly Forces Information Requirement – Information the commander and staff need about the forces available for the operation. This includes personnel, maintenance, supply, ammunition, petroleum, oils, and lubricants status, and experience and leadership capabilities.

FLE/B – Forward Logistics Element/Base

FLS – Forward Landing Strip

FMC – Full Mission Capable, Material condition of an aircraft or training device indicating that it can perform all of its missions.

FSC – Forward Support Company

IPB – Intelligence Preparation of the Battlefield – A systematic approach to analyzing the enemy, weather, and terrain in a specific geographic area. It integrates enemy doctrine with the weather and terrain as they relate to the mission and the specific battlefield environment. This is done to determine and evaluate enemy capabilities, vulnerabilities, and probable courses of action.

ISR Plan – Intelligence, Surveillance, and Reconnaissance Plan. Term is rescinded and now referred to as the Intelligence Collection Plan (see FM 3-55).

LCOP – Logistics Common Operating Picture

LEW – Logistics Estimate Worksheet

LOC – Lines of Communication – All the routes, land, water, and air, which connect operating military force with a base of operations and along which supplies and military forces move.

LSA – Logistics Support Area – An area normally located in rear and often positioned near air-landing facilities along the main supply route. An LSA often contains Support Maintenance units and Level III medical assets. Typically, a Maneuver Enhancement Brigade (MEB) might be co-located along with a Rear Area Operations Center (RAOC). In contemporary doctrine, what was formally referred to as 'LSAs' are now identified as either Corps or Division Support Areas (CSAs/DSAs)

MCOO – Modified Combined Obstacles Overlay – The MCOO is a graphic terrain analysis on which all other IPB products are based. A MCOO is produced when a combination or terrain overlays are put together. It should contain at a minimum: NO-Go terrain, SLOW-GO terrain, built-up areas, LOCs, river and water obstacles, obstacles, key terrain, AAs and MCs, objectives, and other critical terrain features for a CSB.

MC – Mobility corridor. Usually composed of two or more Avenues of Approach (AA)

MEB – Maneuver Enhancement Brigade.

MDMP – Military Decision Making Process

MP – Military Police

MSO – Mission Staging Operation. Mission Staging Operations are initiated by Division order, conducted by the BCT/Spt Bde and enabled by the local Sustainment Brigade at a forward location within the Bde AO. MSO tasks are METT-TC based; may include planning, rehearsals, and limited reorganization ICW sustainment tasks required. The Sustainment Brigade provides replenishment to the BSB/FSC's along with field services and/or other services as required.

MSR – Main Supply Route – The route or routes designated within an area of operations upon which the bulk of traffic flows in support of military operations.

MST – Maintenance Support Team – A tailored direct support team that co-locates with a unit maintenance element for a designated period.

NAI – Named Area of Interest – A point or area along a particular avenue of approach through which enemy activity is expected to occur. Activity or lack of activity within an NAI will help to confirm or deny a particular enemy course of action.

OPCON – Operational Control – Transferable command authority that may be exercised by commanders at any echelon at or below the level of combatant command. Operational Control may be delegated and is the authority to perform those functions of command over subordinate forces involving organizing and employing commands and forces, assigning tasks, designative objectives, and giving authoritative direction necessary to accomplish the mission.

OPORD – Operation Order – A directive issues by a commander to subordinate commander for the purpose of effecting the coordinated execution of an operation.

OPLAN – Operation Plan – Any plan, except for the Single Integrated Operation Plan for the conduct of military operations. An operation plan is the draft document used to lay out the requirements for an operation. OPLANs become OPORDs.

PIR – Priority Intelligence Requirements – Those intelligence requirements for which a commander has an anticipated and stated priority in his/her task of planning and decision-making.

RFI – Request for Information

RO – Replenishment Operation. Preplanned sustainment operations that allow combat forces to replenish. They may be immediate, but usually routine. They are however, time sensitive, deliberate sustainment operations conducted by the CSSB or BSB to replenish FSCs, or by the FSC to conduct quick, in-stride replenishment of the maneuver or maneuver support battalion.

ROZ – Restricted operating zone

RSR – Required Supply Rate – The amount of ammunition expressed in terms of rounds per weapon per day for ammunition items fired by weapons, and in terms of other units of measure per day for bulk allotment and other items, estimated to be required to sustain operations of any designated force without restriction for a specified period.

SEAD – Suppression of enemy air defense

SPO – Support Plans Officer

TMR – Transportation Movement Request. A request for movement of personnel, commodities or other items beyond unit capabilities. If reoccurring for same haul mission, it becomes an STMR (Standard Transportation Movement Request)

TOC – Tactical Operations Center – A physical group of those elements of an organization concerned with the current tactical operations and tactical support of an operation. Used in conjunction with the term *Command Post* (CP)

TSC – Theater Sustainment Command. Also designated as SC(T)

Acronyms

AMC	Army Material Command
AO	Area of Operations
AOI	Area of Influence
APOD	Aerial Port of Debarkation
AOR	Area of Responsibility
ARFOR	Army Forces
AFSB	Army Field Support Brigade
AHRS	Army Human Resource System
BAS	Battalion Aid Station
BCS3	Battle Command Sustainment Support System
BFT	Blue Force Tracker
BMO	Battalion Motor Officer
BSA	Brigade Support Area
BSB	Brigade Support Battalion
BTB	Brigade Troops Battalion
C2	Command and Control
CAB	Combined Arms Battalion
CABSA	Combined Arms Battalion Support Area
CAISI	Combat Service Support Automated Information System Interface
-BM	Bridge Module
-CL	Client Module
CENTCOM	Central Command
COCOM	Combatant Commander
CROP	Container Roll-in Roll-out Platform
CSSB	Combat Sustainment Support Battalion
CTASC	Corps Theater Automated Service Center

Acronyms

CTCP	Combat Trains Command Post
DCGS-A	Distributed Common Ground System - Army
DLA	Defense Logistics Agency
ESC	Sustainment Command (Expeditionary)
FBCB2	Force XXI Battle Command, Brigade and Below
FLOT	Forward Line of Own Troops
FHP	Force Health Protection
FLB	Forward Logistical Base
FLE	Forward Logistical Element
FSC	Forward Support Company
HRSC	Human Resources Support Center
HSS	Health Systems Support
ILAP	Intragrated Logistics Analysis Program
ISB	Intermediate Staging Base
IAW	In Accordance With
ITV	In transit Visibility
JOA	Joint Operational Area
JFC	Joint Forces Command
LOC	Lines of Communication
LOGPAC	Logistics Package
LRP	Logistics Release Point
MCB	Movement Control Battalion
MSO	Mission Staging Operations
MTS	Movement Tracking System
OPCON	Operational Control
PLS	Palletized Load System

Acronyms

PBUSE   Property Book Unit Supply-Enhanced

RO   Replenishment Operations

RSOI   Reception Staging Onward Movement and Integration

RCC   Regional Combatant Commander

RFID   Radio Frequency Identification

SAAS-MOD   Standard Army Ammunition System-Modernized

SAMS   Standard Army Maintenance System

SARSS   Standard Army Retail Supply System

SDDC   Surface Deployment and Distribution Command

SP   Supply Point

SPO   Support Operations Officer

SPOD   Sea Port of Debarkation

STB   Special Troops Battalion

SUS Bde   Sustainment Brigade

TACON   Tactical Control

TASMG   Theater Aviation Sustainment Maintenance Group

TAV   Total Asset Visibility

TCAM   TAMMIS Customer Assistance Module

TMIP   Theater Medical Information Program

TSC   Sustainment Command (Theater)

UD   Unit Distribution

UMCP   Unit Maintenance Collection Point

USFK   United States Forces in Korea

USTC   United States Transportation Command

VSAT   Very Small Aperture Terminal